Prayer Book Studies
Volume Eight

Daily Office Revisited, Church Rites, and the
Formal Introduction, Issues 27-29

Edited by
Derek A. Olsen

Copyright © 2026 The Domestic and Foreign Missionary Society of the Protestant Episcopal Church in the United States of America

The English text of the liturgies presented in this book is in the public domain and is freely available for quotation without restriction.

Unless otherwise noted, Scripture quotations are from The New Revised Standard Version Bible, copyright © 1989 National Council of the Churches of Christ in the United States of America. Used by permission. All rights reserved worldwide.

Seabury Books
19 East 34th Street
New York, NY 10016
www.churchpublishing.org

Seabury Books is an imprint of Church Publishing Incorporated.

Cover design by Newgen
Typeset by Integra Software Services Pvt. Ltd.

ISBN 978-1-64065-942-1 (paperback)
ISBN 978-1-64065-943-8 (hardback)
ISBN 978-1-64065-944-5 (eBook)

Library of Congress Control Number: 2025945267

CONTENTS

Introduction vii

Prayer Book Studies 27: The Daily Office Revised

Preface 3

Morning and Evening Prayer 6
  Concerning the Service 6
  First Order 6
  Canticles for Use after Readings 13
  Second Order 25
  Canticles for Use after Readings 32

Additional Directions and Suggestions 43

Orders of Service for Noonday and Close of Day 45
  An Order of Service for Noonday or Other Times 45
  An Order of Service for the Close of Day (Compline) 47

Daily Devotions for Individuals and Families 52
  Concerning the Devotions 52
  In The Morning 53
  At Noon 54
  At The Close Of Day 54

Lectionary for the Daily Office 55
  Concerning the Lectionary 55
  Office Lectionary for Sundays 57
  Office Lectionary for Fixed Holy Days 63
  Office Lectionary for Weekdays and Moveable Feast Days 66

Supplement to Prayer Book Studies 27: An Order of Worship for the Evening

Concerning the Service 103

An Order of Worship for the Evening 103

Additional Directions and Suggestions 107

An Order of Worship for the Evening Commentary 108
Historical background 109
The present service 111

Prayer Book Studies 28: Dedication and Consecration of a Church, and the Celebration of a New Ministry

Preface 115

The Dedication and Consecration of a Church 117
Introduction 117
The Dedication and Consecration of a Church 128
Concerning the Service 128
At the Ministry of the Word 133
The Sermon or Address 133
The Peace 135
At the Celebration of the Eucharist 135
After Communion 135
Additional Directions and Suggestions 135
For the Dedication of Churches and Chapels in Special Cases 137
For the Dedication of Furnishings, or Parts of a Church or Chapel 137
For a Church or Chapel Long in Use 138
A Litany of Thanksgiving for a Church 138

The Celebration of a New Ministry 139
Introduction 139
Letter of Institution 144
Concerning the Service 144
Celebration of a New Ministry 145
The Institution 145
The Ministry of the Word 146
The Sermon 147
The Induction 148
At the Celebration of the Eucharist 149
After Communion 149
Additional Directions and Suggestions 150

Prayer Book Studies 29: Introducing the Proposed Book

I. Perspectives on the Proposed Book ... 156

II. Limits and Guidelines of Judgment ... 159
Limits ... 159
Criteria for Judgment ... 160

III. Survey of the Contents ... 161

IV. General Observations ... 163
Use of Contemporary Language ... 163
Variety and Flexibility ... 165
Maximum Participation ... 167
Place of the Eucharist ... 168
International Consultation on English Texts ... 169
Theological Emphases ... 171

V. Analysis of the Contents ... 177
The Church Year (The Calendar) ... 177
Morning and Evening Prayer ... 179
The Great Litany ... 181
Collects ... 182
Proper Liturgies for Special Days ... 188
Holy Baptism and Confirmation ... 190
The Holy Eucharist ... 197
Pastoral Offices ... 206
Episcopal Services ... 213
The Psalter ... 219
Prayers and Thanksgivings ... 220
An Outline of the Faith ... 221
Historical Documents of the Church ... 223
Tables and Lectionaries ... 224

VI. Conclusions ... 225

INTRODUCTION

The Series as a Whole

The *Prayer Book Studies* (PBS) series documents the 26-year process of study and conversation that led to the adoption of the American 1979 Book of Common Prayer. It falls broadly into two parts, distinguished by the use of Roman numerals and Arabic numerals. PBS I-XVII were published by the members of the Standing Liturgical Commission between 1950 and 1966 to communicate research and draft liturgies leading toward a revision process; PBS 18-29 were published by the various drafting committees between 1970 and 1976 once the revision process was formally begun and the earlier drafts were being transformed into new usable liturgies leading up to the adoption of the new prayer book in 1979. Finally, PBS 30 and its commentary were added in 1989 to discuss inclusive and expansive language for God for further liturgical efforts.

Context of these Studies

These studies belong to the Second Series of the *Prayer Book Studies*, those using Arabic numerals for their numbering (PBS 18-29), and that followed the kickoff of a formal revision process with the 1967 General Convention. Within these eleven studies, the first seven (PBS 18-24), containing the most critical materials for public worship and pastoral use, were all published in 1970. The rites within these studies, shorn of their exposition, would be printed as *Services for Trial Use*, also known as "the Green Book." The next four (with two supplements) were published in 1973. These would be collected with the preceding materials into *Authorized Services 1973*, also known as "the Zebra Book" for its striped cover. The final study in this Second Series (PBS 29) is the sole publication in 1976 introducing the complete set of new rites to The Episcopal Church.

In contrast with the first series, a wide range of voices are brought into the conversation as both drafters and readers. The preface to the first of the new studies, PBS 18, describes the processes followed by the Standing Liturgical Commission, the drafting committees, reader-consultants, and the Editorial Committee, and should be consulted for full details.

At the same time, the timeline for completing these studies and their liturgies was greatly compressed. While some work on the First Series had been ongoing since the publication of the 1928 Book of Common Prayer, all of the work here—building on and informed by the work of the First Series—had to occur at lightning speed.

One telltale sign of the haste and subsequent disorganization present within this period is the wide range of formatting choices between the studies issued in this period. The choices of fonts for text and headings, the formatting of headings, and the presence or absence of color are entirely inconsistent between studies, leading to an impression of speed and chaos across the material.

Finally—and contributing even more to the pressure on the committees—all of the rites appear in contemporary language (now known as Rite II) rather than the Elizabethan/Jacobean idiom that had been used for all of the preceding liturgical work. Several rites, of course, appear in both (Rites I and II).

These Studies

PBS 27

The first study in this volume revisits the Daily Office to accomplish two important tasks. First, it takes all of the Daily Office material from PBS 22 and rearranges it in a manner that is easier to use. While even the final book never fully achieves that goal, this does represent a step in the right direction. Second, it presents a full two-year Daily Office lectionary that matches the new shape of the calendar.

PBS 27 Supplement

The second study in this volume is a brief supplement to introduce a completely new kind of Daily Office material: the Order of Worship for the Evening. An interesting attempt to resurrect a 4th-century concept as an intimate alternative to Evening Prayer, it has not seen wide use in the decades since its creation.

PBS 28

The third study in this volume completes the final liturgies needed for a full prayer book. After going through all of the rites of public worship, the pastoral rites for individuals and communities, we arrive at the rites for buildings. In keeping with the emphases of the new rites overall, The Dedication and Consecration of a Church takes place within the explicit context of a Eucharist. The material from PBS XIV which had been an institution of rectors is expanded to encompass any form of new priestly ministry.

PBS 29

The fourth and final study of both this volume and this series is essential reading for anyone wishing to truly understand the aims and intentions of the 1979 American Book of Common Prayer as it arrived in its particular historical moment. While written in the voice of a single member of the Standing Liturgical Commission, Charles P. Price, it "has been accepted by the Commission as the consensus of its members." It identifies the general guiding principles that have directed the work and provides an analysis of each portion of the new book, comparing it to previous works and explaining the changes. This study is the capstone and final summarization of the revision process that created the 1979 prayer book.

PRAYER BOOK STUDIES 27:
THE DAILY OFFICE REVISED

1973

PREFACE

The Orders of service contained in this study are essentially identical with those published in *Prayer Book Studies 22*. Thus, the rationale set forth in the introduction to that publication[1] applies to this Study as well. Trial use has demonstrated the desirability of rearranging the various elements of each Order of Service, namely the Opening Sentences, Invitatory Antiphons, and Canticles, in consecutive sequence within each Order so as to minimize the need to turn pages back and forth. This, rather than the contents or the contents of the Office, occasioned the bulk of the criticism from those who attempted to give trial use to the Daily Office. The Standing Liturgical Commission is indebted to all who sent in their comments and criticisms of the earlier arrangement, and especially to all those who made constructive suggestions. It is hoped that the new arrangement will make the Offices, as printed here, easier to follow, without obscuring their structure.

There were three other sources of difficulty in giving trial use to the Daily Office: First, the absence of a new lectionary, which made it necessary to be constantly referring to, and adapting, the lectionary of the Book of Common Prayer, and this made it difficult to take full advantage of the themes and collects of the new Church Year; secondly, the absence of a complete Psalter; and thirdly, the delay in the publication of "Prayers, Thanksgivings, and Litanies" (*Prayer Book Studies* 25). The delay in producing all these materials was unavoidable, but these defects have now been remedied: "The Prayer Book Psalter Revised" containing a contemporary translation of all 150 Psalms has been published; "Prayers, Thanksgivings, and Litanies" is now available and has been well received; and the present publication should meet the need for a lectionary geared to the new Church Year for Daily Morning and Evening Prayer and for Sundays and other Holy Days, and of tables of appointed Psalms.

It is only fair to add that in a number of places where the use of trial services was carefully planned and the congregations were adequately prepared and instructed, the forms in *Prayer Book Studies* 22, reprinted in *Services for Trial Use*, received favorable comment.

---

1. "The Daily Office" (*Prayer Book Studies* 22, reprinted in *Prayer Book Studies Volume Six*), prepared by the Standing Liturgical Commission, published by the Church Hymnal Corporation, New York, 1970. The Orders of Service contained in it were authorized for trial use by the General Convention of 1970 and reprinted in *Services for Trial Use*.

As was pointed out in *Prayer Book Studies* 22, the basic core of the Daily Office, as the Church's daily worship of Almighty God, is the regular, systematic recitation of the Psalter and the reading and hearing of passages from the Scriptures in a regular order.[2]

The lectionary now presented to the Church is based upon the new arrangement of the Church Year, as set forth in *Prayer Book Studies* 19 and reprinted in *Services for Trial Use*.[3] It differs from the Prayer Book lectionary particularly with regard to Sundays, where the Office Readings were thematically related to the Prayer Book Epistles and Gospels; but the difference extends also to weekdays, as a result of the suppression of the Season of Pre-Lent, and a corresponding increase in the length of the Season after Epiphany.

A further factor in the case of weekdays is the permission given in *Services for Trial Use*, pp. 242 and 254 to use the Daily Office in place of the Ministry of the Word at the Eucharist. In order that advantage may be taken of this possibility on weekdays, a passage from the Gospels is included as one of the Readings for each day, and the Gospel reading is available for use at either Morning or Evening Prayer, depending on the time of the eucharistic celebration.

Unlike the eucharistic lectionary for Sundays, which is arranged in a three-year cycle,[4] the proposed lectionary follows a two-year cycle. The basis of the plan is, in structure, but not in content, that which first appeared in England in the proposals of the Interdenominational Joint Liturgical Group; and which is now, in revised form, found in the provisions of *Alternative Services, Second Series [Revised]: Morning and Evening Prayer of the Church of England*. The feature of the English proposal adopted here is that of providing, on a two-year cycle, three Readings for each weekday, one of which is always from the Gospel. For the Holy Days, the Readings are the same in each year.

For Sundays a different arrangement is used which provides two sets of Psalms and Lessons based on themes from the Collects of the new Church Year.

Directions for the use of the proposed lectionary will be found on p. 84 of this book. As is the case with most of the rites prepared under the constitutional provisions for trial use, the conscientious use of the Daily Office in its new format, together with the new lectionary, in situations of actual worship, over a sufficiently prolonged period of time, and in accordance with the directions and suggestions, is the most effective way of discovering both the merits and the

---

2. *Prayer Book Studies* 22 (reprinted in Prayer Book Studies Volume Six), Introduction Vol. 6, pp. 99-102.

3. "The Church Year", *Prayer Book Studies* 19 (reprinted in *Prayer Book Studies Volume Five*), The Church Hymnal Corporation, New York, 1970. The Introduction, Vol. 5, pp. 34-67, contains a detailed rationale.

4. This three-year cycle is also basically the plan in current experimental use in the Roman, Lutheran, and Presbyterian churches, though each has its own set of variations. [Ed. note: This plan would become the framework for the Common Lectionary (1983) and subsequently the Revised Common Lectionary (1992).]

inadequacies of the new proposals. The Commission, as always, will welcome all comments, criticisms, and suggestions, and will take these into account in preparing a definitive presentation for the next constitutional action by the General Convention.

The Commission hopes to prepare and to publish during the next period of trial use, a detailed commentary on the new lectionary, together with a synopsis of the proposed lectionary and others of similar design.

In presenting to the Church "The Daily Office Revised", together with the new lectionary, the Commission desires to place on record its deep appreciation to the Chairman, the Rev. Dr. Charles W.F. Smith and to all members of his Drafting Committee — the Rev. Dr. Edward R. Hardy, the Rev. Benjamin Minifie, Sister Mary Clare, O.S.A., the Rev. William Sydnor, Mr. David Johnson, and the Rt. Rev. Morgan Porteus. Special thanks are due to Mr. Sydnor who is primarily responsible for preparing the lectionary for Sundays, and to Sister Mary Clare who has prepared with diligence and patience the synopsis referred to above. To Captain Howard Galley, C.A., Editorial Assistant on the staff of the Co-ordinator for Prayer Book Revision, the Commission is indebted not only for the eight-week Psalter plan, for which he is largely responsible, but also for the painstaking care with which he has scrutinized all the material prepared by the Drafting Committee for inconsistencies and repetitions. If any remain, it is hoped that they will not be so great as to interfere with the devout, regular, and profitable use of "The Daily Office Revised."

Finally, the Commission desires to restate the pledge it has repeatedly made to the whole Church, to keep all the material it has prepared open to constant review and reconsideration. All the members of the Church are invited to comment and to offer suggestions. As the Commission has stated in its Report on the progress of Prayer Book Revision to the 64th General Convention, "no one is excluded from sharing in the process, no one's comments will fail of consideration, and no part of its proposals has yet reached the stage where it may no longer be revised."

— The Standing Liturgical Commission

Morning and Evening Prayer

Concerning the Service

In the Offices of Morning and Evening Prayer, the term "Minister" is used to denote the person, whether a clergyman or a lay person, leading the service.

The Proper Antiphons on page 10 may be used as refrains with either of the Invitatory Psalms.

Antiphons drawn from the Psalms themselves, or from the opening Sentences given in the Offices, or from other passages of Scripture may be used with the Psalms and Biblical Canticles.

The Apostles' Creed is normally recited at both Morning and Evening Prayer on Sundays and other major Feasts (except when the Eucharist with its own Creed is to follow). It is desirable that the Creed be recited in at least one of the Offices on other days.

At celebrations of the Holy Eucharist, the Order for Morning or Evening Prayer may be used in place of all that precedes the Offertory, provided that a Lesson from the Gospel is always included and that the Intercession conforms to the directions on pages 44-45.

Additional Directions and Suggestions are on pages 43-45.

First Order

The Minister begins the service with one or more of these Sentences of Scripture.

The Sentences in italics may be used as responses by the People or as separate Sentences.

The most frequently used Sentences are printed on page 8, facing the Confession of Sin.

Advent Season
In the wilderness prepare the way of the Lord: make straight in the desert a highway for our God.
The glory of the Lord shall be revealed, and all flesh shall see it together. (Isaiah 40:3,5)

Rejoice: The Lord is at hand. (Philippians 4:5)
Amen, Come, Lord Jesus. (Revelation 22:20)

Christmas Season
Behold, I bring good news of great joy which will come to all the people: for to you is born in the city of David a Savior, who is Christ the Lord. (Luke 2:10,11)
Glory to God in the highest and on earth peace among men. (Luke 2:14)

Behold, the dwelling of God is with men. He will dwell with them, and they shall be his people:
God himself shall be with them, and be their God. (Revelation 21:3)

Epiphany Season
I will give you as a light to the nations, that my salvation may reach to the end of the earth. (Isaiah 49:6
Nations shall come to your light, and kings to the brightness of your rising. (Isaiah 60:3)

If we walk in the light, as he is in the light, we have fellowship with one another:
And the blood of Jesus his Son cleanses us from all sin. (1 John 1:7)

Lent and Holy Week
Jesus said, If any man would come after me, let him deny himself and take up his cross and follow me.
For whoever would save his life will lose it; and whoever loses his life for my sake and the gospel's will save it. (Mark 8:34, 35)

All we like sheep have gone astray; we have turned every one to his own way;
And the Lord has laid on him the iniquity of us all. (Isaiah 53:6)

Easter Season Including Ascension Day and the Day of Pentecost
Alleluia! Christ is risen. (*cf.* Mark 16:6)
The Lord is risen indeed. Alleluia! (Luke 24:34)

Worthy is the Lamb who was slain, to receive power and wealth and wisdom and might and honor and glory and blessing.
To him who sits on the throne and to the Lamb be blessing and honor and glory and might for ever and ever. (Revelation 5:12, 13)

God's love has been poured into our hearts,
Through the Holy Spirit who has been given to us. (Romans 5:5)

All Saints and Other Festivals
Since we are surrounded by so great a cloud of witnesses, let us lay aside every weight, and sin which clings so closely,
And let us run with perseverance the race which is set before us, looking to Jesus, the pioneer and perfecter of our faith. (Hebrews 12:1,2)

National Observances
Let the nations be glad and sing for joy;
For God judges the peoples with equity, and guides all the nations upon earth. (Psalm 67:4)

General Sentences
The Lord is in his holy temple:
Let all the earth keep silence before him. (Habakkuk 2:20)

O worship the Lord in the beauty of holiness;
Let the whole earth stand in awe of him. (Psalm 96:9)

God is spirit, and those who worship him must worship in spirit and truth. (John 4:24)
Let the words of my mouth and the meditation of my heart be acceptable in thy sight, O Lord, my strength and my redeemer. (Psalm 19:14)

Morning
Grace to you and peace from God our Father and the Lord Jesus Christ. (Romans 1:7)
Thanks be to God who gives us the victory through our Lord Jesus Christ. (1 Corinthians 15:57)

Evening
Lord, I love the house in which thou dwellest, and the place where thy glory abides. (Psalm 26:8)
Let my prayer be accounted in thy sight as incense, the lifting up of my hands as the evening sacrifice. (Psalm 141:2)

Occasions of Thanksgiving
Give thanks to the Lord, and call upon his Name; make known his deeds among the peoples.
Sing to him, sing praises to him, and speak of all his marvelous works. (Psalm 105:1,2)

Penitential
Seek the Lord while he wills to be found; call upon him when he draws near. Let the wicked forsake his ways, and the evil man his thoughts;

And let him turn to the Lord, and he will have compassion, and to our God, for he will richly pardon. (Isaiah 55:6,7)

The following Confession of Sin, or the form on page 28, may then be said; or the Office may continue at once with "O Lord, open thou our lips", all still standing.

CONFESSION OF SIN

Minister

Let us humbly confess our sins unto Almighty God.

Silence may be kept
Minister and People together, all kneeling

Almighty and most merciful Father, We have erred and strayed from thy ways like lost sheep. We have followed too much the devices and desires of our own hearts. We have offended against thy holy laws. We have left undone those things which we ought to have done; And we have done those things which we ought not to have done. But thou, O Lord, have mercy upon us; Spare thou those who confess their faults; Restore thou those who are penitent; According to thy promises declared unto mankind in Christ Jesus our Lord; And grant that hereafter we may live a godly, righteous and sober life, To the glory of thy holy Name. Amen.

The Priest alone stands and says

Almighty God have mercy on you, forgive you all your sins, through our Lord Jesus Christ; strengthen you in all goodness, and by the power of the Holy Spirit, keep you in eternal life. *Amen.*

A Deacon or Lay person using the preceding form remains kneeling, and substitutes "us" for "you".

The Psalter

All stand
Minister

O Lord, open thou our lips,

People

And our mouth shall show forth thy praise.

Minister and People

Glory be to the Father, and to the Son, and to the Holy Spirit: as it was in the beginning, is now and ever shall be, world without end. Amen.

Except in Lent

Alleluia.

In the morning there follows, and in the evening there may follow, one of the Invitatory Psalms, Venite or Jubilate.

In the seasons and on the days named, one of the following Antiphons may be sung or said with the Invitatory Psalm:

In Advent
Our King and Savior now draws near: Come let us adore him. Alleluia.

In Christmas Season
Unto us a child is born: Come let us adore him. Alleluia.

In the Epiphany Season and on Transfiguration
The Lord has shown forth his glory: Come let us adore him. Alleluia.

In Easter Season
Alleluia. The Lord is risen indeed: Come let us adore him. Alleluia.

On Ascension Day
Alleluia. Christ the Lord is ascended to heaven: Come let us adore him. Alleluia.

On the Day of Pentecost
Alleluia. The Spirit of the Lord renews the face of the earth: Come let us adore him. Alleluia.

On Trinity Sunday
Father, Son, and Holy Spirit, one God: holy is his Name: Come let us adore him. Alleluia.

In Easter Season, the Alleluia in parentheses is added. In Lent, both Alleluias are omitted.

On Feasts of the Incarnation
(Alleluia.) The Word was made flesh and dwelt among us: Come let us adore him. Alleluia.

On Other Festivals
(Alleluia.) The Lord is glorious in his saints: Come let us adore him. Alleluia.

VENITE *(Psalm 95:1-7; 96:9,13)*

O come let us sing unto the Lord;
    let us heartily rejoice in the strength of our salvation.
Let us come before his presence with thanksgiving;
    and show ourselves glad in him with psalms.

For the Lord is a great God;
    and a great King above all gods.
In his hand are all the corners of the earth;
    and the strength of the hills is his also.
The sea is his and he made it;
    and his hands prepared the dry land.

O come let us worship and fall down
    and kneel before the Lord our Maker.
For he is the Lord our God;
    and we are the people of his pasture,
    and the sheep of his hand.
O worship the Lord in the beauty of holiness;
    let the whole earth stand in awe of him.
For he cometh, for he cometh to judge the earth;
    and with righteousness to judge the world,
    and the peoples with his truth.

JUBILATE *(Psalm 100)*

O be joyful in the Lord all ye lands:
    serve the Lord with gladness,
    and come before his presence with a song.

Be ye sure that the Lord he is God;
it is he that hath made us and not we ourselves;
    we are his people and the sheep of his pasture.

O go your way into his gates with thanksgiving,
and into his courts with praise;
    be thankful unto him and speak good of his Name.

For the Lord is gracious, his mercy is everlasting;
    and his truth endureth from generation to generation.

> *In the evening, for the Invitatory, the Hymn "O Gracious Light" may be used.*

O GRACIOUS LIGHT—Phos hilaron

O gracious light,
pure brightness of the everliving Father in heaven,
O Jesus Christ, holy and blessed!

Now as we come to the setting of the sun,
and our eyes behold the vesper light,
we sing your praises, O God: Father, Son, and Holy Spirit.

You are worthy at all times to be praised by happy voices,
O Son of God, O Giver of life,
and to be glorified through all the worlds.

During Easter Season, the Canticle "Christ Our Passover" may be used for the Invitatory both in the morning and in the evening.

CHRIST OUR PASSOVER
(*Corinthians 5:7 - 8; Romans 6:9 - 11;
1 Corinthians 15:20 - 22*)

Christ our Passover is sacrificed for us:
    therefore let us keep the feast,
Not with old leaven,
neither with the leaven of malice and wickedness;
    but with the unleavened bread of sincerity and truth.

Christ being raised from the dead dieth no more;
    death hath no more dominion over him.
For in that he died, he died unto sin once:
    but in that he liveth, he liveth unto God.
Likewise reckon ye also yourselves
to be dead indeed unto sin,
    but alive unto God through Jesus Christ our Lord.

Christ is risen from the dead,
    and become the first fruits. of them that slept.
For since by man came death,
    by man came also the resurrection of the dead.
For as in Adam all die,
    even so in Christ shall all be made alive.

Then follows the

PSALM OR PSALMS APPOINTED.

At the end of the Psalms is sung or said

Glory be to the Father, and to the Son,
    and to the Holy Spirit:
As it was in the beginning, is now and ever shall be,
    world without end. Amen.

The Word of God

Then is read a selection from the Old Testament and a selection from the New Testament. [See pages 43-44 for forms of announcing Readings.]

1. Silence may be kept after each reading;
2. One of the readings may be omitted;
3. A Canticle from those which follow may be sung or said after each reading; but there is always one at the conclusion of the Scripture.

Canticles for Use after Readings

1

THE FIRST SONG OF ISAIAH—Ecce, Deus.
(Isaiah 12:2 - 6)

Surely, it is God who saves me;
    I will trust in him and not be afraid.
For the Lord is my stronghold and my sure defense,
    and he will be my Savior.
Therefore you shall draw water with rejoicing
    from the springs of salvation.
And on that day you shall say,
    Give thanks to the Lord, and call upon his Name;
Make his deeds known among the peoples;
    see that they remember that his Name is exalted.
Sing the praises of the Lord, for he has done great things,
    and this is known in all the world.
Cry aloud, ring out your joy, inhabitants of Zion,
    for the great one in the midst of you
    is the Holy One of Israel.
Glory be to the Father, and to the Son,
    and to the Holy Spirit:

As it was in the beginning, is now, and ever shall be,
    world without end. Amen.

2

THE SECOND SONG OF ISAIAH—Quaerite Dominum *(Isaiah 55:6 - 11)*

The Second Song of Isaiah is suggested for use on Fridays, and in the Season of Lent.

Seek the Lord while he wills to be found;
    call upon him when he draws near.
Let the wicked forsake his way,
    and the evil man his thoughts;
And let him turn to the Lord, and he will have compassion,
    and to our God, for he will richly pardon.
For my thoughts are not your thoughts,
    not your ways my ways, says the Lord.
For as the heavens are higher than the earth,
    so are my ways higher than your ways,
    and my thoughts than your thoughts.
For as rain and snow fall from the heavens,
    and return not again, but water the earth,
Bringing forth life, and giving growth,
    seed for sowing and bread for eating,
So is my word that goes forth from my mouth:
    it will not return to me empty;
But it will accomplish that which I have purposed,
    and prosper in that for which I sent it.
Glory be to the Father, and to the Son,
    and to the Holy Spirit:
As it was in the beginning, is now, and ever shall be,
    world without end. Amen.

3

THE SONG OF THE THREE YOUNG MEN
Benedictus es, Domine
(verses 29 - 34)

Blessed art thou, O Lord God of our fathers:
    praised and exalted above all for ever.
Blessed art thou for the Name of thy Majesty:
    praised and exalted above all for ever.

Blessed art thou in the temple of thy holiness:
    praised and exalted above all for ever.
Blessed art thou that beholdest the depths,
and dwellest between the Cherubim:
    praised and exalted above all for ever.
Blessed art thou on the glorious throne of thy kingdom:
    praised and exalted above all for ever.
Blessed art thou in the firmament of heaven:
    praised and exalted above all for ever.
Blessed art thou, O Father, Son, and Holy Spirit:
    praised and exalted above all for ever.

4

A SONG OF CREATION
Benedicite, omnia opera Domini
(Song of the Three Young Men: verses 35 - 65)

O all ye works of the Lord, bless ye the Lord:
    praise him and magnify him for ever.
O ye angels of the Lord, bless ye the Lord:
    praise him and magnify him for ever.

O ye heavens, bless ye the Lord;
O ye waters that be above the firmament, bless ye the Lord;
O all ye powers of the Lord, bless ye the Lord:
    praise him and magnify him for ever.

O ye sun and moon, bless ye the Lord;
O ye stars of heaven, bless ye the Lord;
O ye showers and dew, bless ye the Lord:
    praise him and magnify him for ever.

O ye winds of God, bless ye the Lord;
O ye fire and heat, bless ye the Lord;
O ye winter and summer, bless ye the Lord:
    praise him and magnify him for ever.

O ye dews and frosts, bless ye the Lord;
O ye frost and cold, bless ye the Lord;
O ye ice and snow, bless ye the Lord:
    praise him and magnify him for ever.

O ye nights and days, bless ye the Lord;
O ye light and darkness, bless ye the Lord;

O ye lightnings and clouds, bless ye the Lord:
    praise him and magnify him for ever.

O let the earth bless the Lord;
O ye mountains and hills, bless ye the Lord;
O all ye green things upon the earth, bless ye the Lord;
    praise him and magnify him for ever.

O ye wells, bless ye the Lord;
O ye seas and floods, bless ye the Lord;
O ye whales and all that move in the waters, bless ye the Lord:
    praise him and magnify him for ever.

O all ye fowls of the air, bless ye the Lord;
O all ye beasts and cattle, bless ye the Lord;
O ye children of men, bless ye the Lord:
    praise him and magnify him for ever.

O ye people of God, bless ye the Lord;
O ye priests of the Lord, bless ye the Lord;
O ye servants of the Lord, bless ye the Lord:
    praise him and magnify him for ever.

O ye spirits and souls of the righteous, bless ye the Lord;
O ye holy and humble men of heart, bless ye the Lord.
Let us bless the Father, the Son, and the Holy Spirit:
    praise him and magnify him for ever.

5

THE SONG OF MARY—Magnificat
(Luke 1:46 - 55)

My soul doth magnify the Lord,
    and my spirit hath rejoiced in God my Savior.
For he hath regarded
    the lowliness of his handmaiden.
For behold from henceforth
    all generations shall call me blessed.
For he that is mighty hath magnified me;
    and holy is his Name.
And his mercy is on them that fear him
    throughout all generations.

He hath showed strength with his arm;
    he hath scattered the proud
        in the imagination of their hearts.
He hath put down the mighty from their seat,
    and hath exalted the humble and meek.
He hath filled the hungry with good things;
    and the rich he hath sent empty away.
He remembering his mercy hath holpen his servant Israel;
    as he promised to our forefathers,
        Abraham and his seed for ever.
Glory be to the Father, and to the Son,
    and to the Holy Spirit:
As it was in the beginning, is now, and ever shall be,
    world without end. Amen.

6

THE SONG OF ZECHARIAH —Benedictus
(Luke 1:68 - 79)

Blessed be the Lord God of Israel;
    for he hath visited and redeemed his people;
And hath raised up a mighty salvation for us,
    in the house of his servant David;
As he spake by the mouth of his holy Prophets,
    which have been since the world began;
That we should be saved from our enemies,
    and from the hand of all that hate us.

To perform the mercy promised to our forefathers,
    and to remember his holy covenant;
To perform the oath
which he sware to our forefather Abraham,
    that he would give us;
That we being delivered out of the hand of our enemies
    might serve him without fear;
In holiness and righteousness before him,
    all the days of our life.

And thou, child, shalt be called the prophet of the Highest:
    for thou shalt go before the face of the Lord
        to prepare his ways;

To give knowledge of salvation unto his people
    for the remission of their sins,
Through the tender mercy of our God;
    whereby the day-spring from on high hath visited us;
To give light to them that sit in darkness,
and in the shadow of death,
    and to guide our feet into the way of peace.
Glory be to the Father, and to the Son,
    and to the Holy Spirit:
As it was in the beginning, is now, and ever shall be,
    world without end. Amen.

7

THE SONG OF SIMEON —Nunc Dimittis (Luke 2:29 - 32)

Lord, now lettest thou thy servant depart in peace,
    according to thy word;
For mine eyes have seen thy salvation,
    which thou has prepared before the face of all people;
To be a light to lighten the Gentiles,
    and to be the glory of thy people Israel.
Glory be to the Father, and to the Son,
    and to the Holy Spirit:
As it was in the beginning, is and ever shall be,
    world without end. Amen.

8

A SONG TO THE LAMB —Dignus es
(*Revelation 4:11; 5:9 - 10, 13*)

Splendor and honor and kingly power
are yours by right, O Lord our God,
    for you created everything that is,
    and by your will they were created and have their being.
And yours by right, O Lamb that was slain,
for with your Blood you have redeemed for God,
    from every family, language, people, and nation,
    a kingdom of priests to serve our God.
And so, to him who sits upon the throne,
and to Christ the Lamb, be worship and praise, dominion and splendor,
    for ever, and for evermore.

9

THE SONG OF THE REDEEMED —Magna et mirabilia
(*Revelation 15:3 - 4*)

O ruler of the universe, Lord God,
    great deeds are they that you have done,
    surpassing human understanding.
Your ways are ways of righteousness and truth,
    O King of all the ages.
Who can fail to do you homage, Lord,
    and sing the praises of your Name?
    for you only are the holy One.
All nations will draw near, and fall down before you,
    because your just and holy works have been revealed.

10

GLORY BE TO GOD—Gloria in excelsis

Glory be to God on high,
    and on earth peace, good will towards men.
We praise thee, we bless thee, we worship thee,
    we glorify thee, we give thanks to thee
    for thy great glory,
O Lord God, heavenly King,
    God the Father Almighty.

O Lord, the only-begotten Son, Jesus Christ;
    O Lord God, Lamb of God, Son of the Father,
that takest away the sins of the world,
    have mercy upon us.
Thou that takest away the sins of the world,
    receive our prayer.
Thou that sittest at the right hand of God the Father, have mercy upon us.

For thou only art holy;
    thou only art the Lord;
thou only, O Christ, with the Holy Ghost,
    art most high in the glory of God the Father. Amen.

11

WE PRAISE THEE —Te Deum laudamus

We praise thee, O God; we acknowledge thee to be the Lord.
    All the earth doth worship thee, the Father everlasting.
To thee all Angels cry aloud:
the Heavens and all the Powers therein;
    To thee Cherubim and Seraphim continually do cry,
Holy, Holy, Holy, Lord God of Sabaoth;
    Heaven and earth are full of the Majesty of thy glory.
The glorious company of the Apostles praise thee.
    The goodly fellowship of the Prophets praise thee.
The noble army of Martyrs praise thee.
    The holy Church throughout all the world
    doth acknowledge thee;
The Father of an infinite Majesty;
Thine adorable, true, and only Son;
    Also the Holy Ghost the Comforter.
Thou art the King of Glory, O Christ.
    Thou art the everlasting Son of the Father.
When thou tookest upon thee to deliver man,
    thou didst humble thyself to be born of a Virgin.
When thou hadst overcome the sharpness of death,
    thou didst open the Kingdom of Heaven to all believers.
Thou sittest at the right hand of God,
    in the glory of the Father.
We believe that thou shalt come to be our Judge.
    We therefore pray thee, help thy servants,
    whom thou hast redeemed with thy precious blood.
Make them to be numbered with thy Saints,
    in glory everlasting.

Here, or in one of the other places appointed, may follow a SERMON OR MEDITATION

THE APOSTLES' CREED

Minister and People together, all standing

I believe in God, the Father almighty,
    creator of heaven and earth.

I believe in Jesus Christ, his only Son, our Lord.
    He was conceived by the power of the Holy Spirit
        and born of the Virgin Mary.
    He suffered under Pontius Pilate,
        was crucified, died, and was buried.
    He descended to the dead.
    On the third day he rose again.
    He ascended into heaven,
        and is seated at the right hand of the Father.
    He will come again to judge the living and the dead.
I believe in the Holy Spirit,
    the holy catholic Church,
    the communion of saints,
    the forgiveness of sins,
    the resurrection of the body,
    and the life everlasting.

The Prayers

The prayers follow, the People standing or kneeling.

Minister	The Lord be with you.
People	And with thy spirit.
Minister	Let us pray.

Minister and People

Our Father, who art in heaven, hallowed be thy Name,
    thy Kingdom come,
    thy will be done,
    on earth as it is in heaven.
Give us this day our daily bread.
And forgive us our trespasses,
    as we forgive those who trespass against us.
And lead us not into temptation,
    but deliver us from evil.
For thine is the kingdom, and the power,
    and the glory, for ever and ever. Amen.

Then follows one of these sets of Suffrages:

A

V. Show us thy mercy, O Lord:
R. And grant us thy salvation.
V. Clothe thy ministers with righteousness:
R. Let thy people sing with joy.
V. Give peace, O Lord, in all the world:
R. For only in thee can we live in safety.
V. Lord, keep this nation under thy care:
R. And guide us in the way of justice and truth.
V. Let thy way be known upon earth:
R. Thy saving health among all nations.
V. Let not the needy, O Lord, be forgotten:
R. Nor the hope of the poor be taken away.
V. Create in us clean hearts, O God:
R. And sustain us with thy Holy Spirit.

B

V. Save thy people, Lord, and bless thine inheritance:
R. Govern and uphold them, now and always.
V. Day by day we bless thee.
R. We praise thy Name for ever.
V. Lord, keep us from all sin today.
R. Have mercy on us, Lord, have mercy.
V. Lord, show us thy love and mercy;
R. For we put our trust in thee.
V. In thee, Lord, is our hope:
R. May we never be confounded.

The Minister then says

THE COLLECT OF THE DAY

On Fridays and Saturdays, not being Holy Days, the Collect for Good Friday and Holy Saturday, respectively, may be used instead.[i]

In the morning, one of the following is then said

---

[i] [Ed. note: These are the "revised collects" and the Good Friday and Holy Saturday collects from *Prayer Book Studies* 19 (reprinted in *Prayer Book Studies Volume Five*). The first is: "Almighty God, we beseech thee graciously to behold this thy family, for which our Lord Jesus Christ was content to be betrayed, and given up into the hands of sinful men, and to suffer death upon the Cross: who now liveth and reigneth with thee and the Holy Spirit, one God, for ever and ever. Amen."

O heavenly Father, in whom we live and move and have our being: We humbly pray thee so to guide and govern us by thy Holy Spirit, that in all the cares and occupations of life, we may never forget thee, but remember that we are ever walking in thy sight; through Jesus Christ our Lord. *Amen.*

O Lord, our heavenly Father, Almighty and Everlasting God, who hast safely brought us to the beginning of this day: Defend us in the same with thy mighty power; and grant that this day we fall into no sin, neither run into any kind of danger; but that we, being ordered by thy governance, may always do what is righteous in thy sight; through Jesus Christ our Lord. *Amen.*

In the evening, one of the following is said

O God, from whom all holy desires, all good counsels, and all just works do proceed: Give unto thy servants that peace which the world cannot give; that our hearts may be set to obey thy commandments, and also that by thee, we, being defended from the fear of enemies, may pass our time in rest and quietness, through the merits of Jesus Christ our SaVior. *Amen.*

Lighten our darkness, we beseech thee, O Lord; and by thy great mercy defend us from all perils and dangers of this night; for the love of thy only Son, our Savior, Jesus Christ. *Amen.*

The following Collect is always added, both in the morning and in the evening.

Almighty and everlasting God, by whose Spirit the whole body of the Church is governed and sanctified: Receive our supplications and prayers, which we offer before thee for all members of thy holy Church, that every member of the same, in his vocation and ministry, may truly and godly serve thee; through our Lord and Savior Jesus Christ. Amen.

Here may be sung a Hymn or Anthem.

Authorized Intercessions and Thanksgivings may follow. Suitable texts will be found in "Prayers, Thanksgivings, and Litanies"(Prayer Book Studies 25).

Before the close of the Office one or both of the following may be used:

The General Thanksgiving

Minister and People

The second is: "Most Gracious God, who hast baptized us into the death of your Son our Savior Jesus Christ: Grant in thy mercy that we, being dead to sin, may be buried with him; that through the grave and gate of death, we may be raised up with him unto newness of life; through Jesus Christ our Lord. Amen."]

Almighty God, Father of all mercies,
we thine unworthy servants
do give thee most humble and hearty thanks
for all thy goodness and loving-kindness to us
and to all men.
We bless thee for our creation, preservation,
and all the blessings of this life;
but above all for thine inestimable love
in the redemption of the world by our Lord Jesus Christ;
for the means of grace, and for the hope of glory.
And, we beseech thee,
give us that due sense of all thy mercies,
that our hearts may be unfeignedly thankful;
and that we show forth thy praise,
not only with our lips, but in our lives,
by giving up our selves to thy service,
and by walking before thee
in holiness and righteousness all our days;
through Jesus Christ our Lord,
to whom, with thee and the Holy Spirit,
be all honor and glory, world without end. Amen.

A Prayer of St. Chrysostom

   Minister and People

Almighty God,
who hast given us grace at this time with one accord
to make our common supplications unto thee;
and dost promise, through thy well-beloved Son,
that when two or three shall agree in his Name
thou wilt grant their requests:
Fulfill now, O Lord,
the desires and petitions of thy servants,
as may be best for them;
Granting us in this world knowledge of thy truth,
and in the world to come life everlasting;
Through the same thy Son, Jesus Christ our Lord. Amen.

   Then may be said

Let us bless the Lord.
Thanks be to God.

From Easter Day through the Day of Pentecost, "Alleluia, alleluia" may be added to the preceding Versicle and Response.

The Minister then concludes the Office with one of the following:

The grace of our Lord Jesus Christ, and the love of God, and the fellowship of the Holy Spirit, be with us all evermore. *Amen.* (2 Corinthians 13:4)

May the God of hope fill us with all joy and peace in believing through the power of the Holy Spirit. *Amen.* (Romans 15:13)

Glory to God whose power, working in us, can do infinitely more than we can ask or imagine: Glory to him from generation to generation, in the Church, and in Christ Jesus, for ever and ever. *Amen.* (Ephesians 3:20, 21)

Concerning the Service

In the Offices of Morning and Evening Prayer, the term "Minister" is used to denote the person, whether a clergyman or a lay person, leading the service.

The Proper Antiphons on pages 29-30 may be used as refrains with either of the Invitatory Psalms.

Antiphons drawn from the Psalms themselves, or from the opening Sentences given in the Offices, or from other passages of Scripture may be used with the Psalms and Biblical Canticles.

The Apostles' Creed is normally recited at both Morning and Evening Prayer on Sundays and other major Feasts (except when the Eucharist with its own Creed is to follow). It is desirable that the Creed be recited in at least one of the Offices on other days.

At celebrations of the Holy Eucharist, the Order for Morning or Evening Prayer may be used in place of all that precedes the Offertory, provided that a Lesson from the Gospel is always included and that the Intercession conforms to the directions on pages 44-45.

Additional Directions and Suggestions are on pages 43-45.

Second Order

The Minister begins the service with one or more of these Sentences of Scripture.

The Sentences in italics may be used as responses by the people or as separate Sentences.

The most frequently used Sentences are printed on page 27, facing the Confession of Sin.

Advent Season
In the wilderness prepare the way of the Lord: make straight in the desert a highway for our God.
The glory of the Lord shall be revealed, and all flesh shall see it together. (Isaiah 40:3, 5)

Rejoice: the Lord is at hand. (Philippians 4:5)
Amen, Come, Lord Jesus. (Revelation 22:20)

Christmas Season
Behold, I bring good news of great joy which will come to all the people: for to you is born in the city of David a Savior, who is Christ the Lord. (Luke 2:10, 11)
Glory to God in the highest and on earth peace among men. (Luke 2:14)

Behold, the dwelling of God is with men. He will dwell with them, and they shall be his people:
God himself shall be with them, and be their God. (Revelation 21:3)

Epiphany Season
I will give you as a light to the nations, that my salvation may reach to the end of the earth. (Isaiah 49:6)
Nations shall come to your light, and kings to the brightness of your rising. (Isaiah 60:3)

If we walk in the light, as he is in the light, we have fellowship with one another:
And the blood of Jesus his Son cleanses us from all sin. (1 John 1:7)

Lent and Holy Week
Jesus said, If any man would come after me, let him deny himself and take up his cross and follow me.
For whoever would save his life will lose it; and whoever loses his life for my sake and the gospel's will save it. (Mark 8:34, 35)

All we like sheep have gone astray; we have turned every one to his own way;
And the Lord has laid on him the iniquity of us all. (Isaiah 53:6)

Easter Season Including Ascension Day and the Day of Pentecost
Alleluia! Christ is risen. (cf. Mark 16:6)
The Lord is risen indeed. Alleluia! (Luke 24:34)

Worthy is the Lamb who was slain, to receive power and wealth and wisdom and might and honor and glory and blessing.
To him who sits on the throne and to the Lamb be blessing and honor and glory and might for ever and ever. (Revelation 5:12, 13)
God's love has been poured into our hearts,
Through the Holy Spirit who has been given to us. (Romans 5:5)

All Saints and Other Festivals
Since we are surrounded by so great a cloud of witnesses, let us lay aside every weight, and sin which clings so closely,
And let us run with perseverance the race which is set before us, looking to Jesus, the pioneer and perfecter of our faith. (Hebrews 12:1, 2)

National Observances
Let the nations be glad and sing for joy;
For God judges the peoples with equity, and guides all the nations upon earth. (Psalm 67:4)

General Sentences
The Lord is in his holy temple:
Let all the earth keep silence before him. (Habakkuk 2:20)

Worship the Lord in the beauty of holiness;
Let the whole earth tremble before him. (Psalm 96:9)

God is spirit, and those who worship him must worship in spirit and truth. (John 4:24)
Let the words of my mouth and the meditation of my heart be acceptable in your sight, O Lord, my strength and my redeemer. (Psalm 19:14)

Morning
Grace to you and peace from God our Father and the Lord Jesus Christ. (Romans 1:7)
Thanks be to God who gives us the victory through our Lord Jesus Christ. (1 Corinthians 15:57)

Evening
Lord, I love the house in which you dwell, and the place where your glory abides. (Psalm 26:8)
Let my prayer be accounted in your sight as incense, the lifting up of my hands as the evening sacrifice. (Psalm 141:2)

Occasions of Thanksgiving
Give thanks to the Lord, and call upon his Name; make known his deeds among the peoples.
Sing to him, sing praises to him, and speak of all his marvelous works. (Psalm 105:1,2)

Penitential
Seek the Lord while he wills to be found; call upon him when he draws near. Let the wicked forsake his ways, and the evil man his thoughts;
And let him turn to the Lord, and he will have compassion, and to our God, for he will richly pardon. (Isaiah 55:6,7)

The following Confession of Sin, or the form on page 9 may then be said; or the Office may continue at once with "Lord, open our lips," all still standing.

CONFESSION OF SIN

Minister

Dear friends in Christ, here in the presence of Almighty God, let us kneel in silence, and with humble and obedient hearts confess our sins, so that we may obtain forgiveness by his infinite goodness and mercy.

Silence may be kept

Minister and People together, all kneeling

Most merciful God,
we confess that we have sinned against you
in thought, word, and deed:
we have not loved you with our whole heart;
we have not loved our neighbors as ourselves.
We pray you of your mercy
    forgive what we have been,
    amend what we are,
    direct what we shall be;
that we may delight in your will,
and walk in your ways,
through Jesus Christ our Lord. Amen.

The Priest alone stands and says

Almighty God have mercy on you, forgive you all your sins, through our Lord Jesus Christ; strengthen you in all goodness, and by the power of the Holy Spirit, keep you in eternal life. *Amen.*

A Deacon or Lay person using the preceding form remains kneeling, and substitutes "us" for "you".

The Psalter

All stand

Minister

Lord, open our lips.

People

And our mouth shall proclaim your praise.

Minister and People

Glory to the Father, and to the Son, and to the Holy Spirit: as in the beginning, so now, and for ever. Amen.

Except in Lent

Alleluia.

In the morning there follows, and in the evening there may follow, one of the Invitatory Psalms, Venite or Jubilate.

In the seasons and on the days named, one of the following Antiphons may be sung or said with the Invitatory Psalm:

In Advent
Our King and Savior now draws near: Come let us adore him. Alleluia.

In Christmas Season
Unto us a child is born: Come let us adore him. Alleluia.

In the Epiphany Season and on Transfiguration
The Lord has shown forth his glory: Come let us adore him. Alleluia.

In Easter Season
Alleluia. The Lord is risen indeed: Come let us adore him. Alleluia.

On Ascension Day
Alleluia. Christ the Lord is ascended to heaven: Come let us adore him. Alleluia.

On the Day of Pentecost
Alleluia. The Spirit of the Lord renews the face of the earth: Come let us adore him. Alleluia.

On Trinity Sunday
Father, Son, and Holy Spirit, one God: holy is his Name: Come let us adore him. Alleluia.

In Easter Season, the Alleluia in parentheses is added. In Lent, both Alleluias are omitted.

On Feasts of the Incarnation
(Alleluia.) The Word was made flesh and dwelt among us: Come let us adore him. Alleluia.

On Other Festivals
(Alleluia.) The Lord is glorious in his saints: Come let us adore him. Alleluia.

VENITE (Psalm 95:1 - 7)

Come, let us sing to the Lord;
    let us shout for joy to the Rock of our salvation.
Let us come before his presence with thanksgiving, and raise a loud shout to him with psalms.

For the Lord is a great God,
    and a great King above all gods.
In his hand are the caverns of the earth,
    and the heights of the hills are his also.
The sea is his, for he made it,
    and his hands have molded the dry land.

Come, let us bow down, and bend the knee,
    and kneel before the Lord our Maker.
For he is our God, and we are the people of his pasture,
and the sheep of his hand.
    Oh, that today you would hearken to his voice!

JUBILATE (Psalm 100)

Be joyful in the Lord, all you lands;
    serve the Lord with gladness,
    and come before his presence with a song.

Know this: The Lord himself is God;
> he himself has made us, and we are his;
> we are his people and the sheep of his pasture.

Enter his gates with thanksgiving;
go into his courts with praise;
> give thanks to him and call upon his Name.

For the Lord is good;
his mercy is everlasting;
> and his faithfulness endures from age to age.

> *In the evening, for the Invitatory, the Hymn "O Gracious Light" may be used.*

O GRACIOUS LIGHT — Phos hilaron

O gracious light,
pure brightness of the everliving Father in heaven,
O Jesus Christ, holy and blessed!

Now as we come to the setting of the sun,
and our eyes behold the vesper light,
we sing your praises, O God: Father, Son, and Holy Spirit.

You are worthy at all times to be praised by happy voices,
O Son of God, O Giver of life,
and to be glorified through all the worlds.

> *During Easter Season, the Canticle "Christ Our Passover" may be used for the Invitatory both in the morning and in the evening.*

CHRIST OUR PASSOVER
(1 Corinthians 5:7 - 8; Romans 6:9 - 11; 1 Corinthians 15:20 - 22)

Alleluia. Alleluia.
Christ our Passover has been sacrificed for us;
> therefore let us celebrate the feast,
Not with the old leaven, the leaven of malice and evil,
> but with the unleavened bread of sincerity and truth.
> Alleluia.

Christ being raised from the dead will never die again;
> death no longer has dominion over him.
The death that he died, he died to sin, once for all;
> but the life he lives, he lives to God.

So also consider yourselves dead to sin,
> and alive to God in Jesus Christ our Lord.
> Alleluia.

Christ has been raised from the dead,
> the first fruits of those who have fallen asleep.

For since by a man came death,
> by a man has come also the resurrection of the dead.

For as in Adam all die,
> so also in Christ shall all be made alive.
> Alleluia.

Then follows the

PSALM OR PSALMS APPOINTED

At the end of the Psalms is sung or said:

Glory to the Father, and to the Son, and to the Holy Spirit:
> as in the beginning, so now, and for ever. Amen.

The Word of God

> *Then is read a selection from the Old Testament and a selection from the New Testament. [See pages 43-44 for forms of announcing Readings]*
> *1. Silence may be kept after each reading;*
> *2. One of the readings may be omitted;*
> *3. A Canticle from those which follow may be sung or said after each reading; but there is always one at the conclusion of the Scripture.*

Canticles for Use after Readings

1

THE FIRST SONG OF ISAIAH—Ecce, Deus (*Isaiah 12:2 - 6*)

Surely, it is God who saves me;
> I will trust in him and not be afraid.

For the Lord is my stronghold and my sure defense,
> and he will be my Savior.

Therefore you shall draw water with rejoicing
> from the springs of salvation.

And on that day you shall say,
> Give thanks to the Lord, and call upon his Name;

Make his deeds known among the peoples;
see that they remember that his Name is exalted.

Sing the praises of the Lord, for he has done great things,
    and this is known in all the world.
Cry aloud, ring out your joy, inhabitants of Zion,
    for the great one in the midst of you
    is the Holy One of Israel.
Glory to the Father, and to the Son, and to the Holy Spirit:
    as in the beginning, so now, and for ever. Amen.

2

THE SECOND SONG OF ISAIAH—Quaerite Dominum
(*Isaiah 55:6 - 11*)

The Second Song of Isaiah is suggested for use on Fridays, and in the Season of Lent.

Seek the Lord while he wills to be found;
    call upon him when he draws near.
Let the wicked forsake his way,
    and the evil man his thoughts;
And let him turn to the Lord, and he will have compassion,
    and to our God, for he will richly pardon.
For my thoughts are not your thoughts,
    not your ways my ways, says the Lord.
For as the heavens are higher than the earth,
    so are my ways higher than your ways,
    and my thoughts than your thoughts.
For as rain and snow fall from the heavens,
    and return not again, but water the earth,
Bringing forth life, and giving growth,
    seed for sowing and bread for eating,
So is my word that goes forth from my mouth:
    it will not return to me empty;
But it will accomplish that which I have purposed,
    and prosper in that for which I sent it.
Glory to the Father, and to the Son, and to the Holy Spirit:
    as in the beginning, so now, and for ever. Amen.

3

THE SONG OF THE THREE YOUNG MEN
Benedictus es, Domine
(*verses 29 - 34*)

Lord God of our fathers, you are blest and adored,
    praised and exalted above all for ever.
For the glory of your holy Name you are blest and adored,
    praised and exalted above all for ever.
In the splendor of your Temple you are blest and adored,
    praised and exalted above all for ever.
On the throne of your majesty you are blest and adored,
    praised and exalted above all for ever.
Throned upon Cherubim, plumbing the depths,
you are blest and adored,
    praised and exalted above all for ever.
In the high vault of heaven you are blest and adored,
    praised and exalted above all for ever.
Father, Son, and Holy Spirit, you are blest and adored,
    praised and exalted above all for ever.

4

A SONG OF CREATION
Benedicite, omnia opera Domini
(*Song of the Three Young Men: verses 35-65*)

Let all the works of the Lord celebrate the Lord,
    praise him and exalt him above all for ever.
You angels of the Lord, celebrate the Lord,
    praise him and exalt him above all for ever.

You heavens and all waters above the heavens, celebrate the Lord;
All powers—sun and moon, stars of the sky—celebrate the Lord;
    praise him and exalt him above all for ever.

Each shower of rain and fall of dew, celebrate the Lord;
All winds, and fire and heat, celebrate the Lord;
    praise him and exalt him above all for ever.

Chill and cold, drops of dew and flakes of snow, celebrate the Lord;
Frost and cold, ice and sleet, celebrate the Lord;
    praise him and exalt him above all for ever.

Nights and days, light and darkness, celebrate the Lord;
Storm clouds and thunderbolts, celebrate the Lord;
>   praise him and exalt him above all for ever.

Let the earth celebrate the Lord;
Mountains and hills and all that grows upon the earth, celebrate the Lord;
>   praise him and exalt him above all for ever.

O springs of water, seas and streams, celebrate the Lord;
O whales, and all that move in the waters, celebrate the Lord;
>   praise him and exalt him above all for ever.

All birds of the air, celebrate the Lord;
Cattle and wild animals, and sons of men, celebrate the Lord;
>   praise him and exalt him above all for ever.

Let Israel celebrate the Lord;
O priests and servants of the Lord, celebrate the Lord;
>   praise him and exalt him above all for ever.

O spirits and souls of the righteous, celebrate the Lord;
>   praise him and exalt him above all for ever.
O holy and humble-hearted men, celebrate the Lord;
>   praise him and exalt him above all for ever.

Let us celebrate the Father and the Son and the Holy Spirit;
>   let us praise him and exalt him above all for ever.

5

THE SONG OF MARY —Magnificat
(*Luke 1:46 - 55*)

My soul proclaims the greatness of the Lord,
>   my spirit rejoices in God my Savior;
for he has looked with favor on his lowly servant,
>   and from this day all generations will call me blessed.
The Almighty has done great things for me:
>   holy is his Name.
He has mercy on those who fear him
>   in every generation.
He has shown the strength of his arm,
>   he has scattered the proud in their conceit.
He has cast down the mighty from their thrones,
>   and has lifted up the lowly.

He has filled the hungry with good things,
> and sent the rich away empty-handed.
He has come to the help of his servant Israel,
> for he remembered his promise of mercy,
the promise he made to our fathers,
> to Abraham and his children for ever.
Glory to the Father, and to the Son, and to the Holy Spirit:
> as in the beginning, so now, and for ever. Amen.

6

THE SONG OF ZECHARIAH —Benedictus (*Luke 1:68 - 79*)

Blessed be the Lord, the God of Israel;
> he has come to his people and set them free.
He has raised up for us a mighty savior,
> born of the house of his servant David.
Through his holy prophets he promised of old,
that he would save us from our enemies,
> from the hands of all who hate us.

He promised to show mercy to our fathers
> and to remember his holy covenant.
This was the oath he swore to our father Abraham,
> to set us free from our enemies' hand,
free to worship him without fear,
> holy and righteous in his sight
> all the days of our life.

And you, my child, shall be called the prophet of the Most High,
> for you will go before the Lord to prepare his way,
to give his people knowledge of salvation
> by forgiveness of their sins.
In the tender compassion of our God
> the dawn from on high shall break upon us,
to shine on those who dwell in darkness and the shadow of death,
> and to guide our feet on the road to peace.
Glory to the Father, and to the Son, and to the Holy Spirit:
> as in the beginning, so now, and for ever. Amen.

7

THE SONG OF SIMEON —Nunc dimittis
(*Luke 2:29 32*)

Lord, you have fulfilled your word;
    now let your servant depart in peace.
With my own eyes I have seen the salvation,
    which you have prepared in the sight of every people:
A Light to reveal you to the nations,
    and the glory of your people Israel.
Glory to the Father, and to the Son, and to the Holy Spirit:
    as in the beginning, so now, and for ever. Amen.

8

A SONG TO THE LAMB —Dignus es (Revelation 4:11; 5:9 - 10, 13)

Splendor and honor and kingly power
are yours by right, O Lord our God,
    for you created everything that is,
    and by your will they were created and have their being.
And yours by right, O Lamb that was slain,
for with your Blood you have redeemed for God,
    from every family, language, people, and nation,
    a kingdom of priests to serve our God.

And so, to him who sits upon the throne,
and to Christ the Lamb,
    be worship and praise, dominion and splendor,
    for ever, and for evermore.

9

THE SONG OF THE REDEEMED—Magna et mirabilia (*Revelation 15:3 - 4*)

O ruler of the universe, Lord God,
    great deeds are they that you have done,
    surpassing human understanding.
Your ways are of righteousness and truth,
    O King of all the ages.
Who can fail to do you homage, Lord,
    and sing the praises of your Name?
    for you only are the holy One.

All nations will draw near, and fall down before you,
> because your just and holy works have been revealed.

10

GLORY TO GOD—Gloria in excelsis

Glory to God in the highest,
> and peace to his people on earth.
Lord God, heavenly King,
almighty God and Father,
> we worship you, we give you thanks,
> we praise you for your glory.

Lord Jesus Christ, only Son of the Father,
Lord God, Lamb of God,
you take away the sin of the world:
> have mercy on us;
you are seated at the right hand of the Father:
> receive our prayer.

For you alone are the Holy One,
you alone are the Lord,
you alone are the Most High,
> Jesus Christ,
> with the Holy Spirit,
> in the glory of God the Father. Amen.

11

YOU ARE GOD —Te Deum laudamus

You are God: we praise you;
You are the Lord: we acclaim you;
You are the eternal Father:
All creation worships you.
To you all angels, all the powers of heaven,
Cherubim and Seraphim, sing in endless praise:
> Holy, holy, holy Lord, God of power and might,
> heaven and earth are full of your glory.
The glorious company of apostles praise you.
The noble fellowship of prophets praise you.
The white-robed army of martyrs praise you.

Throughout the world the holy Church acclaims you:
    Father, of majesty unbounded,
    your true and only Son, worthy of all worship,
    and the Holy Spirit, Advocate and Guide.
You, Christ, are the king of glory,
eternal Son of the Father.
When you became man to set us free
you did not disdain the Virgin's womb.
You overcame the sting of death
and opened the Kingdom of heaven to all believers.
You are seated at God's right hand in glory.
We believe that you will come and be our judge.
    Come then, Lord, sustain your people,
    bought with the price of your own blood,
    and bring us with your saints
    to glory everlasting.

Here, or in one of the other places appointed, may follow a SERMON OR MEDITATION

THE APOSTLES' CREED

Minister and People together, all standing

I believe in God, the Father almighty,
    creator of heaven and earth.
I believe in Jesus Christ, his only Son, our Lord.
    He was conceived by the power of the Holy Spirit
        and born of the Virgin Mary.
    He suffered under Pontius Pilate,
        was crucified, died, and was buried.
    He descended to the dead.
    On the third day he rose again.
    He ascended into heaven,
        and is seated at the right hand of the Father.
    He will come again to judge the living and the dead.
I believe in the Holy Spirit,
    the holy catholic Church,
    the communion of saints,
    the forgiveness of sins,
    the resurrection of the body,
    and the life everlasting.

The Prayers

The prayers follow, the People standing or kneeling.

Minister   The Lord be with you.
People   And also with you.
Minister   Let us pray.

Minister and People

Our Father, who art in heaven,
  hallowed be thy Name,
  thy kingdom come,
  thy will be done,
    on earth as it is in heaven.
Give us this day our daily bread.
And forgive us our trespasses,
  as we forgive those
    who trespass against us.
And lead us not into temptation,
  but deliver us from evil.
For thine is the kingdom,
  and the power, and the glory,
  for ever and ever. Amen.
	Our Father in heaven,
	  holy be your Name,
	  your kingdom come,
	  your will be done,
	    on earth as in heaven.
	Give us today our daily bread.
	Forgive us our sins
	  as we forgive
	    those who sin against us.
	Do not bring us to the test
	  but deliver us from evil.
	For the kingdom, the power,
	  and the glory are yours,
	now and for ever. Amen.

Then follows one of these sets of Suffrages:

A

V. Show us your mercy, O Lord:
R. And grant us your salvation.
V. Clothe your ministers with righteousness:
R. Let your people sing with joy.
V. Give peace, O Lord, in all the world:
R. For only in you can we live in safety.
V. Lord, keep this nation under your care:
R. And guide us in the way of justice and truth.
V. Let your way be known upon earth:
R. Your saving health among all nations.
V. Let not the needy, O Lord, be forgotten:
R. Nor the hope of the poor be taken away.
V. Create in us clean hearts, O God:
R. And sustain us with your Holy Spirit.

B

V. Save your people, Lord, and bless your inheritance:
R. Govern and uphold them, now and always.
V. Day by day we bless you.
R. We praise your Name for ever.
V. Lord, keep us from all sin today.
R. Have mercy on us, Lord, have mercy.
V. Lord, show us your love and mercy;
R. For we put our trust in you.
V. In you; Lord, is our hope:
R. May we never be confounded.

The Minister then says

THE COLLECT OF THE DAY

On Fridays and Saturdays, not being Holy Days, the Collect for Good Friday and Holy Saturday, respectively, may be used instead.

In the morning, one of the following is then said

Heavenly Father, in you we live and move and have our being: We humbly pray you so to guide and govern us by your Holy Spirit, that in all the cares and occupations of our life we may not forget you, but remember that we are ever walking in your sight; through Jesus Christ our Lord. *Amen.*

Lord God, almighty and everlasting Father, you have brought us in safety to this new day: Preserve us with your might power, that we may not fall into sin, nor be overcome in adversity; and in all we do, direct us to the fulfilling of your purpose; through Jesus Christ our Lord. *Amen.*

In the evening is said

Most holy God, the source of all good desires, all right judgments, and all just works: Give to us, your servants, that peace which the world cannot give, so that our minds may be fixed on the doing of your will, and that we, being delivered from the fear of enemies, may live in peace and quietness; through the mercies of Christ Jesus our Savior. *Amen.*

The following Collect is always added, both in the morning and in the evening.

Almighty and everlasting God, by whose Spirit the whole company of your faithful people is governed and sanctified: Receive our prayers which we now offer before you for all members of your holy Church, that in their vocation and ministry they may truly and devoutly serve you, to the glory of your Name; through ourLordand Savior Jesus Christ. Amen.

Here may be sung a Hymn or Anthem.

Authorized Intercessions and Thanksgivings may follow. Suitable texts will be found in "Prayers, Thanksgivings, and Litanies" [Prayer Book Studies 25].

Before the close of the Office one or both of the following may be used:

The General Thanksgiving

Minister and People

Almighty God, Father of all mercies,
we your unworthy servants give you humble thanks
for all your goodness and loving-kindness to us
and to all men.
We bless you for our creation, preservation,
and all the blessings of this life;
but above all for your incomparable love
in the redemption of the world by our Lord Jesus Christ;
for the means of grace, and for the hope of glory.
And, we pray, give us such an awareness of your mercies,
that with truly thankful hearts
we may make known your praise,
not only with our lips, but in our lives,
by giving up our selves to your service,
and by walking before you in holiness and righteousness
all our days;
through Jesus Christ our Lord,
to whom, with you and the Holy Spirit,
be all honor and glory throughout all ages. Amen.

A Prayer of St. Chrysostom

Minister and People

Almighty God,
by your grace we have come together at this time
to offer you our common petitions;
and you have promised by your Son Jesus Christ
that when two or three are gathered in his Name
he will be in the midst of them.

Fulfill now, O Lord, our desires and petitions,
as may be best for us;
granting us in this world knowledge of your truth,
and in the world to come life everlasting;
through your Son, Jesus Christ our Lord. Amen.

> *Then may be said*

Let us bless the Lord.
Thanks be to God.

> *From Easter Day through the Day of Pentecost, "Alleluia, alleluia" may be added to the preceding Versicle and Response.*

> *The Minister then concludes the Office with one of the following:*

The grace of our Lord Jesus Christ, and the love of God, and the fellowship of the Holy Spirit, be with us all evermore. *Amen.* (2 Corinthians 13:4)

May the God of hope fill us with all joy and peace in believing through the power of the Holy Spirit. *Amen.* (Romans 15:13)

Glory to God whose power, working in us, can do infinitely more than we can ask or imagine: Glory to him from generation to generation, in the Church, and in Christ Jesus, for ever and ever. *Amen.* (Ephesians 3:20, 21)

Additional Directions and Suggestions

Any of the opening Sentences of Scripture, including those listed for specific Seasons or Days, may be used at any time according to the discretion of the Minister.

A metrical version of the Invitatory Psalm "Jubilate" will be found in The Hymnal 1940, number 278.

Metrical versions of the Hymn "O Gracious Light" will be found at numbers 173 and 176. Other versions of it may also be used.

The Psalms and Readings to be used at the Office, together with directions for their use, will be found on pages 55-99 of this book.

Gloria Patri is always sung or said at the conclusion of the entire portion of the Psalter, and may be used after each Psalm, and after each section of Psalm 119.

Readings are announced in one of the following forms (the titles are given by way of illustration):

Old Testament:

The (First) Reading is from . . .
. . . the book of Genesis

... the first Book of Kings
... the Book of the prophet Amos

New Testament: The (Second) Reading is from ...
... The Gospel according to Matthew
... The Acts of the Apostles
... The Epistle of Paul to the Romans
... The Epistle to the Hebrews
... The first Epistle of Peter
... The Revelation of John

>Or, except in the case of Readings from the Apocrypha,
>Hear the Word of God from ...

At the end of each Reading may be said: Here ends the Reading.

One or two versions of each of the Canticles to be used after Readings are providedin the Orders of Service. Other translations may be used when they are associated with particular musical settings.

The following form of the Gloria Patri may be used with contemporary settings of the Canticles:

>Glory to the Father, and the Son, and the Holy Spirit: as in the beginning, so now, and for ever. Amen.

In musical settings of Canticle 4 (Benedicite), the grouping of verses and the frequency of the refrain are at the discretion of the composer or musical editor.

A metrical version of Canticle 9 (Magna et mirabilia) will be found in The Hymnal 1940, number 260.

In special circumstances, in place of a Canticle, a Hymn may be sung.

The Sermon or Meditation is optional. One place for it is indicated in the text. Other appropriate places are

>After the Hymn or Anthem after
>The Prayers (the Lord's Prayer and Collects)
>After the Intercessions and Thanksgivings (see pages 23 and 42).
>After the Office

The Meditation may, on occasion, take the form of readings from non-Biblical Christian literature.

When Morning or Evening Prayer is used as the Ministry of the Word at the Eucharist, the Nicene Creed may take the place of the Apostles' Creed; and the Intercessions shall include prayer for

The Universal Church, its members, and its mission
The Nation and all in authority
The welfare of the world
The concerns of the local community
Those who suffer and those in any trouble
The departed (with commemoration of a saint when appropriate).

The forms of the Intercession given in *Services for Trial Use* (pages 93-112) are recommended.

When Communion is not to follow, an Offering may be received and presented at the time of the Hymn or Anthem which precedes the Intercessions and Thanksgivings; or immediately before the devotions which conclude the Office (see pages 23 and 42).

In the Intercessions and Thanksgivings, opportunity may be given for the members of the congregation to express intentions or objects of prayer and thanksgiving, either at the bidding, or in the course of the prayer; and opportunity may be given for silent prayer.

Orders of Service for Noonday and Close of Day

An Order of Service for Noonday or Other Times

Leader

Our help is in the Name of the Lord:

People

The maker of heaven and earth.

Leader and People

Glory to the Father, and to the Son, and to the Holy Spirit: as in the beginning, so now, and for ever. Amen.

Except in Lent Alleluia.

Then follows a Hymn or a Psalm, or both.
[Psalm 67 or a section of Psalm 119 is suggested.]

One of the following, or some other passage of Scripture, is then read:

To the king of ages, immortal, invisible, the only God, be honor and glory for ever and ever. (1 Timothy 1:17)

If anyone is in Christ he is a new creation; the old has passed away, behold, the new has come. All this is from God, who through Christ reconciled us to himself and gave us the ministry of reconciliation. (2 Corinthians 5:17-18)

From the rising of the sun to its going down, let the name of the Lord be praised! The Lord is high above all nations, and his glory above the heavens. (Psalm 113:3-4)

People   Thanks be to God.

A Meditation, silent or spoken, may follow.

The Leader then says to the People

The Lord be with you.

People

And also with you.

Leader

Let us pray.

Lord, have mercy.
Christ, have mercy.
Lord, have mercy.

Leader and People

Our Father, who art in heaven,
    hallowed be thy Name,
    thy kingdom come,
    thy will be done,
        on earth as it is in heaven.
Give us this day our daily bread.
And forgive us our trespasses,
    as we forgive those
        who trespass against us.
And lead us not into temptation,
    but deliver us from evil.
	Our Father in heaven,
	    holy be your Name,
	    your kingdom come,
	    your will be done,
	        on earth as in heaven.
	Give us today our daily bread.
	Forgive us our sins
	    as we forgive
	        those who sin against us.
	Do not bring us to the test
	    but deliver us from evil.

The Collect of the Day may then be said, and one or more of the following:

Blessed Savior, at this hour you hung upon upon the cross, stretching out your loving arms: Grant that all the peoples of the earth may look to you and be saved; for your mercies' sake. *Amen.*

Almighty Savior, who at noonday called your servant Saint Paul to be an apostle to the Gentiles: We pray you to illumine the world with the radiance of your glory, that all nations may come and worship you, who with the Father and the Holy Spirit live and reign, one God, for ever and ever. *Amen.*

Lord Jesus Christ, you said to your Apostles, "Peace I give to you; my own peace I leave with you": Regard not our sins, but the faith of your Church, and give to us the peace and unity of that heavenly city, where the Father and the Holy Spirit you live and reign, now and for ever. *Amen.*

Free intercessions may be offered.

The Service concludes as follows:

Leader

Let us praise the Lord.

Answer

Thanks be to God.

An Order of Service for the Close of Day (Compline)

When the people are assembled the Leader says

The Lord Almighty grant us a peaceful night and a perfect end. *Amen.*

Leader

Lord, you are in the midst of us, and we are called by your Name:

People

Do not forsake us, O Lord our God.

Leader

Be pleased, O Lord, to deliver us:

People

O Lord, make haste to help us.

Leader

Our help is in the Name of the Lord:

People

The maker of heaven and earth.

The Leader may then say

Let us ask God's pardon for our failures and shortcomings this day.

Silence may be kept for a time.

Leader and People

Almighty God, our heavenly Father:
We have sinned against you,
through our own fault,
in thought, and word, and deed,
and in what we have left undone.
For your Son our Lord Jesus Christ's sake,
forgive us all our offenses;
and giant that we may serve you
in newness of life,
to the glory of your Name. Amen.

Leader

May the Almighty God grant us forgiveness of all our sins, and the grace and comfort of the Holy Spirit. *Amen.*

The Leader and People then say together

Glory to the Father, and to the Son, and to the Holy Spirit: as in the beginning, so now, and for ever. Amen.

Except in Lent

Alleluia.

One or more of the following Psalms is then sung or said [for other suitable selections from the Psalter]:

Psalm 4

1 Answer me when I call, O God, defender of my cause;
 you set me at liberty when I am hard-pressed;
 have mercy on me, and hear my prayer.
2 O man, how long will you dishonor my Glory?
 how long will you worship dumb idols,

       and run after false gods?
3   Know that the Lord does wonders for him who is faithful:
       when I call upon the Lord, he will hear me.
4   Tremble, then, and do not sin;
       speak to your heart, in silence, upon your bed.
5   Offer the rightful sacrifices,
       and put your trust in the Lord.
6   Many are saying, "Oh, that we might see better times!"
       Lift up the light of your countenance upon us, O Lord.
7   You have put gladness in my heart,
       more than when grain and wine and oil increase.
8   I lie down in peace; at once I fall asleep;
       for you, Lord, only, make me dwell in safety.

From Psalm 33

1   Rejoice in the Lord, you righteous;
       to sing praises is becoming to the upright.
2   Praise the Lord with the harp;
       play to him upon the psaltery and lyre.
3   Sing for him a new song;
       sound a fanfare with all your skill upon the trumpet.
4   For the word of the Lord is right,
       and all his works are sure.
5   He loves righteousness and justice;
       the loving-kindness of the Lord fills the whole earth.
12   Happy is the nation whose God is the Lord!
       happy the people he has chosen to be his own!
13   The Lord looks down from heaven,
       and beholds all the children of men.
14   From where he sits enthroned he turns his gaze
       on all who dwell on the earth.
18   Behold, the eye of the Lord is upon those who fear him,
       on those who wait upon his love,
19   To pluck their lives from death,
       and to keep them in the time of dearth.
20   Our soul waits for the Lord;
       he is our help and our shield.
21   Indeed, our heart rejoices in him,
       for in his holy Name we put our trust.
22   Let your loving-kindness, O Lord, be upon us,
       as we have put our trust in you.

Psalm 134

1   Behold now, bless the Lord, all you servants of the Lord,
     you that stand by night in the house of the Lord.
2   Lift up your hands to the holy place, and bless the Lord.
     The Lord who made heaven and earth
     bless you out of Zion.

The following Psalms are also suggested: Psalms 31:1-5, 34, 77, 91

At the end of the Psalms is sung or said

Glory to the Father, and to the Son, and to the Holy Spirit:
as in the beginning, so now, and for ever. Amen.

One of the following, or some other short passage of Scripture, is then read.

Come to me, all who labor and are heavy-laden, and I will give you rest. Take my yoke upon you, and learn from me; for I am gentle and lowly in heart, and you will find rest for your souls. For my yoke is easy, and my burden is light. (Matthew 11:28-30)

May the God of peace who brought again from the dead our Lord Jesus, the great shepherd of the sheep, by the blood of the eternal covenant, equip you with everything good that you may do his will, working in you that which is pleasing in his sight, through Jesus Christ; to whom be glory for ever and ever. (Hebrews 13:20-21)

People

Thanks be to God.

A Hymn suitable for the evening may then be sung or said.

Then follows

V. Into your hands, O Lord, I commend my spirit:
R. For you have redeemed me, O Lord, 0 God of truth.
V. Keep us, O Lord, as the apple of your eye:
R. Hide us under the shadow of your wings.
V. Lord, hear our prayer:
R. And let our cry come to you.
V. Let us pray.

   Lord, have mercy.
   Christ, have mercy.
   Lord, have mercy.

Leader and People

Our Father, who art in heaven,	Our Father in heaven,
hallowed be thy Name,	holy be your Name,
thy kingdom come,	your kingdom come,
thy will be done,	your will be done,
on earth as it is in heaven.	on earth as in heaven.
Give us this day our daily bread.	Give us today our daily bread.
And forgive us our trespasses,	Forgive us our sins
as we forgive those	as we forgive
who trespass against us.	those who sin against us.
And lead us not into temptation,	Do not bring us to the test
but deliver us from evil.	but deliver us from evil.

Intercession may be offered in the following form:

Eternal God, to you, our heavenly Father, the darkness and the light are both alike, and the night is as clear as the day. We therefore pray you to be with those who watch and work throughout the night on behalf of others:

Here the Leader or members of the congregation may mention specific persons and occupations.

Grant them courage in danger, diligence in emergencies, and the presence of your Holy Spirit in the long and lonely hours. When we awake may we be thankful for their labors and take thought in turn for their needs: through Jesus Christ our ever-reigning Lord. *Amen.*

Silence may be kept; and free intercessions and thanksgivings may be offered.

One of the following Collects is then said:

Lighten our darkness, Lord, we pray; and in your mercy defend us from all the dangers of the night; for the love of your only Son, Jesus Christ. *Amen.*

Be present, O merciful God, and protect us through the hours of this night, so that we who are wearied by the changes and chances of this life may rest in your eternal changelessness; through Jesus Christ our Lord. *Amen.*

Look down, O Lord, from your heavenly throne, and illumine the darkness of this night with your celestial brightness; and from the children of light banish the deeds of darkness; through Jesus Christ our Lord. *Amen.*

The Service concludes with the Song of Simeon with this Antiphon, which is sung or said by all.

Antiphon

Guide us waking, O Lord, and guard us sleeping; that awake we may watch with Christ, and asleep we may rest in peace.

In Easter Season add

Alleluia, Alleluia, Alleluia.

Lord, you have fulfilled your word;
  now let your servant depart in peace.
With my own eyes I have seen the salvation,
  which you have prepared in the sight of every people;
A Light to reveal you to the nations,
  and the glory of your people Israel.

All repeat the Antiphon

Guide us waking, O Lord, and guard us sleeping; that awake we may watch with Christ, and asleep we may rest in peace.

In Easter Season add

Alleluia, Alleluia, Alleluia.

Leader

Let us praise the Lord.

People

Thanks be to God.

Leader

The almighty and merciful Lord, Father, Son, and Holy Spirit, bless us and keep us. Amen.

Daily Devotions for Individuals and Families

Concerning the Devotions

When more than one person is present, the devotions, except for the Reading, may be said in unison. Individuals may find it helpful, when possible, to say the devotions aloud.

The Readings may be taken from:

The Psalms or Readings for the day listed on pages 55-99 of this book

The Psalms or Lessons for the day listed in the Prayer Book Lectionary (pages x to xli)

The Lessons or Gospels for Sundays and Holy Days listed in *Services for Trial Use* (Pages 473-601)

The Lessons or Gospels for Sundays and Holy Days in the Book of Common Prayer (pages 90-269)

Some other manual of devotion which provides daily selections for the Church Year

In The Morning

An Act of Praise (Psalm 103:1-4, 22)

Bless the Lord, O my soul;
    and all that is within me, bless his holy Name.
Bless the Lord, O my soul;
    and forget not all his benefits.
He forgives all my sins,
    and heals all my infirmities;
He redeems my life from the grave,
    and crowns me with mercy and loving-kindness.
Bless the Lord, all you works of his,
    in all places of his dominion.
Bless the Lord, O my soul.

A Reading

followed, when possible, by silent meditation.

A Hymn or Canticle may follow.

The Apostles' Creed may be recited.

The Prayers

Heavenly Father, in you we live and move and have our being: We humbly pray you so to guide and govern us by your Holy Spirit, that in all the cares and occupations of our life we may not forget you, but remember that we are ever walking in your sight; through Jesus Christ our Lord. *Amen.*

Remember today, O Lord, especially . . .

[Here may be mentioned names and particular concerns]

We ask this in the Name of Jesus Christ. Amen.

The Lord's Prayer

At Noon

An Act of Recollection

O God, you will keep him in perfect peace,
>   whose mind is steadfast in you;
For in returning and rest we shall be saved;
>   in quietness and trust shall be our strength.
>   (Isaiah 26:3, 30:15)

The Reading

From the rising of the sun to its going down, let the Name of the Lord be praised! The Lord is high above all nations, and his glory above the heavens. (Psalm 113:3-4)

The Prayers

Either or both of the following:

Blessed Savior, at this hour you hung upon the cross, stretching out your loving arms: Grant that all the peoples of the earth may look to you and be saved; for your mercies' sake. *Amen.*

Lord Jesus Christ, you said to your Apostles, "Peace I give to you; my own peace I leave with you": Regard not our sins, but the faith of your Church, and give to us the peace and unity of that heavenly city, where with the Father and the Holy Spirit you live and reign, now and for ever. *Amen.*

Other prayers may be added.

The Lord's Prayer

At The Close Of Day

An Act of Praise (Psalm 67:1-3)

God be merciful to us, and bless us;
>   show us the light of his countenance, and come to us.
Let your ways be known upon earth,
>   your saving health among all nations.
Let the peoples praise you, O God;
>   let all the peoples praise you.

A Reading

Followed, when possible, by silent meditation.

The Song of Simeon may be said:
Lord, you have fulfilled your word;
> now let your servant depart in peace.
With my own eyes I have seen the salvation,
> which you have prepared in the sight of every people.
A Light to reveal you to the nations,
> and the glory of your people Israel.

The Prayers
Most holy God, the source of all good desires, all right judgments, and all just works: Give to us, your servants, that peace which the world cannot give, so that our minds may be fixed on the doing of your will; and that we, being delivered from the fear of enemies, may live in peace and quietness; through the mercies of Christ Jesus our Savior. *Amen.*

> *Other prayers may be added. Those from the Service for the Close of Day are suggested [page 51].*

> *The Lord's Prayer*

Conclusion
Let me lie down and sleep in peace, O Lord; for you, Lord, only, make me dwell in safety.

Lectionary for the Daily Office

Concerning the Lectionary[ii]

The Lectionary for the Daily Office is arranged in a two-year cycle. Year One begins on the First Sunday of Advent preceding odd-numbered years, and Year Two begins on the First Sunday of Advent preceding even-numbered years. (Thus, on the First Sunday of Advent, 1973, the Lectionary for Year Two is begun.)

Sundays

On Sundays, the Psalms and Readings for the current year are used at Morning Prayer, and those of the alternate year at Evening Prayer.

[ii] [Ed. note: The lectionary presented here is very similar to what is printed in the 1979 Book of Common Prayer. The two largest differences both appear in the Season After Pentecost. First, the weeks are identified specifically as "Week of X Pentecost" in this lectionary; in the '79 Lectionary, they are identified by Propers which do not shift from year to year with the date of Easter. Second, the Post-Pentecost readings appointed for Year One are shifted to Year Two in the '79 Lectionary and vice-versa. There are a number of less important differences which are beyond the scope of this note.]

On all Sundays, however, and on major Holy Days, the Psalms and Lessons appointed for the Eucharist may be substituted for those cited in the following tables. If desired, all three Eucharistic lections may be read at the Office. One or both of the Psalms appointed for the Eucharist may be used, and when only selected verses are cited in the Proper, the entire Psalm, or a longer portion of the Psalm, may be used.

Holy Days

Three Readings are provided for use at the Office on each of the fixed Holy Days, two of which may be used in the morning and one in the evening. If, however, the Office is read only once in the day, all three Readings may be used. In the citations of the Psalms, those for morning are given first, and then—after the slash—those for the evening.

Proper Psalms and Readings are also provided for the Eves of the major Feasts of the Lord.

Weekdays

Three Readings are provided for each weekday in each of the two years. Two of the Readings may be used in the morning and one in the evening, or, if the Office is read only once in the day, all three Readings may be used. When the Office is read twice in the day, it is suggested that the Gospel Reading be used in the evening in Year One, and in the morning in Year Two. If two Readings are desired at both Offices, the Old Testament Reading for the alternate year is used as the First Reading at Evening Prayer.

As in the Table for Holy Days, morning Psalms are separated from evening Psalms by a slash. At the discretion of the Minister, however, any of the Psalms appointed for a given day may be used in the morning or in the evening. Likewise, Psalms appointed for any weekday may be used on any other weekday in the same week, except on major Holy Days.

On weekdays (except in the weeks from 4 Advent to 1 Epiphany, Palm Sunday to 2 Easter, and in the weeks of 6 Easter and Pentecost), the Psalms are arranged in an eight-week pattern which recurs throughout the year, except for appropriate variations in Lent and Easter Season. Brackets and parentheses are used

[ ] in the case of whole Psalms
( ) in the case of verses

to indicate Psalms and verses of Psalms which may be omitted. In some instances, the entire portion of the Psalter assigned to a given Office has been bracketed, and alternative Psalmody suggested. Those who desire to recite the Psalter in its entirety should, in each instance, use the bracketed Psalms rather than the alternatives.

In individual recitation of the Office, other arrangements of the Psalter for daily use may be followed.

Special Occasions
On Special Occasions, the Minister may select such Psalms and Readings as may be suitable. (For suggestions, see the Prayer Book, pages ix and xlii, and *Services for Trial Use*, pages 612-639.)[iii]

Notes
The verse numbering of Psalms in these tables is that of *The Prayer Book Psalter Revised*, which in many instances is not identical to the numeration in *The Book of Common Prayer*. In the Psalm citations for Sundays, however, the Prayer Book verses are shown in brackets.

Antiphons drawn from the Psalms themselves, or from the opening Sentences given in the Office, or from other passages of Scripture may be used with the Psalms and Biblical Canticles. The antiphons may be sung or said at the beginning and end of each Psalm or Canticle, or may be used as refrains after each verse or group of verses.

The First Readings in these tables include passages from the Apocrypha and from the Acts of the Apostles.

Any Reading may be lengthened or shortened at the discretion of the Minister.

Office Lectionary for Sundays

YEAR ONE	YEAR TWO
First Sunday Of Advent	
Psalm 82	Psalm 1
Malachi 3:1-6; 4:4-6	Isaiah 55
Luke 1:5-25	Luke 12:35-43
Second Sunday Of Advent	
Psalm 9	Psalm 63
Amos 7:4-15	Isaiah 62:6-12
Luke 1:57-80	Matthew 9:35-10:7

[iii] [Ed. note: The three page locations mentioned in this line are as follows:

BCP page ix - This is the "Selections of Psalms" that provides 28 thematic collections of psalms starting with "God the Creator", "God the Redeemer", etc.

BCP page xlii - This is the "Psalms and Lessons for Special Occasions" that includes occasions like the Dedication of a Church and patronal festivals of various kinds.

STU pages 612-639 - This is the "Special Occasions" section containing 22 occasions starting wth "Of the Holy Trinity", "Of the Holy Spirit", "Of the Holy Angels", etc. that entered the 1979 BCP as "Various Occasions."

Third Sunday Of Advent
Psalm 98
Isaiah 65:17-25
Luke 1:39-56 or Philippians 4:4-9
Fourth Sunday Of Advent
Psalm 2
Wisdom 5:1-16
Luke 12:35-43

Psalm 99
Jeremiah 23:3-8
Revelation 22:6-17, 20

Psalm 113
Isaiah 6:1-8
Revelation 21:1-7

For Christmas Eve, Christmas Day, and the Holy Days following, see pages 68-69.

YEAR ONE

YEAR TWO

First Sunday After Christmas
Psalm 8
1 Samuel 1:1a, 2, 7b-28
Luke 2:22-40
Second Sunday After Christmas
Psalm 111
Isaiah 40:25-31
Hebrews 1:1-12

Psalm 147
Isaiah 49:7-13
Luke 4:16-21

Psalm 146
Jeremiah 31:7-14
John 9:1-3, 6-21, 24-25, 33-38

For the Eve and Feast of Epiphany, see page 70

First Sunday After The Epiphany
Psalm 102:15-27 (16-28 BCP)
Isaiah 41:1-10
Mark 3:13-30
Second Sunday After The Epiphany
Psalm 22:22-30 (23-32 BCP)
Zechariah 8:1-8, 20-23
1 John 5:1-12
Third Sunday After The Epiphany
Psalm 33
1 Kings 18:21-39
Matthew 10:1-15
Fourth Sunday After The Epiphany
Psalm 119:1-16
Jeremiah 26:1-13
2 Timothy 2:8-15
Fifth Sunday After The Epiphany
Psalm 126
Isaiah 60:15-22
John 8:12-20
Sixth Sunday After The Epiphany
Psalm 57
Jeremiah 14:2-9
Hebrews 12:18-29

Psalm 47
Ezekiel 2:1-7
Acts 1:15-26

Psalm 18:1-20
Ezekiel 39:21-29
Luke 19:1-10

Psalms 42, 43
Amos 2:6-8; 3:1-8
Acts 26:1, 9-18

Psalm 119:89-104
Isaiah 35
John 5:36-47

Psalm 112
Isaiah 60:1-9
Colossians 1:21-29

Psalm 31
Zechariah 10:6-12
Matthew 22:1-14

Seventh Sunday After The Epiphany
Psalm 25
1 Samuel 24:1-17
Matthew 18:21-35

Psalm 71
Hosea 11:1-9
1 Corinthians 13

Eighth Sunday After The Epiphany
Psalm 63
Deuteronomy 7:6-13
1 Corinthians 10:1-13

Psalm 62
Lamentations 3:22-33
Mark 9:14-29

Last Sunday After The Epiphany
Psalm 97
Ezekiel 1:3-5a, 22, 26-2:7
John 12:20-33

Psalm 84
Exodus 34:29-35
2 Peter 1:12-19

For Ash Wednesday, see page 75.

First Sunday In Lent
Psalm 119:17-32
2 Samuel 11:2-4a;
12:1-7, 9-10, 12-13a
Hebrews 2:14-18

Psalm 50
Numbers 13:25-14:4,
11-14, 19
Luke 22:1-34

Second Sunday In Lent
Psalm 32
Jonah 3:10-4:11
Ephesians 2:1-10

Psalm 56
Deuteronomy 6:1-13
Luke 10:25-37

Third Sunday In Lent
Psalm 51
1 Samuel 17:37-50
Mark 10:17-31

Psalm 142
1 Kings 21:1-20
Romans 7:14-25

Fourth Sunday In Lent
Psalm 78:12-39 (13-40 BCP)
Exodus 12:1-14a
1 Corinthians 10:16-17;
11:27-32"

Psalm 116
Exodus 17:1-7
John 6:27-40

Fifth Sunday In Lent
Psalm 27
Genesis 8:6-12, 15-16; 9:8-16
Luke 20:9-19

Psalm 34
2 Esdras 2:42-47
Philippians 3:8-14

Sunday of The Passion
Psalm 138
Isaiah 42:1-9
John 18:1-14, 19-23, 25-40;
19:1-16, 23-30

Psalm 23
Isaiah 52:13-53:12
For the second reading, use one of the Passion Gospels not read at the Eucharist that year

For Holy Week, see page 78

Easter Day
Psalm 118
Isaiah 12
Luke 24:13-35
or John 20:11-18

Psalm 111
Isaiah 51:9-16
John 20:1-9**
or John 20:11-18
or Luke 24:13-35

** *If not read at the Eucharist*

Second Sunday Of Easter
Psalm 30
2 Samuel 12:15b-23
John 14:1-14

Psalm 103
Exodus 14:5b-31
1 Corinthians 15:1-14, 20-22

Third Sunday Of Easter
Psalm 68:1-20
Ezekiel 39:21-29
Acts 2:36-47

Psalm 107:1-31 (1-32 BCP)
Exodus 15:1-18
John 6:4-14, 35

Fourth Sunday Of Easter
Psalm 145
Isaiah 43:1-7
1 Peter 5:1-11

Psalm 121
Jeremiah 25:1-9
Mark 6:30-44

Fifth Sunday Of Easter
Psalm 36
Isaiah 2:1-5
John 1:1-5, 10-14

Psalm 7
Proverbs 4:10-18
2 Corinthians 4:11-18

Sixth Sunday Of Easter
Psalm 119:65-80
Genesis 17:1-8
Revelation 7:9-17

Psalm 49
Ecclesiasticus 2:1-2, 6-18
Matthew 25:1-13

For the Eve and Feast of the Ascension, see page 82

Seventh Sunday Of Easter
Psalm 108
Daniel 7:9-14
Hebrews 4:14-5:10

Psalm 93
2 Kings 2:1-15
Ephesians 1:15-23

The Day Of Pentecost
Psalm 48
Isaiah 11:1-9
John 14:15-27

Psalm 104
Isaiah 44:1-8
Acts 4:18-21, 23-33

Trinity Sunday
Psalm 29
Job 38:1-7; 42:1-5
Revelation 19:5-16

Psalm 99
Genesis 1:1-2:3
John 1:1-18

Second Sunday After Pentecost
Psalm 85
Exodus 3:16-18a; 4:1-17
Matthew 26:1-13
Third Sunday After Pentecost
Psalm 130
2 Kings 5:1-15
1 Peter 2:1-10
Fourth Sunday After Pentecost
Psalm 96
1 Kings 22:1-23
Mark 14:53-64
Fifth Sunday After Pentecost
Psalm 146
Daniel 6:1-23

Acts 16:16-34
Sixth Sunday After Pentecost
Psalms,124, 125
2 Kings 4:8-37
Mark 4:35-5:20
Seventh Sunday After Pentecost
Psalm 89:1-18 (1-19 BCP)
Leviticus 19:1-2, 9-18
Romans 12:9-21
Eighth Sunday After Pentecost
Psalm 144
Ruth 2:1-13, 17-18, 20a
Acts 12:117
Ninth Sunday After Pentecost
Psalm 46
Daniel 5:1-9, 13-30
Mark 4:1-9, 14-20
Tenth Sunday After Pentecost
Psalm 119:33-48
Isaiah 30:15-21
1 Corinthians 4:2-10
Eleventh Sunday After Pentecost
Psalm 38
1 Kings 8:22-30
John 4:46-54

Psalm 92
1 Kings 3:4-15
Acts 17:1-15

Psalm 61
Genesis 32:3-13, 21; 33:1-4
John 16:12-24

Psalm 91
Amos 5:1-7, 10-15
Acts 26:1-8, 22-32

Psalm 73
Genesis 41:1-16, 25b-26,
   32-38, 41
Mark 9:14-27 (28-32)

Psalm 33
Deuteronomy 30:15-20
1 John 2:1-11

Psalm 15
Genesis 45:1-15
John 15: 1-17

Psalm 62
Exodus 13:1-3, 11-16, 21-22
Luke 9:1-17

Psalm 143
Exodus 6:1-13
1 Peter 3:8-15

Psalm 19
Proverbs 3:1-18
Matthew 5:1-12

Psalm 32
1 Samuel 28:3-25
2 Corinthians 12:1-10

Twelfth Sunday After Pentecost
Psalm 50
Genesis 32:22-31
Ephesians 6:10-20

Psalm 37:1-25 (1-24 BCP)
Amos 5:18-24
Luke 22:28-46

Thirteenth Sunday After Pentecost
Psalm 25
Wisdom 5:1-16
Mark 2:18-28

Psalm 86
Isaiah 57:14-21
1 Thessalonians 5:12-24

YEAR ONE

YEAR TWO

Fourteenth Sunday After Pentecost
Psalm 116
Jeremiah 3:12-18
Ephesians 2:11-22

Psalm 118
Isaiah 28:9-16
John 15:18-27

Fifteenth Sunday After Pentecost
Psalm 23
Isaiah 50:4-10
John 10:1-11

Psalm 80
Ezekiel 34:11-16, 30-31
1 Peter 2:19-25

Sixteenth Sunday After Pentecost
Psalm 100
Ezekiel 36:22-28
Acts 11:1-18

Psalm 138
Deuteronomy 30:1-10
Luke 14:15-24

Seventeenth Sunday After Pentecost
Psalm 36
Jeremiah 13:15-21
Luke 18:9-14

Psalm 75
Proverbs 16:18-24, 32
Philippians 2:3-13

Eighteenth Sunday After Pentecost
Psalm 3
Micah 6:1-4, 6-8
Titus 2:1-15

Psalm 4
Ecclesiasticus 38:1-14
Luke 15:11-32

Nineteenth Sunday After Pentecost
Psalm 1
Jeremiah 1:4-19
Luke 5:1-11

Psalm 43
Isaiah 6:1-8
Acts 9:1-19

Twentieth Sunday After Pentecost
Psalm 11
Genesis 37:2-35
Colossians 3:12-24

Psalm 48
Deuteronomy 10:12-15, 17-11:1
Matthew 5:1-16

Twenty-First Sunday After Pentecost
Psalm 10
2 Kings 5:19b-27
Matthew 19:16-30

Psalm 5
Wisdom 11:14-22
Galatians 5:16-24

Twenty-Second Sunday After Pentecost
Psalm 119:81-96
Genesis 45:16-20, 25-46:7
Romans 15:4-13

Psalm 38
Isaiah 40:1-11
Matthew 15:21-28

Twenty-Third Sunday After Pentecost
Psalm 33
Tobit 4:5-11, 16
Matthew 6:1-6, 16-21

Psalm 57
Hosea 14:1-9
Ephesians 4:25-5:10

Twenty-Fourth Sunday After Pentecost
Psalm 42
1 Samuel 18:1-16
Ephesians 5:1-14

Psalm 90
2 Samuel 9:1-13
Mark 9:33-50

Twenty-Fifth Sunday After Pentecost
Psalm 96
Genesis 41:1-16, 25b-26, 32-38, 41
Luke 24:36-47

Psalm 86
Daniel 3:1-30

Acts 26:1-5, 9, 12-29

**Twenty-Sixth Sunday After Pentecost
[Or Third Before Advent]**
Psalm 73
Jeremiah 32:6-10, 15-23, 26, 36-41
Acts 5:12a, 17-22, 25-39

Psalm 97
2 Kings 6:8-23

Matthew 10:16-28

**Twenty-Seventh Sunday After Pentecost
[Or Second Before Advent]**
Psalm 94
2 Esdras 8:63-9:13
John 3:13-21

Psalm 27
Jeremiah 17:5-14
1 John 3:9-18

Sunday Before Advent
Psalm 145
Ecclesiastes 11:9-12:8, 13-14
2 Corinthians 3:4-11

Psalm 138
Isaiah 25:1-9
Matthew 6:24-33

Office Lectionary for Fixed Holy Days

Years One and Two

The slash separates the Morning Psalms from the Evening Psalms.
Nov. 30, St. Andrew, 34 / 87
Isa. 49:1-6   1 Cor. 4:1-16   John 1:35-42
Dec. 21, St. Thomas, 120, 121 / 139:1-17v
Job 42:1-6   1 Peter 1:3-9   John 11:1-16

Jan. 18, Confession of St. Peter, 66, 67 / 30
Ezek. 34:12-16　　　　Acts 10:34-44　　　　　　Luke 5:1-11
Jan. 25, Conversion of St. Paul, 50, 18:21-33 / 119:41-56
Ecclus. 39:1-10　　　　2 Cor. 12:1-9　　　　　　Matt. 13:44-52
or Jer. 1:1-4
For Christmas Eve, Christmas Day, and the Holy Days following, see pages 68-69
Feb. 1, Eve of the Presentation --- / 134, 135:1-9, 13-21
1 Sam. 1:20-28a　　　　Heb. 10:1-10
Feb. 2, Presentation, 42,43 / 122, [123]
1 Sam. 2:1-10　　　　　Gal. 3:21-29　　　　　　John 8:31-36"
Feb. 24, St. Matthias, 33 / 80
1 Sam. 16:1-13　　　　 1 John 2:18-25　　　　　Matt. 7:15-21
Mar. 19, St. Joseph, 37 / 34
2 Chron. 6:12-17　　　　Eph. 3:14-21　　　　　　Matt. 1:18-25
Mar. 24, Eve of the Annunciation --- / 38
Gen. 3:8-15　　　　　　Gal. 4:1-7
Mar. 25, Annunciation, 8, 85 / 111
Isa. 52:7-12　　　　　　Heb. 2:5-10　　　　　　 John 1:9-14
Apr. 25, St. Mark, 145 / 96
Ecclus. 2:1-11　　　　　2 Tim. 4:1-11　　　　　　Mark 8:34-38
or Isa. 6
May 1, St. Philip & St. James, 27 / 119:137-152
Job 23:1-12　　　　　　Acts 1:10-14　　　　　　 John 12:20-26
May 30, Eve of the Visitation --- / 62
Isa. 11:1-10　　　　　　Heb. 2:11-17
May 31, Visitation, 72 / 63:1-8
1 Sam. 1:1-20　　　　　Heb. 3:1-6　　　　　　　John 3:25-30
June 11, St. Barnahas, 100, 101 / 15
Isa. 58:1-8　　　　　　 Acts 4:32-37　　　　　　 Matt. 5:13-20
June 23, Eve of St. John Baptist --- / 20, 21:1-7
Ecclus. 48:1-10　　　　 John 3:22-30
June 24, St. John Baptist, 103 / 80
Mal. 4　　　　　　　　 1 Thess. 5:1-9　　　　　　Matt. 11:2-19
June 29, St. Peter & St. Paul, 66, 71 / 97
Ezek. 2:1-7　　　　　　Gal. 2;1-9　　　　　　　 Matt. 10:24-39
or Acts 5:12-33
July 4, Independence Day, 33 / 107 or 77
Deut. 10:12-22　　　　 Rom. 8:14-23　　　　　　John 8:31-36
July 22, St. Mary Magdalene, 30 / 57
Zeph. 3:14-20　　　　　2 Cor. 1:3-7　　　　　　 Mark 15:36-16:7

July 25, St. James, 29 / 94
Jer. 16:14-21　　　　Rom. 9:14-26　　　　Mark 1:14-20
Aug. 5, Eve of the Transfiguration --- / 97
1 Kings 19:1-12　　　2 Cor. 3:1-9,18
Aug. 6, Transfiguration, 2:1-8, 29 / 72
Exod. 24:12-18　　　2 Cor. 4:1-6　　　　John 12:27-36a
Aug. 15, St. Mary the Virgin, 113, 115 / 138
Zech. 2:10-13　　　　Acts 1:6-14　　　　John 2:1-12
　　　　　　　　　　　　　　　　　　　or John 19:23-27

Aug. 24, St. Bartholomew, 86 / 15
Isa. 55:6-11　　　　　Acts 4:23-31　　　　Mark 13:28-37
Sept. 13, Eve of Holy Cross --- / 40:1-14
Isa. 52:13-15　　　　1 Cor. 1:17-25
Sept. 14, Holy Cross, 42, 43 / 25
Num. 21:4-9　　　　Gal. 2:15-3:1　　　　John 3:11-17
Sept. 21, St. Matthew, 119:89-104 / 25
Isa. 8:11-20　　　　　Rom. 10:1-13　　　　Matt. 7:21-29
Sept. 29, St. Michael, 34, 150 / 91
Job 38:1-7　　　　　Heb. 1:1-14　　　　　Mark 13:21-27
Oct. 18, St. Luke, 103 / 119:105-112, 121-128
Lam. 3:19-26　　　　Acts 1:1-8　　　　　Luke 10:25-37
Oct. 23, St. James of Jerusalem, 11 / 26
Gen. 32:22-29　　　　Gal. 1:11-24　　　　Matt. 11:25-30
Oct. 28, St. Simon & St. Jude, 101:1-6 / 119:1-16
Isa. 63:15-64:11　　　1 Cor. 14:1-12　　　John 15:18-27
or Isa. 28:9-17
Oct. 31, Eve of All Saints --- / 121, 122
Wisdom 3:1-9　　　　Rev. 19:1,4-10
Nov. 1, All Saints, 111, 112 / 148, 150
2 Esdras 2:42-47　　　Heb. 11:32-12:2　　　Luke 9:57-62
Thanksgiving Day, 104 / 145
Deut. 8:1-3, 11-20　　1 Thess. 5:12-24　　　Luke 12:15-21(22-31)

Office Lectionary for Weekdays and Moveable Feast Days

YEAR ONE

WEEK OF 1 ADVENT
Monday, 1, 2:1-8(9-13), 3 / 4, 10
Isa. 1:1-9   1 Thess. 1   Luke 20:1-8
Tuesday, 5, 6 / 7, 8
Isa. 1:10-20   1 Thess. 2:1-12   Luke 20:9-18
Wednesday, 119:1-24 / 11, 12, 13
Isa. 1:21-28   1 Thess. 2:13-20   Luke 20:19-26
Thursday, 9 / [14], 15, 16
Isa. 2:1-11   1 Thess. 3   Luke 20:27-40
Friday, 18:1-20 / 18:21-50
Isa. 2:12-22   1 Thess. 4:1-12   Luke 20:41-21:4
Saturday, 17, 21:1-7(8-13) / 104
Isa. 4:2-6   1 Thess. 4:13-18   Luke 21:5-19

WEEK OF 2 ADVENT
Monday, 19, 20 / 23, 27
Isa. 5:1-7   1 Thess. 5:1-11   Luke 21:20-28
Tuesday, 26, 28 / 24, 25
Isa. 5:8-12,18-23   1 Thess.   Luke 21:29-37
                          5:12-24(25-28)
Wednesday, 119:25-48 / 29, 30
Isa. 6   2 Thess. 1   John 7:53-8:11

YEAR TWO

WEEK OF 1 ADVENT
Monday, 1, 2:1-8(9-13), 3 / 4, 10
Amos 1:1-5,13-2:8   2 Peter 1:1-11   Matt. 21:1-11
Tuesday, 5, 6 / 7, 8
Amos 2:6-16   2 Peter 1:12-21   Matt. 21:12-22
Wednesday, 119:1-24 / 11, 12, 13
Amos 3:1-11   2 Peter 3:1-10   Matt. 21:23-32
Thursday, 9 / [14], 15, 16
Amos 3:12-4:5   2 Peter 3:11-18   Matt. 21:33-45
Friday, 18:1-20 / 18:21-50
Amos 4:6-13   Jude 1-16   Matt. 22:1-14
Saturday, 17, 21:1-7(8-13) / 104
Amos 5:1-17   Jude 17-25   Matt. 22:15-22

WEEK OF 2 ADVENT
Monday, 19, 20 / 23, 27
Amos 5:18-27   Rev. 1:1-8   Matt. 22:23-33
Tuesday, 26, 28 / 24, 25
Amos 6   Rev. 1:9-16   Matt. 22:34-46
Wednesday, 119:25-48 / 29, 30
Amos 7:1-8;8:1-3   Rev. 1:17-2:7   Matt. 23:1-12

Thursday, 33 / 34
Isa. 7:1-9 — 2 Thess. 2:1-12 — Luke 22:1-13
Friday, 32, 36 / 22
Isa. 7:10-20 — 2 Thess. 2:13-3:5 — Luke 22:14-30
Saturday, 31 / 110:1-5(6)7, 116
Isa. 8:1-8 — 2 Thess. 3:6-16 — Luke 22:31-38

WEEK OF 3 ADVENT
Monday, 37:1-23 / 37:24-42
Isa. 8:6-9:1 — 2 Peter 1:1-11 — Luke 22:39-53
Tuesday, [35] or 117, 118 / 39, 41
Isa. 5:13-17, 24-25 — 2 Peter 1:12-21 — Luke 22:54-69
Wednesday, 119:49-72 / 42, 43
Isa. 9:8-17 — 2 Peter 3:1-10 — Mark 1:1-8
Thursday, 40:1-14(15-19) / 45, 46
Isa. 9:18-10:4 — 2 Peter 3:11-18 — Matt. 3:1-12
Friday, 38:1-4(5-8)9-22 / 51
Isa. 10:5-19 — Jude 17-25 — Matt. 11:2-15
Saturday, 44 / 146, 147
Isa. 10:20-27a — Rev. 19:11-16 — Luke 3:1-9

WEEK OF 4 ADVENT
Dec. 19 or M. 47, 48 / 112, 115
Isa. 9:1-7 — Rev. 20:1-6, 11-15 — John 5:30-47
Dec. 20 or T. 49 / 116, 117
Isa. 11:1-9 — Rev. 21:1-8 — Luke 1:5-25

Thursday, 33 / 34
Amos 8:4-12(13-14) — Rev. 2:8-17 — Matt. 23:16-26
Friday, 32, 36 / 22
Amos 9:1-10 — Rev. 2:18-29 — Matt. 23:29-39
Saturday, 31 / 110:1-5(6)7, 116
Amos 7:10-17 — Rev. 3:1-6 — Matt. 24:1-14

WEEK OF 3 ADVENT
Monday, 37:1-23 / 37:24-42
Haggai 1 — Rev. 3:7-13 — Matt. 24:15-31
Tuesday, [35] or 117, 118 / 39, 41
Haggai 2:1-9 — Rev. 3:14-22 — Matt. 24:32-44
Wednesday, 119:49-72 / 42, 43
Zech. 1:7-17 — Rev. 4:1-8 — Matt. 24:45-51
Thursday, 40:1-14(15-19) / 45, 46
Zech. 2 — Rev. 4:9-5:5 — Matt. 25:1-13
Friday, 38:1-4(5-8)9-22 / 51
Zech. 7:8-8:8 — Rev. 5:6-14 — Matt. 25:14-30
Saturday, 44 / 146, 147
Zech. 8:9-17 — Rev. 7 — Matt. 25:31-46

WEEK OF 4 ADVENT
Dec. 19 or M. 47, 48 / 112, 115
Isa. 33:17-22 — Titus 1 — Matt. 3:1-6
Dec. 20 or T. 49 / 116, 117
Isa. 35 — Titus 2:1-10 — Matt. 3:7-12

YEAR ONE

Dec. 21 or W. 50 / 110:1-5(6)7, 111		
Isa. 11:10-16	Rev. 21:9-21	Luke 1:26-38
Dec. 22 or Th. 61, 62 / 146, 147		
Isa. 28:9-22	Rev. 21:22-22:5	Luke 1:39-56
Dec. 23 or F. 66, 67 / 148, 150		
Isa. 29:13-24	Rev. 22:6-11,18-20	Luke 1:57-66
Dec. 24 or S. 45, 46 / ---		
Isa. 35	Rev. 22:12-17	Luke 1:67-80
Christmas Eve --- / 89:1-29		
Isa. 59:15b-21	Phil. 2:5-11	
Dec. 25, CHRISTMAS DAY, 85 / 132		
Zech. 2:10-13	1 John 4:7-16	John 3:31-36
Dec. 26, St. Stephen, 119:17-24, 161-168 / 88		
1 Sam. 7:4-13	Acts 6:1-7	John 15:20-16:4a
or Acts 7:44-51		
Dec. 27, St. John, 97 / 145		
Exod. 33:12-23	1 John 2:1-7	John 21:20-25
		or John 17:1-8
Dec. 28, Holy Innocents, 8 / 123, 131		
Isa. 49:13-23	1 Cor. 1:26-29	Mark 10:13-16
December 29. 18:1-20 / 18:21-50		
Isa. 12	Rev. 1:1-8	John 7:37-52
December 30. 19, 20 / 23, 27		
Isa. 25:1-9	Rev. 1:9-20	John 7:53-8:11

YEAR TWO

Dec. 21 or W. 50 / 110:1-5(6)7, 111		
2 Sam. 7:1-17	Titus 2:11-3:8a	Luke 1:26-38
Dec. 22 or Th. 61, 62 / 146, 147		
2 Sam. 7:18-29	Gal. 3:1-14	Luke 1:39-56
Dec. 23 or F. 66, 67 / 148, 150		
Baruch 4:21-29	Gal. 3:15-22	Luke 1:57-66
Dec. 24 or S. 45, 46 / ---		
Baruch 4:36-5:9	Gal. 3:23-4:7	Luke 1:67-80
Christmas Eve --- / 89:1-29		
Isa. 59:15b-21	Phil. 2:5-11	
Dec. 25, CHRISTMAS DAY, 85 / 132		
Zech. 2:10-13	1 John 4:7-16	John 3:31-36
Dec. 26, St. Stephen, 119:17-24, 161-168 / 88		
1 Sam. 7:4-13	Acts 6:1-7	John 15:20-16:4a
or Acts 7:44-51		
Dec. 27, St. John, 97 / 145		
Exod. 33:12-23	1 John 2:1-7	John 21:20-25
		or John 17:1-8
Dec. 28, Holy Innocents, 8 / 123, 131		
Isa. 49:13-23	1 Cor. 1:26-29	Mark 10:13-16
December 29. 18:1-20 / 18:21-50		
2 Sam. 23:13-17b*	2 John	John 2:1-11
December 30. 19, 20 / 23, 27		
1 Kings 17:17-24	3 John	John 4:46-54

The Daily Office Revised

Dec. 31, [New Year's Eve] 46 / 90#
Isa. 26:1-9   2 Cor. 5:16-6:2   John 8:12-19
Eve of Holy Name --- / 143:1-11
Exod. 3:1-14   John 8:52-58

\# May be used in place of the Psalm appointed for the Eve of Holy Name. Readings for Dec. 31 may also be used in the evening.

January 1, Holy Name, 103 / 148
Isa. 62:1-5, 10-12   Acts 4:5-12   John 5:30-44
January 2. 33 / 34
Gen. 12:1-7   Heb. 11:1-12   John 6:35-42, 48-51
January 3. 68 / 72
Gen. 28:10-22   Heb. 11:13-22   John 10:7-17
January 4. 85, 87 / 89:1-29
Exod. 3:1-12   Heb. 11:23-31   John 14:6-14
January 5. 2, 110:1-5(6)7 / ---
Joshua 1:1-9   Heb. 11:32-12:2   John 15:1-16

Eve of Epiphany --- / 98
Isa. 49:1-6   Rom. 15:7-13
January 6, EPIPHANY, 96 / 97
Isa. 61:1-4, 8-9   Rev. 21:22-27   Matt. 12:14-21
*January 7. 103 / 104
Isa. 52:3-6   Rev. 2:1-7   John 2:1-11
January 8. 117, 118 / 112, 113
Isa. 59:15-21   Rev. 2:8-17   John 4:46-54

Dec. 31, [New Year's Eve] 46 / 90#
1 Kings 3:5-14   James 4:13-17; 5:7-11   John 5:1-15
Eve of Holy Name --- / 143:1-11
Exod. 3:1-14   John 8:52-58

\# May be used in place of the Psalm appointed for the Eve of Holy Name. Readings for, Dec. 31 may also be used in the evening.

January 1, Holy Name, 103 / 148
Isa. 62:1-5, 10-12   Acts 4:5-12   John 5:30-44
January 2. 33 / 34
1 Kings 19:1-8   Eph. 1:1-14   John 6:1-14
January 3. 68 / 72
1 Kings 19:9-18   Eph. 1:15-23   John 6:15-27
January 4. 85, 87 / 89:1-29
Joshua 3:14-4:7   Eph. 2:1-10   John 9:1-12, 35-38
January 5. 2, 110:1-5(6)7 / ---
Jonah 2:2-9   Eph. 2:11-22   John 11:17-27, 38-44

Eve of Epiphany --- / 98
Isa. 49:1-6   Rom. 15:7-13
January 6, EPIPHANY, 96 / 97
Isa. 61:1-4, 8-9   Rev. 21:22-27   Matt. 12:14-21
*January 7. 103 / 104
Deut. 8:1-3   Eph. 3:1-13   John 6:35-51
January 8. 117, 118 / 112, 113
Exod. 17:1-7   Eph. 3:14-21   John 7:37-52

YEAR ONE

January 9. 121, 122, 123 / 131, 132		
Isa. 63:1-5	Rev. 2:18-29	John 5:1-15
January 10. 138, 139:1-17(18-23) / 147		
Isa. 65:1-9	Rev. 3:1-6	John 6:1-14
January 11. 148, 150 / 91, 92		
Isa. 65:13-16	Rev. 3:7-13	John 6:15-27
January 12. 98, 99, [100] / ---		
Isa. 66:1-2,22-23	Rev. 3:14-22	John 9:1-12, 35-38
Eve of 1 Epiphany --- / 72 or 23, 24		
Isa. 49:5-13	Gal. 3:23-29; 4:4-7	

* The Psalms and Readings for the dated days after Epiphany are used only until the following Saturday evening.

WEEK OF 1 EPIPHANY

Monday, 1, 2:1-8(9-13), 3 / 4, 10
Isa. 40:1-11	Eph. 1:1-14	Mark 1:1-13
Tuesday, 5, 6 / 7, 8		
Isa. 40:12-17	Eph. 1:15-23	Mark 1:14-28
Wednesday, 119:1-24 / 11, 12, 13		
Isa. 40:18-23	Eph. 2:1-10	Mark 1:29-45
Thursday, 9 / [14], 15, 16		
Isa. 41:1-20	Eph. 2:11-22	Mark 2:1-12
Friday, 18:1-20 / 18:21-50		
Isa. 41:21-29	Eph. 3:1-13	Mark 2:13-22
Saturday, 17, 21:1-7(8-13) / 104		
Isa. 42:1-9	Eph. 3:14-21	Mark 2:22-3:6

YEAR TWO

January 9. 121, 122, 123 / 131, 132		
Isa. 45:14-19	Eph. 4:1-16	John 8:12-19
January 10. 138, 139:1-17(18-23) / 147		
Jer. 23:1-8	Eph. 4:17-32	John 10:7-17
January 11. 148, 150 / 91, 92		
Isa. 55:3-9	Eph. 5:1-20	John 14:6-14
January 12. 98, 99, [100] / ---		
Genesis; 49:1-2,8-12	Eph. 6:10-20	John 15:1-16
Eve of 1 Epiphany --- / 72 or 23, 24		
Isa. 49:5-13	Gal. 3:23-29; 4:4-7	

* The Psalms and Readings for the dated days after Epiphany are used only until the following Saturday evening.

WEEK OF 1 EPIPHANY

Monday, 1, 2:1-8(9-13), 3 / 4, 10
Gen. 1:1-2:3	Heb. 1	John 1:1-18
Tuesday, 5, 6 / 7, 8		
Gen. 2:4b-9, 16-25	Heb. 2:1-10	John 1:19-28
Wednesday, 119:1-24 / 11, 12, 13		
Gen. 3:1-24	Heb. 2:11-18	John 1:29-34
Thursday, 9 / [14], 15, 16		
Gen. 4:1-16	Heb. 3:1-11	John 1:35-43
Friday, 18:1-20 / 18:21-50		
Gen. 4:17-26	Heb. 3:12-19	John 1:43-51
Saturday, 17, 21:1-7(8-13) / 104		
Gen. 6:1-8	Heb. 4:1-13	John 2:1-12

WEEK OF 2 EPIPHANY
Monday, 19, 20 / 23, 27
Isa. 42:10-17　　Eph. 4:1-16　　Mark 3:7-19a　　John 2:13-22
Tuesday, 26, 28 / 24, 25
Isa. 43:1-13　　Eph. 4:17-32　　Mark 3:20-35　　John 2:23-3:15
Wednesday, 119:25-48 / 29, 30
Isa. 43:13-44:5　　Eph. 5:1-14　　Mark 4:1-20　　John 3:16-21
Thursday, 33 / 34
Isa. 44:6-8, 21-23　　Eph. 5:15-33　　Mark 4:21-34　　John 3:22-36
Friday, 32, 36 / 22
Isa. 44:9-20　　Eph. 6:1-9　　Mark 4:35-41　　John 4:1-26
Saturday, 31 / 110:1-5(6)7, 116
Isa. 44:24-45:7　　Eph. 6:10-24　　Mark 5:1-20　　John 4:27-42

WEEK OF 3 EPIPHANY
Monday, 37:1-23 / 37:24-42
Isa. 45:5-19　　Gal. 1:1-5,11-17　　Mark 5:21-43　　John 4:43-5:1
Tuesday, [35] or 117, 118 / 39, 41
Isa. 45:20-25　　Gal. 1:18-2:10　　Mark 6:1-16　　John 5:2-18
Wednesday, 119:49-72 / 42, 43
Isa. 46　　Gal. 2:11-21　　Mark 6:30-46　　John 5:19-29
Thursday, 40:1-14(15-19) / 45, 46
Isa. 47　　Gal. 3:1-14　　Mark 6:47-56　　John 5:30-47
Friday, 38:1-4(5-8)9-22 / 51
Isa. 48:1-11　　Gal. 3:15-22　　Mark 7:1-23　　John 6:1-15
Saturday, 44 / 146, 147
Isa. 48:12-21　　Gal. 3:23-29　　Mark 7:24-37　　John 6:16-27

WEEK OF 2 EPIPHANY
Monday, 19, 20 / 23, 27
Gen. 6:9-22　　Heb. 4:14-5:6
Tuesday, 26, 28 / 24, 25
Gen. 7:1,7-10,17-23　　Heb. 5:7-14
Wednesday, 119:25-48 / 29, 30
Gen. 8:6-22　　Heb. 6:1-12
Thursday, 33 / 34
Gen. 9:8-17　　Heb. 6:13-20
Friday, 32, 36 / 22
Gen. 11:1-9　　Heb. 7:1-17
Saturday, 31 / 110:1-5(6)7, 116
Gen. 11:27-12:8　　Heb. 7:18-28

WEEK OF 3 EPIPHANY
Monday, 37:1-23 / 37:24-42
Gen. 13:2,5-18　　Heb. 8
Tuesday, [35] or 117, 118 / 39, 41
Gen. 15:1-11,17-21　　Heb. 9:1-14
Wednesday, 119:49-72 / 42, 43
Gen. 16:1-14　　Heb. 9:15-28
Thursday, 40:1-14(15-19) / 45, 46
Gen. 16:15-17:14　　Heb. 10:1-10
Friday, 38:1-4(5-8)9-22 / 51
Gen. 17:15-22　　Heb. 10:11-25
Saturday, 44 / 146, 147
Gen. 18:1-16　　Heb. 10:26-39

YEAR ONE

WEEK OF 4 EPIPHANY
Monday, 47, 48 / 49
Isa. 49:1-12　　Gal. 4:1-11　　Mark 8:1-10
Tuesday, 50 / [52, 53, 54] or 148, 150
Isa. 49:13-23　　Gal. 4:12-20　　Mark 8:11-21
Wednesday, 119:73-88 / 55:1-15(16)17-26
Isa. 51:1-8　　Gal. 4:21-31　　Mark 8:22-33
Thursday, 56, 57, [58] / [59, 60] or 114, 115
Isa. 51:9-16　　Gal. 5:1-14　　Mark 8:34-9:1
Friday, 61, 62 / 69:1-23(24-30)31-38
Isa. 52:1-2,7-12　　Gal. 5:16-24　　Mark 9:2-13
Saturday, 63:1-8(9-11), 64 / 111, 112, 113
Isa. 54:1-10　　Gal. 5:25-6:10　　Mark 9:14-29

WEEK OF 5 EPIPHANY
Monday, 67, 72 / 65, 66
Isa. 55:1-5　　Gal. 6:11-18　　Mark 9:30-41
Tuesday, [70], 71 / 68:1-20(21-23)24-35
Isa. 55:6-13　　2 Tim. 1:1-14　　Mark 9:42-50
Wednesday, 119:89-112 / 73
Isa. 56:1-7　　2 Tim. 2:1-13　　Mark 10:1-16
Thursday, 74 / 77, [79]
Isa. 57:14-21　　2 Tim. 3:10-17　　Mark 10:17-31

YEAR TWO

WEEK OF 4 EPIPHANY
Monday, 47, 48 / 49
Gen. 18:16-33　　Heb. 11:1-12　　John 6:28-40
Tuesday, 50 / [52, 53, 54] or 148, 150
Gen. 19:1-3,12-17, Heb. 11:13-22　　John 6:41-51
24-28
Wednesday, 119:73-88 / 55:1-15(16)17-26
Gen. 21:1-4,8-21　　Heb. 11:23-31　　John 6:52-59
Thursday, 56, 57, [58] / [59, 60] or 114, 115
Gen. 22:1-14　　Heb. 11:32-12:2　　John 6:60-71
Friday, 61, 62 / 69:1-23(24-30)31-38
Gen. 24:1-27　　Heb. 12:3-11　　John 7:1-13
Saturday, 63:1-8(9-11), 64 / 111, 112, 113
Gen. 24:28-38,49-51 Heb. 12:12-29　　John 7:14-31

WEEK OF 5 EPIPHANY
Monday, 67, 72 / 65, 66
Gen. 24:52-67　　Heb. 13:1-6　　John 7:31-52
Tuesday, [70], 71 / 68:1-20(21-23)24-35
Gen. 25:19-34　　Heb. 13:7-21　　John 7:53-8:11
Wednesday, 119:89-112 / 73
Gen. 27:1-29　　Rom. 12:1-8　　John 8:12-20
Thursday, 74 / 77, [79]
Gen. 27:30-45　　Rom. 12:9-21　　John 8:21-32

The Daily Office Revised 73

Friday, 78:1-39 / 78:40-72
Isa. 58:1-12   2 Tim. 4:1-8   Mark 10:32-45   John 8:33-47
Saturday, 75, 76 / 114, 115
Isa. 60:1-17   2 Tim. 4:9-18   Mark 10:46-52   John 8:47-59

WEEK OF 6 EPIPHANY
Monday, [82, 83] or 104 / 80, 81
Isa. 61:1-9   1 Tim. 1:1-17   Mark 11:1-11   John 9:1-17
Tuesday, 84, 85 / 86, 87
Isa. 61:10-62:5   1 Tim. 2:1-8   Mark 11:11-26   John 9:18-38
Wednesday, 119:113-128 / [88] or 134, 135
Isa. 62:6-12   1 Tim. 3   Mark 11:27-12:12   John 9:34-41; 10:19-30
Thursday, 89:1-18 / 89:19-52
Isa. 63:7-14   1 Tim. 4   Mark 12:13-27   John 10:1-18
Friday, 90, 93 / 91, 92
Isa. 63:15-64:9   1 Tim. 5:17-22   Mark 12:28-34   John 10:30-42
Saturday, 94, [95] / 117, 118
Isa. 65:17-25   1 Tim. 6:11-16   Mark 12:35-44   John 11:1-16

WEEK OF 7 EPIPHANY
Monday, 96, 97 / 98, 99, [100]
Deut. 6:1-9   2 Cor. 5:11-15   Matt. 5:1-12   John 11:17-29
Tuesday, 105:1-22 / 105:23-45
Deut. 7:6-11   2 Cor. 5:16-21   Matt. 5:13-20   John 11:30-44

Friday, 78:1-39 / 78:40-72
Gen. 27:46-28:4, 10-22   Rom. 13
Saturday, 75, 76 / 114, 115
Gen. 29:1-20   Rom. 14

WEEK OF 6 EPIPHANY
Monday, [82, 83] or 104 / 80, 81
Gen. 32:3-21   1 John 1
Tuesday, 84, 85 / 86, 87
Gen. 32:22-31   1 John 2:1-11
Wednesday, 119:113-128 / [88] or 134, 135
Gen. 35:1-7, 16-20   1 John 2:12-17
Thursday, 89:1-18 / 89:19-52
Prov. 1:20-33   1 John 2:18-29
Friday, 90, 93 / 91, 92
Prov. 3:11-20   1 John 3:1-10
Saturday, 94, [95] / 117, 118
Prov. 4   1 John 3:11-18

WEEK OF 7 EPIPHANY
Monday, 96, 97 / 98, 99, [100]
Prov. 8:1-21   1 John 3:19-4:6
Tuesday, 105:1-22 / 105:23-45
Prov. 8:22-26   1 John 4:7-21

YEAR ONE

Wednesday, 119:129-152 / 102
Deut. 10:10-15　　2 Cor. 6:1-10　　Matt. 5:21-26
Thursday, 106:1-18 / 106:19-48
Deut. 10:17-11:1　　2 Cor. 8:1-15　　Matt. 5:27-37
Friday, 103 / 107:1-31
Deut. 11:13-21　　2 Cor. 8:16-24　　Matt. 5:38-48
Saturday, 107:32-42, 108:1-6(7-13) / 134, 135
Deut. 11:22-28　　2 Cor. 9　　Matt. 6:1-6

WEEK OF 8 EPIPHANY

Monday, 101, 109:1-4(5-19)20-30 / [120], 121, 122, 123
Ruth 1:1-14　　2 Cor. 10　　Matt. 6:7-15
Tuesday, 124, 125, 126, [127] / 128, 129, 130
Ruth 1:15-22　　2 Cor. 11:1-21a　　Matt. 6:16-23

Wednesday, 119:153-176 / 131, 132, [133]
Ruth 2:1-13　　2 Cor. 11:21b-30　　Matt. 6:24-34
Thursday, 136, 137:1-6(7-9) / 138, 139:1-17(18-23)
Ruth 2:14-23　　2 Cor. 12:1-10　　Matt. 7:1-12
Friday, 145 / 140:1-8(9-11)12-13, 141, 142
Ruth 3　　2 Cor. 12:11-21　　Matt. 7:13-21
Saturday, 143, 144 / 148, 149, 150
Ruth 4:1-17　　2 Cor. 13　　Matt. 7:22-29

YEAR TWO

Wednesday, 119:129-152 / 102
Prov. 10:1-12　　1 John 5:1-12　　John 11:45-54
Thursday, 106:1-18 / 106:19-48
Prov. 14:27-35　　1 John 5:13-21　　John 11:55-12:8
Friday, 103 / 107:1-31
Prov. 15:16-33　　Philemon　　John 12:9-19
Saturday, 107:32-42, 108:1-6(7-13) / 134, 135
Prov. 16:18-32　　2 Tim. 1:1-14　　John 12:20-26

WEEK OF 8 EPIPHANY

Monday, 101, 109:1-4(5-19)20-30 / [120], 121, 122, 123
Prov. 20:9-12,17-22　　2 Tim. 2:1-13　　John 12:27-36a
Tuesday, 124, 125, 126, [127] / 128, 129, 130
Prov. 21:30-22:6　　2 Tim. 3:1-9　　John 12:44-50, 36b-43
Wednesday, 119:153-176 / 131, 132, [133]
Prov. 23:19-21, 29-35　　2 Tim. 3:10-17　　John 13:1-20
Thursday, 136, 137:1-6(7-9) / 138, 139:1-17(18-23)
Prov. 25:15-28　　2 Tim. 4:1-8　　John 13:21-30
Friday, 145 / 140:1-8(9-11)12-13, 141, 142
Prov. 27:1-6,10-12　　2 Tim. 4:9-22　　John 13:31-38
Saturday, 143, 144 / 148, 149, 150
Prov. 30:1-9　　Phil. 1:1-11　　John 18:1-14

LAST WEEK OF EPIPHANY
Monday, 1, 2:1-8(9-13), 3 / 4, 10
Deut. 4:7-12   Heb. 1   John 1:1-18

Tuesday, 5, 6 / 7, 8
Deut. 4:15-24   Heb. 2:1-10   John 1:19-28

ASH WEDNESDAY, 51:1-18 or 102 / 31:15-24, 32
Isa. 58:1-12   Heb. 12:1-14   Luke 18:9-14
Thursday, 9 / [14], 15, 16
Deut. 4:32-39   Titus 1:4-2:10   John 1:29-34
Friday, 18:1-20 / 18:21-50
Deut. 5:1-22   Titus 2:11-3:8   John 1:35-43
Saturday, 17, 21:1-7(8-13) / 119:89-112
Deut. 5:23-33   Titus 3:9-15   John 1:43-51

WEEK OF 1 LENT
Monday, 19, 20 / 23, 27
Deut. 6:10-16   Heb. 2:11-18   John 2:1-11
Tuesday, 26, 28 / 24, 25
Deut. 8:1-5   Heb. 3:1-11   John 2:13-22
Wednesday, 119:25-48 / 29, 30
Deut. 8:11-18   Heb. 3:12-19   John 2:23-3:15
Thursday, 33 / 34
Deut. 9:6-12   Heb. 4:1-10   John 3:16-21
Friday, 32, 36 / 22
Dent. 9:25-29   Heb. 4:11-16   John 3:22-36

LAST WEEK OF EPIPHANY
Monday, 1, 2:1-8(9-13), 3 / 4, 10
Isa. 56:1-7   Phil 2:1-13   John 18:15-18, 25-27

Tuesday, 5, 6 / 7, 8
Isa. 58:1-12   Phil. 3:1-11   John 18:28-38

ASH WEDNESDAY, 51:1-18 or 102 / 31:15-24, 32
Amos 5:6-15   Heb. 12:1-14   Luke 18:9-14
Thursday, 9 / [14], 15, 16
Deut. 8:1-6   Phil. 3:12-21   John 17:1-8
Friday, 18:1-20 / 18:21-50
Deut. 6:4-13   Phil. 4:1-9   John 17:9-19
Saturday, 17, 21:1-7(8-13) / 119:89-112
Deut. 6:14-25   Phil. 4:10-20   John 17:20-26

WEEK OF 1 LENT
Monday, 19, 20 / 23, 27
Gen. 37:1-11   1 Cor. 1:1-19   Mark 1:1-13
Tuesday, 26, 28 / 24, 25
Gen. 37:12-24   1 Cor. 1:20-31   Mark 1:14-28
Wednesday, 119:25-48 / 29, 30
Gen. 37:25-36   1 Cor. 2:1-13   Mark 1:29-45
Thursday, 33 / 34
Gen. 39:1-6a   1 Cor. 2:14-3:15 Mark 2:1-12
Friday, 32, 36 / 22
Gen. 39:6b-23   1 Cor. 3:16-23   Mark 2:13-22

YEAR ONE

Saturday, 31 / 119:113-128
Deut. 30:11-14　　Heb. 5:1-10　　John 4:1-26

WEEK OF 2 LENT
Monday, 37:1-23 / 37:24-42
Jer. 1:1-10　　Rom. 1:1-17　　John 4:27-42
Tuesday, [35] or 117, 118 / 39, 41
Jer. 1:11-19　　Rom. 1:18-32　　John 4:43-54
Wednesday, 119:49-72 / 42, 43
Jer. 2:4-13　　Rom. 2:1-16　　John 5:2-18
Thursday, 40:1-14(15-19) / 45, 46
Jer. 3:6-18　　Rom. 2:17-29　　John 5:19-29
Friday, 38:1-4(5-8)9-22 / 51
Jer. 4:9-10,19-28　　Rom. 3:1-20　　John 5:30-47
Saturday, 44 / 119:129-152
Jer. 5:1-9　　Rom. 3:21-31　　John 7:1-13

WEEK OF 3 LENT
Monday, 47, 48 / 49
Jer. 5:20-31　　Rom. 4:1-12　　John 7:14-30
Tuesday, 50 / [52, 53, 54] or 148, 150
Jer. 6:9-15　　Rom. 4:13-25　　John 7:31-52
Wednesday, 119:73-88 / 55:1-15(16)17-26
Jer. 7:1-15　　Rom. 5:1-11　　John 8:12-20
Thursday, 56, 57, [58] / [59, 60] or 114, 115
Jer. 7:21-28*　　Rom. 5:12-21　　John 8:21-32

YEAR TWO

Saturday, 31 / 119:113-128
Gen. 40　　1 Cor. 4:1-7　　Mark 2:22-3:6

WEEK OF 2 LENT
Monday, 37:1-23 / 37:24-42
Gen. 41:1-13　　1 Cor. 4:8-20 (21)　　Mark 3:7-19a
Tuesday, [35] or 117, 118 / 39, 41
Gen. 41:14-45　　1 Cor. 5:1-8　　Mark 3:20-35
Wednesday, 119:49-72 / 42, 43
Gen. 41:46-57　　1 Cor. 5:9-6:8　　Mark 4:1-20
Thursday, 40:1-14(15-19) / 45, 46
Gen. 42:1-17　　1 Cor. 6:9-20　　Mark 4:21-34
Friday, 38:1-4(5-8)9-22 / 51
Gen. 42:18-28　　1 Cor. 7:1-9　　Mark 4:35-41
Saturday, 44 / 119:129-152
Gen. 42:29-38　　1 Cor. 7:10-24　　Mark 5:1-20

WEEK OF 3 LENT
Monday, 47, 48 / 49
Gen. 43:1-15　　1 Cor. 7:25-31　　Mark 5:21-43
Tuesday, 50 / [52, 53, 54] or 148, 150
Gen. 43:16-34　　1 Cor. 7:32-40　　Mark 6:1-16
Wednesday, 119:73-88 / 55:1-15(16)17-26
Gen. 44:1-17　　1 Cor. 8　　Mark 6:30-46
Thursday, 56, 57, [58] / [59, 60] or 114, 115
Gen. 44:18-34　　1 Cor. 9:1-15　　Mark 6:47-56

The Daily Office Revised 77

Friday, 61, 62 / 69:1-23(24-30)31-38
Jer. 8:18-9:3   Rom. 6:1-11   John 8:33-47
Saturday, 63:1-8(9-11), 64 / 119:153-176
Jer. 10:11-24   Rom. 6:12-23   John 8:47-59

WEEK OF 4 LENT
Monday, 67, 72 / 65, 66
Jer. 11:1-8   Rom. 7:1-12   John 6:1-15
Tuesday, [70], 71 / 68:1-20(21-23)24-35
Jer. 11:14-20   Rom. 7:13-25   John 6:16-27
Wednesday, 119:89-112 / 73
Jer. 14:1-9   Rom. 8:1-11   John 6:27-40
Thursday, 74 / 77, [79]
Jer. 14:17-22   Rom. 8:12-27   John 6:41-51
Friday, 78:1-39 / 78:40-72
Jer. 16:10-21   Rom. 8:28-39   John 6:52-59
Saturday, 75, 76 / 119:1-24
Jer. 17:19-27   Rom. 9:1-18   John 6:60-71
* Duplicates the First Lesson appointed for the Eucharist in Lesser Feasts and Fasts. Jer. 8:4-13 may be substituted.

WEEK OF 5 LENT
Monday, [82, 83] or 104 / 80, 81
Jer. 18:1-11   Rom. 9:19-26   John 9:1-17
Tuesday, 84, 85 / 86, 87
Jer. 23:1-8   Rom. 10:1-13   John 9:18-38

Friday, 61, 62 / 69:1-23(24-30)31-38
Gen. 45:1-15   1 Cor. 9:16-27   Mark 7:1-23
Saturday, 63:1-8(9-11), 64 / 119:153-176
Gen. 45:16-28   1 Cor. 10:1-13   Mark 7:24-37

WEEK OF 4 LENT
Monday, 67, 72 / 65, 66
Gen. 46:1-7,28-34 1 Cor. 10:14-11:1   Mark 8:1-10
Tuesday, [70], 71 / 68:1-20(21-23)24-35
Gen. 47:1-26   1 Cor. 11:17-34   Mark 8:11-21
Wednesday, 119:89-112 / 73
Gen. 47:27-48:7   1 Cor. 12:1-11   Mark 8:22-33
Thursday, 74 / 77, [79]
Gen. 48:8-22   1 Cor. 12:12-26   Mark 8:34-9:1
Friday, 78:1-39 / 78:40-72
Gen. 49:29-50:14   1 Cor. 12:27-13:3   Mark 9:2-13
Saturday, 75, 76 / 119:1-24
Gen. 50:15-26   1 Cor. 13:1-13   Mark 9:14-29

WEEK OF 5 LENT
Monday, [82, 83] or 104 / 80, 81
Exod. 1:6-17,22   1 Cor. 14:1-19   Mark 9:30-41
Tuesday, 84, 85 / 86, 87
Exod. 2:1-22   1 Cor. 14:20-33a,39-40   Mark 9:42-50

YEAR ONE

Wednesday, 119:113-128 / [88] or 134, 135

Jer. 23:16-32	Rom. 10:14-21	John 9:34-41; 10:19-30

Thursday, 89:1-18 / 89:19-52

Jer. 24	Rom. 11:1-12	John 10:1-18

Friday, 90, 93 / 91, 92

Jer. 26:1-16	Rom. 11:13-24	John 10:30-39*

Saturday, 94, [95] / 119:25-48

Jer. 29:1, 4-13	Rom. 11:25-36	John 11:45-57*

HOLY WEEK

Monday, 42, 43 / 71

Lam. 1:1–2,6-12	2 Cor. 1:1-7	Mark 11:12-25

Tuesday, 51:1-18(19-20) / 6, 12

Jer:15:10-21	Phil. 3:15-21	John 12:20-26

Wednesday, 88 / 74

Jer. 17:9-10,14-17	Phil. 4:1-13	John 12:27-36

Maundy Thursday, 102 / 116

Jer. 20:7-11	1 Cor.John 17:1-11
	10:14-17;11:27-32	

GOOD FRIDAY, 22 / 40:1-14(15-19)

Gen. 22:1-14	1 Peter 1:10-20	John 13:36-38
or Wisdom 2:1, 12-24		or Luke 23:50-56+

Holy Saturday, 27 / 14, 16

Lam. 3:1-6,19-33	Heb. 10:19-25	Rom. 8:1-11#

YEAR TWO

Wednesday, 119:113-128 / [88] or 134, 135

Exod. 3:1-15	2 Cor. 2:14-3:6	Mark 10:1-16

Thursday, 89:1-18 / 89:19-52

Exod. 4:10-17,27-31	2 Cor. 3:7-18	Mark 10:17-31

Friday, 90, 93 / 91, 92

Exod. 5:1-9,19-6:1	2 Cor. 4:1-12	Mark 10:32-45

Saturday, 94, [95] / 119:25-48

Exod. 10:21-11:8	2 Cor. 4:13-18	Mark 10:46-52

HOLY WEEK

Monday, 42, 43 / 71

Jer. 12:1-16	Phil. 3:1-14	John 12:9-19

Tuesday, 51:1-18(19-20) / 6, 12

Lam. 1:17-22	2 Cor. 1:8-22	Mark 11:27-33

Wednesday, 88 / 74

Lam. 2:1-9	2 Cor. 1:23-2:11	Mark 12:1-11 (12)

Maundy Thursday, 102 / 116

Lam. 2:10-18	1	Cor.Mark 14:12-25
	10:14-17;11:27-32	

GOOD FRIDAY, 22 / 40:1-14(15-19)

Lam. 3:1-9,19-33	1 Peter 1:10-20	John 13:36-38
		or Luke 23:50-56+

Holy Saturday, 27 / 14, 16

Lam. 3:37-58	Heb. 10:19-25	Rom. 8:11-11#

The Daily Office Revised 79

* Duplicates the Gospel appointed in Lesser Feasts and Fasts. Readings from Year Two may be substituted.
+ The passage from Luke is intended for use in the evening.
# If a Gospel reading is preferred, see the choices in the Proper of the Day.

EASTER WEEK

Monday, 93, 98 / 111, 114

Isa. 25:1-9	Acts 2:14, 22-32*	John 15:1-11
Exod. 12:1-13	1 Cor. 15:1-11	Mark 16:1-8

Tuesday, 103 / 115:1-3(4-8)9-18

Isa. 30:18-21	Acts 2:36-41(-2-47)*	John 15:12-27
Exod. 12:14-27	1 Cor. 15:12-28	Mark 16:9-19

Wednesday, 97 / 99

Micah 7:7-15	Acts 3:1-10*	John 16:1-15
Exod. 12:28-39	1 Cor. 15:(29)30-41	Matt. 28:1-16

Thursday, 147 / 148

Ezek. 37:1-14	Acts 3:11-26*	John 16:16-33
Exod. 12:40-51	1 Cor. 15:41-50	Matt. 28:16-20

Friday, 123, 124 / 125, 126

Dan. 12:1-4, 13	Acts 4:1-12*	John 14:1-14
Exod. 13:3-10	1 Cor. 15:51-58	Luke 24:1-12

Saturday, 145 / 146

Jonah 2:2-9	Acts 4:13-21*	John 14:15-31
Exod. 13:1-2, 11-16	2 Cor. 4:16-5:10	Mark 12:18-27

WEEK OF 2 EASTER

Monday, 96, 97 / 98, 99, [100]

Deut. 11:1-7	1 John 1	John 17:1-11
Exod. 13:17-14:4	1 Peter 1:1-12	John 15:1-11

Tuesday, 105:1-22 / 105:23-45

Deut. 11:8-12	1 John 2:1-11	John 17:12-19
Exod. 14:5-20	1 Peter 1:13-25	John 15:12-27

YEAR ONE
Wednesday, 104 / 102
Deut. 12:1-11   1 John 2:12-17   John 17:20-26
Thursday, 106:1-18 / 106:19-48
Deut. 13:1-5a#   1 John 2:18-29   Luke 3:1-14
Friday, 103 / 107:1-31
Deut. 16:16-20   1 John 3:1-10   Luke 3:15-20
Saturday, 107:32-42, 108:1-6(7-13) / 134, 135
Deut. 17:14-20   1 John 3:11-18   Luke 3:21-22; 4:1-13

* The readings from Acts duplicate the First Lessons appointed for the Eucharist. Readings from Year Two may be substituted.
# "... commanded you to walk"

WEEK OF 3 EASTER
Monday, 101, 109:1-4(5-19)20-30 / [120], 121, 122, 123
Deut. 26:1-11   1 John 3:19-4:6   Luke 4:14-30
Tuesday, 124, 125, 126, [127] / 128, 129, 130
Deut. 30:1-10   1 John 4:7-21   Luke 4:31-37
Wednesday, 114, 115 / 131, 132, [133]
Deut. 30:11-20   1 John 5:1-12   Luke 4:38-44
Thursday, 136, 137:1-6(7-9) / 138, 139:1-17(18-23)
Deut. 31:1-8   1 John 5:13-20(21) Luke 5:1-11
Friday, 145 / 140:1-8(9-11)12-13, 141, 142
Deut. 31:9-13   2 John   Luke 5:12-26
Saturday, 143, 144 / 148, 149, 150
Deut. 34   3 John   Luke 5:27-39

YEAR TWO
Wednesday, 104 / 102
Exod. 14:21-31   1 Peter 2:1-10   John 16:1-15
Thursday, 106:1-18 / 106:19-48
Exod. 15:1-21   1 Peter 2:11-25   John 16:16-33
Friday, 103 / 107:1-31
Exod. 15:22-16:10   1 Peter 3:13-4:6 John 14:1-14
Saturday, 107:32-42, 108:1-6(7-13) / 134, 135
Exod. 16:10-22   1 Peter 4:7-19   John 14:15-31

WEEK OF 3 EASTER
Monday, 101, 109:1-4(5-19)20-30 / [120], 121, 122, 123
Exod. 16:23-36   1 Peter 5:1-11   Matt. 2:1-12
Tuesday, 124, 125, 126, [127] / 128, 129, 130
Exod. 17:1-13   Col. 1:1-8   Matt. 2:13-23
Wednesday, 114, 115 / 131, 132, [133]
Exod. 18:1-5, 13-27   Col. 1:15-23   Matt 3:1-12
Thursday, 136, 137:1-6(7-9) / 138, 139:1-17(18-23)
Exod. 19:1-16   Col. 1:24-2:7   Matt. 3:13-17
Friday, 145 / 140:1-8(9-11)12-13, 141, 142
Exod. 19:17-20:21   Col. 2:8-23   Matt. 4:1-11
Saturday, 143, 144 / 148, 149, 150
Exod. 24   Col. 3:1-11   Matt. 4:12-17

WEEK OF 4 EASTER
Monday, 67, 72 / 65, 66
Dan. 1　　　　　　　Col. 1:1-14　　　　Luke 6:1-11　　　　　Matt. 4:18-25
Tuesday, [70], 71 / 68:1-20(21-23)24-35
Dan. 2:1-3,10-16　　Col. 1:15-23　　　　Luke 6:12-26　　　　Matt. 5:1-10
Wednesday, 146, 147 / 73
Dan. 2:17-28　　　　Col. 1:24-2:7　　　　Luke 6:27-38　　　　Matt. 5:11-16
Thursday, 74 / 77, [79]
Dan. 2:31-46　　　　Col. 2:8-23　　　　　Luke 6:39-49　　　　Matt. 5:17-20
Friday, 78:1-39 / 78:40-72
Dan. 3:1-2,4-12　　　Col. 3:1-11　　　　　Luke 7:1-17　　　　　Matt. 5:21-26
Saturday, 75, 76 / 114, 115
Dan. 3:13-25　　　　Col. 3:12-17　　　　Luke 7:18-28,31-35　Matt. 5:27-37

WEEK OF 5 EASTER
Monday, [82, 83] or 104 / 80, 81
Dan. 3:26-30　　　　Col. 3:18-4:6　　　　Luke 7:36-50　　　　Matt. 5:38-48
Tuesday, 84, 85 / 86, 87
Dan. 4:1-18　　　　　Rom. 12　　　　　　Luke 8:1-15　　　　　Matt. 6:1-6,16-18
Wednesday, 110:1-5(6)7, 116 / [88] or 134, 135
Dan. 4:19-27　　　　Rom. 13　　　　　　Luke 8:16-25　　　　Matt. 6:7-15
Thursday, 89:1-18 / 89:19-52
Dan. 4:28-37　　　　Rom. 14:1-12　　　　Luke 8:26-39　　　　Matt. 6:19-24
Friday, 90, 93 / 91, 92
Dan. 5:1-12　　　　　Rom. 14:13-23　　　Luke 8:40-56　　　　Matt. 6:25-34

WEEK OF 4 EASTER
Monday, 67, 72 / 65, 66
Exod. 25:1-22　　　　　Col. 3:12-25
Tuesday, [70], 71 / 68:1-20(21-23)24-35
Exod. 28:1-3,30-38　　1 Thess. 1
Wednesday, 146, 147 / 73
Exod. 32:1-8,15-20　　1 Thess. 2:1-12
Thursday, 74 / 77, [79]
Exod. 32:21-24,　　　1 Thess. 2:13-20
30-34
Friday, 78:1-39 / 78:40-72
Exod. 33:7-23　　　　1 Thess. 3
Saturday, 75, 76 / 114, 115
Exod. 34:1-10,29-35　1 Thess. 4:1-12

WEEK OF 5 EASTER
Monday, [82, 83] or 104 / 80, 81
Exod. 40:18-38　　　　1 Thess. 4:13-18
Tuesday, 84, 85 / 86, 87
Lev. 23:1-14　　　　　1 Thess. 5:1-11
Wednesday, 110:1-5(6)7, 116 / [88] or 134, 135
Lev. 23:15-22　　　　1 Thess. 5:12-28
Thursday, 89:1-18 / 89:19-52
Lev. 23:23-32　　　　2 Thess. 1
Friday, 90, 93 / 91, 92
Lev. 23:33-44　　　　2 Thess. 2:13-3:5

YEAR ONE
Saturday, 94, [95] / 117, 118
Dan. 5:13-30 Rom. 15:1-13 Luke 9:1-6,10-17

WEEK OF 6 EASTER
Monday, 104:1-34(35-37) / 65
Deut. 8:1-10 James 1:1-15
Tuesday, 34 / 50:1-15
Deut. 8:11-20 James 1:16-26 Luke 9:7-9,18-27
Wednesday, 111 / ---
Baruch 3:24-37 James 5:13-18 Luke 11:1-13
Eve of Ascension --- / 93
2 Chron. 6:12-21 Rev. 5 Luke 12:22-31

ASCENSION DAY, 47 / 96
2 Kings 2:6-16 Heb. 2:5-18 Matt. 28:16-20
Friday, 145 / 141, 142
Dan. 7:9-14 Heb. 4:14-5:6 Luke 9:28-36
Saturday, 63:1-8(9-11), 64 / 112, 113
Ezek. 1:1-12,26-28a Heb. 5:7-14 Luke 9:37-49

WEEK OF 7 EASTER
Monday, 96, 97 / 98, 99, [100]
Ezek. 1:28b-3:3 Heb. 6:1-12 Luke 9:51-62
Tuesday, 105:1-22 / 105:23-45
Ezek. 3:4-15 Heb. 6:13-20 Luke 10:1-16

YEAR TWO
Saturday, 94, [95] / 117, 118
Lev. 25:1-12 2 Thess. 3:6-16 Matt. 7:1-12

WEEK OF 6 EASTER
Monday, 104:1-34(35-37) / 65
Amos 9:11-15 Col. 1:9-14 Matt. 13:1-16
Tuesday, 34 / 50:1-15
Deut. 26:1-11 Rom. 8:26-33 Matt. 13:18-23
Wednesday, 111 / ---
Baruch 3:24-37 Eph. 1:3-10 Matt. 22:41-45
Eve of Ascension --- / 93
2 Chron. 6:12-21 Rev. 5

ASCENSION DAY, 47 / 96
2 Kings 2:6-16 Heb. 2:5-18 Matt. 28:16-20
Friday, 145 / 141, 142
1 Sam. 2:1-10 Eph. 2:1-10 Matt. 7:13-21
Saturday, 63:1-8(9-11), 64 / 112, 113
Num. 11:16-17,24-29 Eph. 3:14-21 Matt. 7:22-27

WEEK OF 7 EASTER
Monday, 96, 97 / 98, 99, [100]
Exod. 3:1-12 Eph. 2:11-22 Matt. 7:28-8:4
Tuesday, 105:1-22 / 105:23-45
Joshua 1:1-9 Eph. 3:1-13 Matt. 8:5-17

The Daily Office Revised

Wednesday, 117, 118 / 102

Ezek. 3:22-27	Heb. 7:1-17	Luke 10:17-24

Thursday, 106:1-18 / 106:19-48

Ezek. 37:1-14	Heb. 7:18-28	Luke 10:25-37

Friday, 103 / 107:1-31

Ezek. 39:21-29	Heb. 8	Luke 10:38-42

Saturday, 143 / ---

Ezek. 43:1-9	Heb. 9:1-14	Luke 11:14-26

Eve of Pentecost --- / 46, 111

Exod. 19:3-8a,16-20	1 Peter 2:4-10

WEEK OF PENTECOST galley[iv]

Monday, 139:1-17 / 138

Wisdom 1:1-15	Acts 1:1-14	Luke 11:27-36

Tuesday, 148 / 18:1-20

Wisdom 1:16-2:15	Acts 1:15-26	Luke 11:37-52

Wednesday, 8 / 132

Wisdom 2:21-3:9	Acts 2:1-21	Luke 11:53-12:12

Thursday, 145 / 144

Wisdom 5:1-16	Acts 2:22-36	Luke 12:13-31

Friday, 136:1-16(17-22)23-26 / 142

Wisdom 6:1-3,12-21	Acts 2:37-47	Luke 12:32-48

Saturday, 19 / ---

Wisdom 7:1-7,15-22	Acts 4:32-5:11	Luke 12:49-59

Wednesday, 117, 118 / 102

1 Sam. 3:1-9	Eph. 4:1-16	Matt. 8:18-27

Thursday, 106:1-18 / 106:19-48

Isa. 6	Eph. 4:17-32	Matt. 8:28-34

Friday, 103 / 107:1-31

Jer. 1:4-8,13-19	Eph. 5:1-20	Matt. 9:1-8

Saturday, 143 / ---

Ezek. 2:1-7	Eph. 6:10-20	Matt. 9:9-17

Eve of Pentecost --- / 46, 111

Exod. 19:3-8a,16-20	1 Peter 2:4-10

WEEK OF PENTECOST

Monday, 139:1-17 / 138

Zech. 4	Rom. 8:1-11	Matt. 9:35-10:4

Tuesday, 148 / 18:1-20

Haggai 2:1-9	Rom. 8:12-17	Matt. 10:5-15

Wednesday, 8 / 132

1 Sam. 16:1-13a	Rom. 8:18-25	Matt. 10:16-23

Thursday, 145 / 144

Ezek. 36:22-27	Rom. 8:26-30	Matt. 10:24-33

Friday, 136:1-16(17-22)23-26 / 142

Micah 3:1-8	Rom. 8:31-39	Matt. 10:33-11:1

Saturday, 19 / ---

Jer. 31:27-34	Rom. 1:1-15	Matt. 11:2-11

[iv] [Ed. note: This cryptic misprint is, most likely, a reference to Howard Galley who did yeoman's work on the draft prayer books. This inclusion probably indicates that he was the chief editor of this section of the lectionary.]

YEAR ONE

Eve of Trinity Sunday --- / 147
Ecclus. 42:15-25   Eph. 3:14-21 (43:27-33)

WEEK OF 1 PENTECOST

Monday, 1, 2:1-8(9-13), 3 / 4, 10
Wisdom 7:22-8:1   Acts 5:12-26   Luke 13:1-9
Tuesday, 5, 6 / 7, 8
Wisdom 8:21-9:6   Acts 5:27-42   Luke 13:10-17
Wednesday, 119:1-24 / 11, 12, 13
Wisdom 9:7-18   Acts 6:1-15   Luke 13:18-30
Thursday, 9 / [14], 15, 16
Wisdom 10:9-21   Acts 6:15-7:16
Friday, 18:1-20 / 18:21-50
Wisdom 11:21-12:2   Acts 7:17-29   Luke 13:31-35
Saturday, 17, 21:1-7(8-13) / 104
Wisdom 13:1-9   Acts 7:30-43   Luke 14:1-11

WEEK OF 2 PENTECOST

Monday, 19, 20 / 23, 27
Num. 9:15-23   Acts 7:44-8:1   Luke 14:12-24
Tuesday, 26, 28 / 24, 25
Num. 11:1-15   Acts 8:1-13   Luke 14:25-35
Wednesday, 119:25-48 / 29, 30
Num. 11:16-23   Acts 8:14-25   Luke 15:1-10
Thursday, 33 / 34
Num. 11:24-30   Acts 8:26-40   Luke 15:1-2, 11-32
                                 Luke 16:1-9

YEAR TWO

Eve of Trinity Sunday --- / 147
Ecclus. 42:15-25   Eph. 3:14-21 (43:27-33)

WEEK OF 1 PENTECOST

Monday, 1, 2:1-8(9-13), 3 / 4, 10
Isa. 40:12-31   Rom. 1:16-25   Matt. 11:25-30
Tuesday, 5, 6 / 7, 8
Isa. 43:1-13   Rom. 1:28-2:11   Matt. 11:11-24
Wednesday, 119:1-24 / 11, 12, 13
Isa. 44:6-22   Rom. 2:12-24   Matt. 9:18-26
Thursday, 9 / [14] 15, 16
Isa. 45:1-7   Rom. 2:25-3:8   Matt. 9:27-34
Friday, 18:1-20 / 18:21-50
Wisdom 14:27-15:3   Rom. 3:9-20   Matt. 12:1-14
Saturday, 17, 21:1-7(8-13) / 104
Wisdom 16:24-17:1   Rom. 3:21-31   Matt. 12:15-21

WEEK OF 2 PENTECOST

Monday, 19, 20 / 23, 27
1 Sam. 1:1-11   Rom. 4:1-12   Matt. 12:22-32
Tuesday, 26, 28 / 24, 25
1 Sam. 1:12-20   Rom. 4:13-25   Matt. 12:33-42
Wednesday, 119:25-48 / 29, 30
1 Sam. 1:21-28;2:11   Rom. 5:1-11   Matt. 12:43-50
Thursday, 33 / 34
1 Sam. 2:18-26   Rom. 5:12-21   Matt. 13:24-30

Friday, 32, 36 / 22
Num. 13:1-3,21-30　Acts 9:1-9　　　Luke 16:10-17(18)　　Matt. 13:36-43
Saturday, 31 / 110:1-5(6)7, 116
Num. 13:31-14:3,　Acts 9:10-19　　Luke 16:19-31　　　　Matt. 13:31-35
10b-23

Friday, 32, 36 / 22
1 Sam. 3:1-18　　Rom. 6:1-11
Saturday, 31 / 110:1-5(6)7, 116
1 Sam. 4:1b-11　Rom. 6:12-23

WEEK OF 3 PENTECOST
Monday, 37:1-23 / 37:24-42
Num. 16:1-19　　Acts 9:20-31　　　Luke 17:1-10
Tuesday, [35] or 117, 118 / 39, 41
Num. 16:20-35　 Acts 9:32-43　　　Luke 17:11-19
Wednesday, 119:49-72 / 42, 43
Num. 16:41-50　 Acts 10:1-16　　　Luke 17:20-37
Thursday, 40:1-14(15-19) / 45, 46
Num. 17:1-11　　Acts 10:17-33　　Luke 18:1-8
Friday, 38:1-4(5-8)9-22 / 51
Num. 20:1-13　　Acts 10:34-48　　Luke 18:9-14
Saturday, 44 / 146, 147
Num. 20:22-29　 Acts 11:1-18　　　Luke 18:15-30

WEEK OF 3 PENTECOST
Monday, 37:1-23 / 37:24-42
1 Sam. 4:12-22　Rom. 7:1-12　　　　Matt. 13:44-52
Tuesday, [35] or 117, 118 / 39, 41
1 Sam. 5:1-11　　Rom. 7:13-25　　　Matt. 13:53-58
Wednesday, 119:49-72 / 42, 43
1 Sam. 6:1-16　　Rom. 9:1-18　　　 Matt. 14:1-12
Thursday, 40:1-14(15-19) / 45, 46
1 Sam. 9:1-10　　Rom. 9:19-26　　　Matt. 14:13-21
Friday, 38:1-4(5-8)9-22 / 51
1 Sam. 9:11-24a　Rom. 10:1-13　　　Matt. 14:22-36
Saturday, 44 / 146, 147
1 Sam. 9:24b-10:8　Rom. 10:14-21　 Matt. 15:1-20

WEEK OF 4 PENTECOST
Monday, 47, 48 / 49
Num. 21:4-9　　　Acts 11:19-30　　Luke 18:31-43
Tuesday, 50 / [52, 53, 54] or 148, 150
Num. 22:1-12　　 Acts 12:1-17　　 Luke 19:1-10
Wednesday, 119:73-88 / 55:1-15(16)17-26
Num. 22:13-31　 Acts 12:18-25　　Luke 19:11-27

WEEK OF 4 PENTECOST
Monday, 47, 48 / 49
1 Sam. 10:9-16　 Rom. 11:1-12　　　Matt. 15:21-28
Tuesday, 50 / [52, 53, 54] or 148, 150
1 Sam. 11:1-13　 Rom. 11:13-24　　 Matt. 15:29-38
Wednesday, 119:73-88 / 55:1-15(16)17-26
1 Sam. 13:19-14:15　Rom. 11:25-36　Matt. 16:1-12

YEAR ONE

Thursday, 56, 57, [58] / [59, 60] or 114, 115
Num. 22:31-38   Acts 13:1-12   Luke 19:28-40

Friday, 61, 62 / 69:1-23(24-30)31-38
Num. 22:41-23:12   Acts 13:13-25   Luke 19:41-48

Saturday, 63:1-8(9-11), 64 / 111, 112, 113
Num. 23:11-26   Acts 13:26-43   Luke 20:1-8

WEEK OF 5 PENTECOST

Monday, 67, 72 / 65, 66
Num. 24:1-13   Acts 13:44-52   Luke 20:9-18(19)

Tuesday, [70], 71 / 68:1-20(21-23)24-35
Num. 27:12-23   Acts 14:1-18   Luke 20: (19)20-26

Wednesday, 119:89-112 / 73
Num. 32:1-6,16-22   Acts 14:19-28   Luke 20:27-40

Thursday, 74 / 77, [79]
Num. 35:1-3,9-15   Acts 15:1-11   Luke 20:41-21:4

Friday, 78:1-39 / 78:40-72
Deut. 3:18-28   Acts 15:12-21   Luke 21:5-19

Saturday, 75, 76 / 114, 115
Deut. 32:45-52   Acts 15:22-35   Luke 21:20-28

WEEK OF 6 PENTECOST

Monday, [82, 83] or 104 / 80, 81
Joshua 1:1-9   Acts 15:36-16:5   Luke 21:29-36

YEAR TWO

Thursday, 56, 57, [58] / [59, 60] or 114, 115
1 Sam. 14:16-30   Rom. 12:1-8   Matt. 16:13-20

Friday, 61, 62 / 69:1-23(24-30)31-38
1 Sam. 14:36-45   Rom. 12:9-21   Matt. 16:21-28

Saturday, 63:1-8(9-11), 64 / 111, 112, 113
1 Sam. 15:1-3,7-23   Rom. 13:1-7   Matt. 17:1-13

WEEK OF 5 PENTECOST

Monday, 67, 72 / 65, 66
1 Sam. 15:24-35   Rom. 13:8-14   Matt. 17:14-21

Tuesday, [70], 71 / 68:1-20(21-23)24-35
1 Sam. 16:1-13   Rom. 14:1-12   Matt. 17:22-27

Wednesday, 119:89-112 / 73
1 Sam. 17:1-11   Rom. 14:13-23   Matt. 18:1-9

Thursday, 74 / 77, [79]
1 Sam. 17:17-30   Rom. 15:1-13   Math 18:10-20

Friday, 78:1-39 / 78:40-72
1 Sam. 17:31-37, 41-49   Rom. 15:14-24   Matt. 18:21-35

Saturday, 75, 76 / 114, 115
1 Sam. 17:50-18:4   Rom. 15:25-32   Matt. 19:1-12

WEEK OF 6 PENTECOST

Monday, [82, 83] or 104 / 80, 81
1 Sam. 18:5-16   Rom. 16:1-16   Matt. 19:13-22

The Daily Office Revised 87

Tuesday, 84, 85 / 86, 87
Joshua 1:10-18   Acts 16:6-15   Luke 21:37-22:13
Wednesday, 119:113-128 / [88] or 134, 135
Joshua 2:1-14   Acts 16:16-24   Luke 22:14-23
Thursday, 89:1-18 / 89:19-52
Joshua 2:15-23   Acts 16:25-40   Luke 22:24-30
Friday, 90, 93 / 91, 92
Joshua 3:1-13   Acts 17:1-15   Luke 22:31-38
Saturday, 94, [95] / 117, 118
Joshua 3:14-4:7   Acts 17:16-34   Luke 22:39-51

WEEK OF 7 PENTECOST
Monday, 96, 97 / 98, 99, [100]
Joshua 5:13-6:11   Acts 18:1-11   Luke 22:52-62
Tuesday, 105:1-22 / 105:23-45
Joshua 6:12-23   Acts 18:12-28   Luke 22:63-71
Wednesday, 119:129-152 / 102
Joshua 7:1,6-13   Acts 19:1-10   Luke 23:1-12
Thursday, 106:1-18 / 106:19-48
Joshua 8:30-35   Acts 19:11-20   Luke 23:13-25
Friday, 103 / 107:1-31
Joshua 23:1-3, 14-16   Acts 19:21-41   Luke 23:26-31
Saturday, 107:32-42, 108:1-6(7-13) / 134, 135
Joshua 24:1-15   Acts 20:1-16   Luke 23:32-43

WEEK OF 8 PENTECOST
Monday, 101, 109:1-4(5-19)20-30 / [120], 121, 122, 123
Joshua 24:16-28   Acts 20:17-38   Luke 23:44-56a

Tuesday, 84, 85 / 86, 87
1 Sam. 19:1-7,11-18   Rom. 16:17-27   Matt. 19:23-30
Wednesday, 119:113-128 / [88] or 134, 135
1 Sam. 20:1-23   Acts 1:1-14   Matt. 20:1-16
Thursday, 89:1-18 / 89:19-52
1 Sam. 20:24-42   Acts 1:15-26   Matt. 20:17-28
Friday, 90, 93 / 91, 92
1 Sam. 21:1-10   Acts 2:1-21   Matt. 20:29-34
Saturday, 94, [95] / 117, 118
1 Sam. 22:6-23   Acts 2:22-36   Matt. 21:1-11

WEEK OF 7 PENTECOST
Monday, 96, 97 / 98, 99, [100]
1 Sam. 23:7-18   Acts 2:37-47   Matt. 21:12-22
Tuesday, 105:1-22 / 105:23-45
1 Sam. 24   Acts 3:1-11   Matt. 21:23-32
Wednesday, 119:129-152 / 102
1 Sam. 28:3-19   Acts 3:12-26   Matt. 21:33-45
Thursday, 106:1-18 / 106:19-48
1 Sam. 31   Acts 4:1-12   Matt. 22:1-14
Friday, 103 / 107:1-31
2 Sam. 1:1-16   Acts 4:13-31   Matt. 22:15-22
Saturday, 107:32-42, 108:1-6(7-13) / 134, 135
2 Sam. 1:17-27   Acts 4:32-5:11   Matt. 22:23-33

WEEK OF 8 PENTECOST
Monday, 101, 109:1-4(5-19)20-30 / [120], 121, 122, 123
2 Sam. 2:1-11   Acts 5:12-26   Matt. 23:1-12

YEAR ONE

Tuesday, 124, 125, 126, [127] / 128, 129, 130
Judges 2:1-3,11-18   Acts 21:1-14   Luke 23:56b-24:11
Wednesday, 119:153-176 / 131, 132, [133]
Judges 4:1-10   Acts 21:15-26   Luke 24:12-21 (22-24)25-35

Thursday, 136, 137:1-6(7-9) / 138, 139:1-17(18-23)
Judges 4:11-23   Acts 21:27-36   Luke 24:36-51
Friday, 143, 144 / 140:1-8(9-11)12-13, 141, 142
Judges 5:1-18   Acts 21:37-22:16   Mark 1:1-13
Saturday, 145 / 148, 149, 150
Judges 5:19-31   Acts 22:17-29   Mark 1:14-28

WEEK OF 9 PENTECOST

Monday, 1, 2:1-8(9-13), 3 / 4, 10
Judges 6:1-23   Acts 22:30-23:11   Mark 1:29-45
Tuesday, 5, 6 / 7, 8
Judges 6:24-32   Acts 23:12-24   Mark 2:1-12
Wednesday, 119:1-24 / 11, 12, 13
Judges 6:33-40   Acts 23:23-35   Mark 2:13-22
Thursday, 9 / [14], 15, 16
Judges 7:1-8   Acts 24:1-23   Mark 2:23-3:6
Friday, 18:1-20 / 18:21-50
Judges 7:9-23   Acts 24:24-25:12   Mark 3:7-19a
Saturday, 17, 21:1-7(8-13) / 104
Judges 8:22-28,33-35   Acts 25:13-27   Mark 3:20-35

YEAR TWO

Tuesday, 124, 125, 126, [127] / 128, 129, 130
2 Sam. 5:1-10   Acts 5:27-42   Matt. 23:16-26
Wednesday, 119:153-176 / 131, 132, [133]
2 Sam. 6:1-19   Acts 6:1-15   Matt. 23:29-39

Thursday, 136, 137:1-6(7-9) / 138, 139:1-17(18-23)
2 Sam. 7:1-17   Acts 6:15-7:16   Matt. 24:1-14
Friday, 143, 144 / 140:1-8(9-11)12-13, 141, 142
2 Sam. 7:18-29   Acts 7:17-29   Matt. 24:15-31
Saturday, 145 / 148, 149, 150
2 Sam. 9:1-9, 13   Acts 7:30-43   Matt. 24:45-51

WEEK OF 9 PENTECOST

Monday, 1, 2:1-8(9-13), 3 / 4, 10
2 Sam. 11   Acts 7:44-8:1   Matt. 25:1-13
Tuesday, 5, 6 / 7, 8
2 Sam. 12:1-14   Acts 8:1-13   Matt. 25:14-30
Wednesday, 119:1-24 / 11, 12, 13
2 Sam. 12:15b-25   Acts 8:14-25   Matt. 25:31-46
Thursday, 9 / [14], 15, 16
2 Sam. 15:1-12   Acts 8:26-40   Matt. 26:1-16
Friday, 18:1-20 / 18:21-50
2 Sam. 15:13-31   Acts 9:1-9   Matt. 26:17-25
Saturday, 17, 21:1-7(8-13) / 104
2 Sam. 16:15-17:41   Acts 9:10-19   Matt. 26:26-35

WEEK OF 10 PENTECOST
Monday, 26, 28 / 23, 27
Judges 9:1-16,19-21 Acts 26:1-23 Mark 4:1-20
Tuesday, 19, 20 / 24, 25
Judges 9:22-25, 50-57 Acts 26:24-27:8 Mark 4:21-34
Wednesday, 119:25-48 / 29, 30
Judges 11:1-11 Acts 27:9-26 Mark 4:35-41
Thursday, 33 / 34
Judges 11:29-40 Acts 27:27-44 Mark 5:1-20
Friday, 32, 36 / 22
Judges 13:1-14 Acts 28:1-16 Mark 5:21-43
Saturday, 31 / 110:1-5(6)7, 116
Judges 13:15-24 Acts 28:17-31 Mark 6:1-13

WEEK OF 11 PENTECOST
Monday, 37:1-23 / 37:24-42
Judges 14:1, 5-19a Phil. 1:1-11 Mark 6:14-29
Tuesday, [35] or 117, 118 / 39, 41
Judges 14:20-15:8 Phil. 1:12-29 Mark 6:30-46
Wednesday, 119:49-72 / 42, 43
Judges 15:9-20 Phil. 2:1-11 Mark 6:47-56
Thursday, 40:1-14(15-19) / 45, 46
Judges 16:1-14 Phil. 2:12-18 Mark 7:1-23
Friday, 38:1-4(5-8)9-22 / 51
Judges 16:15-22 Phil. 2:19-3:1 Mark 7:24-37

WEEK OF 10 PENTECOST
Monday, 26, 28 / 23, 27
2 Sam. 18:1-17 Acts 9:20-31 Matt. 25:31-46
Tuesday, 19, 20 / 24, 25
2 Sam. 18:19-33 Acts 9:32-43 Matt. 26:47-56
Wednesday, 119:25-48 / 29, 30
2 Sam.19:1-15, 41-43 Acts 10:1-16 Matt 26:57-68
Thursday, 33 / 34
2 Sam 23:8-17 Acts 10:17-33 Matt. 26:69-75
Friday, 32, 36 / 22
2 Sam. 24:1-2,10-25 Acts 10:34-48 Matt. 27:1-10
Saturday, 31 / 110:1-5(6)7, 116
1 Kings 1:5-31 Acts 11:1-18 Matt. 27:11-23

WEEK OF 11 PENTECOST
Monday, 37:1-23 / 37:24-42
1 Kings 1:38-48; Acts 11:19-30 Matt. 27:24-31
2:1-4
Tuesday, [35] or 117, 118 / 39, 41
1 Sam. 8 Acts 12:1-17 Matt. 27:32-44
Wednesday, 119:49-72 / 42, 43
1 Kings 3:1-15 Acts 12:18-25 Matt. 27:45-54
Thursday, 40:1-14(15-19) / 45, 46
1 Kings 8:1-21 Acts 13:1-12 Matt. 27:55-66
Friday, 38:1-4(5-8)9-22 / 51
1 Kings 8:22-30 Acts 13:13-25 Matt. 28:1-10
(31-43)

YEAR ONE

Saturday, 44 / 146, 147
Judges 16:23-31   Phil. 3:2-4:1   Mark 8:1-10

WEEK OF 12 PENTECOST
Monday, 47, 48 / 49
Job 2:11-3:10,20-26   James 2:1-13   Mark 8:11-21
Tuesday, 50 / [52, 53, 54] or 148, 150
Job 4:1-6,12-5:8   James 2:14-26   Mark 8:22-33
Wednesday, 119:73-88 / 55:1-15(16)17-26
Job 6:1-2,8-13,   James 3:1-12   Mark 8:34-9:11
24-28
Thursday, 56, 57, [58] / [59, 60] or 114, 115
Job. 8:1-10,20-22   James 3:13-4:10   Mark 9:2-13
                      (11-12)
Friday, 61, 62 / 69:1-23(24-30)31-38
Job 9:1-12,14-15   James 4:13-5:6   Mark 9:14-29
Saturday, 63:1-8(9-11), 64 / 111, 112, 113
Job 10:1-9,18-22   James 5:7-12   Mark 9:30-41

WEEK OF 13 PENTECOST
Monday, 67, 72 / 65, 66
Job 11:1-6,13-20   2 Cor. 10   Mark 9:42-50
Tuesday, [70], 71 / 68:1-20(21-23)24-35
Job 12:1-4;13:1-12   2 Cor. 11:1-21a   Mark 10:1-16
Wednesday, 119:89-112 / 73
Job 14:1-17   2 Cor. 11:21b-30   Mark 10:17-31

YEAR TWO

Saturday, 44 / 146, 147
1 Kings 8:54-62   Acts 13:26-43   Matt. 28:11-20

WEEK OF 12 PENTECOST
Monday, 47, 48 / 49
1 Kings 9:1-9   Acts 13:44-52   John 1:1-18
Tuesday, 50 / [52, 53, 54] or 148, 150
1 Kings 10:1-13   Acts 14:1-18   John 1:19-28
Wednesday, 119:73-88 / 55:1-15(16)17-26
1 Kings 11:9-12,   Acts 14:19-28   John 1:29-42
26-43
Thursday, 56, 57, [58] / [59, 60] or 114, 115
1 Kings 12:1-20   Acts 15:1-11   John 1:43-51
Friday, 61, 62 / 69:1-23(24-30)31-38
1 Kings 12:21-33   Acts 15:12-21   John 2:1-12
Saturday, 63:1-8(9-11), 64 / 111, 112, 113
1 Kings 16:25-34   Acts 15:22-35   John 2:13-25

WEEK OF 13 PENTECOST
Monday, 67, 72 / 65, 66
1 Kings 17   Acts 15:36-16:5   John 3:1-21
Tuesday, [70], 71 / 68:1-20(21-23)24-35
1 Kings 18:1-19   Acts 16:6-15   John 3:22-36
Wednesday, 119:89-112 / 73
1 Kings 18:20-40   Acts 16:16-24   John 4:1-26

The Daily Office Revised 91

Thursday, 74 / 77, [79]
Job 18:1-7;19:1-9   2 Cor. 12:1-10   Mark 10:32-45
Friday, 78:1-39 / 78:40-72
Job 20:1-9;21:1-16,34;   2 Cor. 12:11-21   Mark 10:46-52
Saturday, 75, 76 / 114, 115
Job 22:1-5,21-23;7   2 Cor. 13   Mark 11:1-11

WEEK OF 14 PENTECOST
Monday, [82, 83] or 104 / 80, 81
Job 23:8-24:1   2 Cor. 1:1-11   Mark 11:11-26
Tuesday, 84, 85 / 86, 87
Job 25:2-6;26:6-14   2 Cor. 1:12-22   Mark 11:27-12:12
Wednesday, 119:113-128 / [88] or 134, 135
Job 29:1-30:1   2 Cor. 1:23-2:17   Mark 12:13-27
Thursday, 89:1-18 / 89:19-52
Job 38:1-11,16-18   2 Cor. 3   Mark 12:28-34
Friday, 90, 93 / 91, 92
Job 38:19-38   2 Cor. 4:1-12   Mark 12:35-44
Saturday, 94, [95] / 117, 118
Job 38:39-39:12   2 Cor. 4:13-5:10   Mark 13:1-13

WEEK OF 15 PENTECOST
Monday, 96, 97 / 98, 99, [100]
Job 39:19-40:1   2 Cor. 5:11-6:2   Mark 13:14-27
Tuesday, 105:1-22 / 105:23-45
Job 40:3-9;41:1-11   2 Cor. 6:3-13;7:2-4   Mark 13:28-37
Wednesday, 119:129-152 / 102
Job 42:1-9   2 Cor. 7:5-16   Mark 14:1-11

Thursday, 74 / 77, [79]
1 Kings 18:41-19:8   Acts 16:25-40   John 4:27-42
Friday, 78:1-39 / 78:40-72
1 Kings 19:8-21   Acts 17:1-15   John 4:43-5:1
Saturday, 75, 76 / 114, 115
1 Kings 21:1-16   Acts 17:16-34   John 5:2-18

WEEK OF 14 PENTECOST
Monday, [82, 83] or 104 / 80, 81
1 Kings 21:17-29   Acts 18:1-11   John 5:19-29
Tuesday, 84, 85 / 86, 87
1 Kings 22:1-28   Acts 18:12-28   John 5:30-47
Wednesday, 119:113-128 / [88] or 134, 135
1 Kings 22:29-45   Acts 19:1-10   John 6:1-15
Thursday, 89:1-18 / 89:19-52
2 Kings 1:2-8,15-17a   Acts 19:11-20   John 6:16-27
Friday, 90, 93 / 91, 92
2 Kings 2:1-15   Acts 19:21-41   John 6:28-40
Saturday, 94, [95] / 117, 118
2 Kings 4:8-37   Acts 20:1-16   John 6:21-51

WEEK OF 15 PENTECOST
Monday, 96, 97 / 98, 99, [100]
2 Kings 5:1-19a   Acts 20:17-38   John 6:52-59
Tuesday, 105:1-22 / 105:23-45
2 Kings 5:19b-27   Acts 21:1-14   John 6:60-71
Wednesday, 119:129-152 / 102
2 Kings 6:8-23   Acts 21:15-26   John 7:1-13

YEAR ONE
Thursday, 106:1-18 / 106:19-48
Job 1　　　　　2 Cor. 8:1-15　　　Mark 14:12-26
Friday, 103 / 107:1-31
Job 2:1-10　　　2 Cor. 8:16-24　　Mark 14:27-32
Saturday, 107:32-42, 108:1-6(7-13) / 134, 135
Job. 42:10-16　　2 Cor. 9　　　　Mark 14:43-52

WEEK OF 16 PENTECOST
Monday, 101, 109:1-4(5-19)20-30 / [120] 121, 122, 123
Job 28:12-28　　1 Cor. 1:1-19　　Mark 14:53-65
Tuesday, 124, 125, 126, [127] / 128, 129, 130
Ecclus. 1:1-10, 18-27 1 Cor. 1:20-31　Mark 14:66-72
Wednesday, 119:153-176 / 131, 132, [133]
Ecclus. 4:11-19　　1 Cor. 2:1-13　　Mark 15:1-11
Thursday, 136, 137:1-6(7-9) / 138, 139:1-17(18-23)
Ecclus. 6:18-31　　1 Cor. 2:14-3:15　Mark 15:12-21
Friday, 145 / 140:1-8(9-11)12-13, 141, 142
Ecclus. 24:1-12　　1 Cor. 3:16-23　　Mark 15:22-32
Saturday, 143, 144 / 148, 149, 150
Ecclus. 51:13-22　1 Cor. 4:1-7　　　Mark 15:33-39

WEEK OF 17 PENTECOST
Monday, 1, 2:1-8(9-13), 3 / 4, 10
2 Chron. 5:2-14　1 Cor. 4:8-20(21)　Mark 15:40-47

YEAR TWO
Thursday, 106:1-18 / 106:19-48
2 Kings 9:1-13　　Acts 21:27-36　　John 7:14-31
Friday, 103 / 107:1-31
2 Kings 9:14-34　Acts 21:37-22:16　John 7:31-52
Saturday, 107:32-42, 108:1-6(7-13) / 134, 135
2 Kings 17:1-18　Acts 22:17-29　　John 8:12-20

WEEK OF 16 PENTECOST
Monday, 101, 109:1-4(5-19)20-30 / [120], 121, 122, 123
2 Kings 18:1-25　Acts 22:30-23:11　John 8:21-32
Tuesday, 124, 125, 126, [127] / 128, 129, 130
2 Kings 19:1-20　Acts 23:12-24　　John 8:33-47
Wednesday, 119:153-176 / 131, 132, [133]
2 Kings 19:21-36　Acts 23:23-35　　John 8:47-59
Thursday, 136, 137:1-6(7-9) / 138, 139:1-17(18-23)
2 Kings 21:1-18　Acts 24:1-23　　John 9:1-17
Friday, 145 / 140:1-8(9-11)12-13, 141, 142
2 Kings 22:1-13　Acts 24:24-25:12　John 9:18-38
Saturday, 143, 144 / 148, 149, 150
2 Kings 22:14-23:3　Acts 25:13-27　John 9:34-41; 10:19-30

WEEK OF 17 PENTECOST
Monday, 1, 2:1-8(9-13), 3 / 4, 10
2 Kings 23:4-25　Acts 26:1-23　　John 10:1-18

The Daily Office Revised   93

Tuesday, 5, 6 / 7, 8
2 Chron. 6:1-11   1 Cor. 5:1-8   Mark 16:1-8(9-19)
Wednesday, 119:1-24 / 11, 12, 13
2 Chron. 6:12-21   1 Cor. 5:9-6:8   Matt. 2:1-12
Thursday, 9 / [14], 15, 16
2 Chron. 6:22-31   1 Cor. 6:9-20   Matt. 2:13-23
Friday, 18:1-20 / 18:21-50
2 Chron. 6:32-42   1 Cor. 7:1-9   Matt. 3:1-12
Saturday, 17, 21:1-7(8-13) / 104
2 Chron. 7:1-10   1 Cor. 7:10-24   Matt. 3:13-17

WEEK OF 18 PENTECOST
Monday, 19, 20 / 23, 27
Hosea 1:1-2:1   1 Cor. 7:25-31   Matt. 4:1-11
Tuesday, 26, 28 / 24, 25
Hosea 2:2-9,14-15   1 Cor. 7:32-40   Matt. 4:12-17
Wednesday, 119:25-48 / 29, 30
Hosea 2:16-23   1 Cor. 8   Matt. 4:18-25
Thursday, 33 / 34
Hosea 4:1-10   1 Cor. 9:1-15   Matt. 5:1-10
Friday, 32, 36 / 22
Hosea 5:8-6:6   1 Cor. 9:16-27   Matt. 5:11-16
Saturday, 31 / 110:1-5(6)7, 116
Hosea 11:1-9   1 Cor. 10:1-13   Matt. 5:17-20

Tuesday, 5, 6 / 7, 8
2 Kings 23:36-24:17   Acts 26:24-27:8   John 10:30-42
Wednesday, 119:1-24 / 11, 12, 13
Jer. 35   Acts 27:9-26   John 11:1-16
Thursday, 9 / [14], 15, 16
Jer. 36:1-10   Acts 27:27-44   John 11:17-29
Friday, 18:1-20 / 18:21-50
Jer. 36:11-26   Acts 28:1-16   John 11:30-44
Saturday, 17, 21:1-7(8-13) / 104
Jer. 36:27-37:2   Acts 28:17-31   John 11:45-54

WEEK OF 18 PENTECOST
Monday, 19, 20 / 23, 27
Jer. 37:3-21   Rev. 7:1-8   John 11:55-12:8
Tuesday, 26, 28 / 24, 25
Jer. 38:1-13   Rev. 7:9-17   John 12:9-19
Wednesday, 119:25-48 / 29, 30
Jer. 38:14-28   Rev. 8   John 12:20-26
Thursday, 33 / 34
2 Kings 25:8-12, 22-26   Rev. 9:1-12   John 12:27-36a
Friday, 32, 36 / 22
Jer. 29:1, 4-14   Rev. 9:13-21   John 12:44-50
Saturday, 31 / 110:1-5(6)7, 116
Jer. 44:1-14   Rev. 10   John 12:36b-43

YEAR ONE

WEEK OF 19 PENTECOST
Monday, 37:1-23 / 37:24-42
Hosea 13:4-14　　1 Cor. 10:14-11:1　Matt. 5:21-26
Tuesday, [35] or 117, 118 / 39, 41
Hosea 14　　1 Cor. 11:1-16　　Matt. 5:27-37
Wednesday, 119:49-72 / 42, 43
Micah (1:1)2:1-13　1 Cor. 11:17-34　Matt. 5:38-48
Thursday, 40:1-14(15-19) / 45, 46
Micah 3:9-4:5　　1 Cor. 12:1-11　　Matt. 6:1-6, 16-18
Friday, 38:1-4(5-8)9-22 / 51
Micah 5:1-5, 10-15　1 Cor. 12:12-26　Matt. 6:7-15

Saturday, 44 / 146, 147
Micah 6:1-8　　1 Cor. 12:27-13:3　Matt. 6:19-24

WEEK OF 20 PENTECOST
Monday, 50 / 49
Jonah 1:1-16　　1 Cor. 13:(1-3)4-13　Matt. 6:25-34
Tuesday, 47, 48 / [52, 53, 54] or 148, 150
Jonah 1:17-2:10　1 Cor. 14:1-12　　Matt. 7:1-12
Wednesday, 119:73-88 / 55:1-15(16)17-26
Jonah 3　　　　1 Cor. 14:13-25　　Matt. 7:13-21
Thursday, 56, 57, [58] / [59, 60] or 114, 115
Jonah 4　　　　1 Cor. 14:26-40　　Matt. 7:22-29

YEAR TWO

WEEK OF 19 PENTECOST
Monday, 37:1-23 / 37:24-42
Ezra 1:1-8　　　Rev. 11:1-14　　Luke 2:25-39
Tuesday, [35] or 117, 118 / 39, 41
Ezra 3　　　　Rev. 11:14-19　　Luke 2:41-52
Wednesday, 119:49-72 / 42, 43
Ezra 4:7, 11-24　Rev. 12:1-6　　Luke 3:1-14
Thursday, 40:1-14(15-19) / 45, 46
Haggai 1　　　Rev. 12:7-17　　Luke 3:15-20
Friday, 38:1-4(5-8)9-22 / 51
Haggai 2:1-9　　Rev. 13:1-10　　Luke 3:21-22; 4:1-13

Saturday, 44 / 146, 147
Zech. 1:7-17　　Rev. 13:11-18　　Luke 4:14-30

WEEK OF 20 PENTECOST
Monday, 50 / 49
Ezra 5:1-2,6-17　Rev. 14:1-13　　Luke 4:31-37
Tuesday, 47, 48 / [52, 53, 54] or 148, 150
Ezra 6;1-15,19-22　Rev. 14:14-20　Luke 4:38-44
Wednesday, 119:73-88 / 55:1-15(16)17-26
Ezra 7:11-26　　Rev. 15　　　　Luke 5:1-11
Thursday, 56, 57, [58] / [59, 60] or 114, 115
Ezra 7:27-28;8:　Rev. 16:1-11　　Luke 5:12-26
15a,21-23

The Daily Office Revised

Friday, 61, 62 / 69:1-23(24-30)31-38
Prayer of Manasseh 1-7 | 1 Cor. 15:1-11 | Matt. 8:1-13
Neh. 1 | Rev. 16:12-21 | Luke 5:27-39

Saturday, 63:1-8(9-11), 64 / 111, 112, 113
Prayer of Manasseh 8-15 | 1 Cor. 15:12-28 | Matt. 8:(14-17)18-27
Neh. 2 | Rev. 17:1-6 | Luke 6:1-11

WEEK OF 21 PENTECOST

Monday, 67, 72 / 65, 66
Ecclus. 2 | 1 Cor. 15:(29)30-41 | Matt. 8:28-34
Neh. 4:6-23 | Rev. 17:7-18 | Luke 6:12-26

Tuesday, [70], 71 / 68:1-20(21-23)24-35
Ecclus. 3:17-31 | 1 Cor. 15:41-50 | Matt. 9:1-8
Neh. 5:1-13 | Rev. 19:1-10 | Luke 6:27-38

Wednesday, 119:89-112 / 73
Ecclus. 4:20-5:7 | 1 Cor. 15:51-58 | Matt. 9:9-17
Neh. 8:1-3,5-18 | Gal. 1:1-17 | Luke 6:39-49

Thursday, 74 / 77, [79]
Ecclus. 5:9-6:1 | 1 Cor. 16:1-9 | Matt. 9:18-26
Neh. 9:1-15 | Gal. 1:18-2:10 | Luke 7:1-17

Friday, 78:1-39 / 78:40-72
Ecclus. 6:5-17 | 1 Cor. 16:10-24 | Matt. 9:27-34
Neh. 9:26-38 | Gal. 2:11-21 | Luke 7:18-28, 31-35

Saturday, 75, 76 / 114, 115
Ecclus. 7:4-14 | Philemon | Matt. 9:35-10:4
Neh. 13:15-22 | Gal. 3:1-14 | Luke 7:36-50

WEEK OF 22 PENTECOST

Monday, [82, 83] or 104 / 80, 81
Ecclus. 10:1-18 | Rev. 1:4-20 | Matt. 10:5-15
Eccles. 1:1-11 | Gal. 3:15-22 | Luke 8:1-15

YEAR ONE
Tuesday, 84, 85 / 86, 87
Ecclus. 11:2-20 Rev. 4 Matt. 10:16-23
Wednesday, 119:113-128 / [88] or 134, 135
Ecclus. 15:9-20 Rev. 5:1-10 Matt. 10:24-33
Thursday, 89:1-18 / 89:19-52
Ecclus. 16:17-30 Rev. 5:11-14 Matt. 10:33-42
Friday, 90, 93 / 91, 92
Ecclus. 17:1-24 Rev. 6:1-7:3 Matt. 11:1-6
Saturday, 94, [95] / 117, 118
Ecclus. 18:1-14 Rev. 7:4, 9-17 Matt. 11:7-15

WEEK OF 23 PENTECOST
Monday, 96, 97 / 98, 99, [100]
Ecclus. 18:19-33 Rev. 10 Matt. 11:16-24
Tuesday, 105:1-22 / 105:23-45
Ecclus. 19:4-17 Rev. 11:1-2, 5-19 Matt. 11:25-30
Wednesday, 119:129-152 / 102
Ecclus. 28:14-26 Rev. 12:1-12 Matt. 12:1-14
Thursday, 106:1-18 / 106:19-48
Ecclus. 31:12-18, Rev. 14:1-13 Matt. 12:15-21
25-32:2
Friday, 103 / 107:1-31
Ecclus. 34:1-17 Rev. 15 Matt. 12:22-32
Saturday, 107:32-42, 108:1-6(7-13) / 134, 135
Ecclus. 34:18-26 Rev. 17:1-14 Matt. 12:33-42

YEAR TWO
Tuesday, 84, 85 / 86, 87
Eccles. 2:1-15 Gal. 3:23-29 Luke 8:16-25
Wednesday, 119:113-128 / [88] or 134, 135
Eccles. 2:16-26 Gal. 4:1-11 Luke 8:26-39
Thursday, 89:1-18 / 89:19-52
Eccles. 3:1-15 Gal. 4:12-20 Luke 8:40-56
Friday, 90, 93 / 91, 92
Eccles. 3:16-4:3 Gal. 4:21-31 Luke 9:1-6, 10-17
Saturday, 94, [95] / 117, 118
Eccles. 5:1-7 Gal. 5:1-14 Luke 9:7-9, 18-27

WEEK OF 23 PENTECOST
Monday, 96, 97 / 98, 99, [100]
Eccles. 5:8-20 Gal. 5:16-24 Luke 9:28-36
Tuesday, 105:1-22 / 105:23-45
Eccles. 6 Gal. 5:25-6:10 Luke 9:37-49
Wednesday, 119:129-152 / 102
Eccles. 8:14-9:10 Gal. 6:11-18 Luke 9:51-62
Thursday, 106:1-18 / 106:19-48
Eccles. 9:11-18 1 Tim. 1:1-17 Luke 10:1-16
Friday, 103 / 107:1-31
Eccles. 11:1-8 1 Tim. 2:1-8 Luke 10:17-24
Saturday, 107:32-42, 108:1-6(7-13) / 134, 135
Eccles. 11:9-12:14 1 Tim. 3 Luke 10:25-37

WEEK OF 24 PENTECOST
Monday, 47, 48 / 49
Ecclus. 35:1-17 Rev. 18:1-8 Matt. 12:43-50

Tuesday, 50 / [52, 53, 54] or 148, 150
Ecclus. 36:1-5,12-17 Rev. 18:9-20 Matt. 13:1-9
Wednesday, 119:73-88 / 55:1-15(16)17-26
Ecclus. 38:1-15 Rev. 18:21-24 Matt. 13:10-17
Thursday, 56, 57, [58] / [59, 60] or 114, 115
Ecclus. 38:24-34 Rev. 19:1-10 Matt. 13:18-23
Friday, 61, 62 / 69:1-23(24-30)31-38
Ecclus. 39:1-11 Rev. 19:11-16 Matt. 13:24-30
Saturday, 63:1-8(9-11), 64 / 111, 112, 113
Ecclus. 42:15-25 Rev. 20:1-6 Matt. 13:31-35

WEEK OF 25 PENTECOST
Monday, 67, 72 / 65, 66
Ecclus. 43:1-22 Rev. 20:7-15 Matt. 13:36-43
Tuesday, [70], 71 / 68:1-20(21-23)24-35
Ecclus. 43:23-33 Rev. 21:1-8 Matt. 13:44-52
Wednesday, 119:89-112 / 73
Ecclus. 44:1-15 Rev.21:9-21 Matt. 13:53-58

WEEK OF 24 PENTECOST
Monday, 47, 48 / 49
Esther 1:1-4,10-13, 1 Tim. 4 Luke 10:38-42
16-19*
Tuesday, 50 / [52, 53, 54] or 148, 150
Esther 2:5-8,15-23* 1 Tim. 5:17-22 Luke 11:1-13
Wednesday, 119:73-88 / 55:1-15(16)17-26
Esther 3:1-13* 1 Tim. 6:11-16 Luke 11:14-26
Thursday, 56, 57, [58] / [59, 60] or 114, 115
Esther 4* James 1:1-15 Luke 11:27-36
Friday, 61, 62 / 69:1-23(24-30)31-38
Esther 5* James 1:16-26 Luke 11:37-52
Saturday, 63:1-8(9-11), 64 / 111, 112, 113
Esther 6* James 2:1-13 Luke 11:53-12:12
* In place of Esther
may be read Judith: Th... 8:9-17,28-35
M... 4 F... 9:1,7-14
T... 5:1-21 S... 10:1-17
W... 6:1-4,10-19

WEEK OF 25 PENTECOST
Monday, 67, 72 / 65, 66
Esther 7* James 2:14-26 Luke 12:13-31
Tuesday, [70], 71 / 68:1-20(21-23)24-35
Esther 8:1-8,15-7* James 3:1-12 Luke 12:32-48
Wednesday, 119:89-112 / 73
1 Macc. 1:1-15 James 3:13-4:10(11-12) Luke 12:49-59

YEAR ONE
Thursday, 74 / 77, [79]
Ecclus. 44:16-45:1 Rev. 21:22-22:5 Matt. 14:1-12
Friday, 78:1-39 / 78:40-72
Ecclus. 50:1,11-17, Rev. 22:641,18-20 Matt. 14:13-21
22-24
Saturday, 75, 76 / 114, 115
Ecclus. 51:1-12 Rev. 22:12-17 Matt. 14:22-36

YEAR TWO
Thursday, 74 / 77, [79]
1 Macc. 1:41-63 James 4:13-5:6 Luke 13:1-9
Friday, 78:1-39 / 78:40-72
1 Macc. 2:1-28 James 5:7-12 Luke 13:10-17
Saturday, 75, 76 / 114, 115
1 Macc. 2:29-43, James 5:13-20 Luke 13:18-30
49-50
*In place of Esther M: Judith 11 T: 13
may be read:

WEEK OF 26 PENTECOST (OR THIRD BEFORE ADVENT)
Monday, [82, 83] or 104 / 80, 81
Joel 1:1-14 1 Tim. 1:147 Matt. 15:1-20
Tuesday, 84, 85 / 86, 87
Joel 1:15-2:2 1 Tim. 2:1-8 Matt.15:21-28
Wednesday, 119:113-128 / [88] or 134, 135
Joel 2:12-19 1 Tim. 3 Matt. 15:29-38
Thursday, 89:1-18 / 89:19-52
Joel 2:21-27 1 Tim. 4 Matt. 16:1-12
Friday, 94, [95] / 91, 92
Joel 2:28-3:8 1 Tim. 5:17-22 Matt. 16:13-20
Saturday, 90, 93 / 117, 118
Joel 3:9-17 1 Tim. 6:11-16 Matt. 16:21-28

WEEK OF 26 PENTECOST (OR THIRD BEFORE ADVENT)
Monday, [82, 83] or 104 / 80, 81
1 Macc. 3:1-12 1 John 1 Luke 13:31-35
Tuesday, 84, 85 / 86, 87
1 Macc. 4:1-25 1 John 2:1-11 Luke 14:1-11
Wednesday, 119:113-128 / [88] or 134, 135
1 Macc. 4:36-59 1 John 2:12-17 Luke 14:12-24
Thursday, 89:1-18 / 89:19-52
Hab. 1:1-4,12-2:1 1 John 2:18-29 Luke 14:25-35
Friday, 94, [95] / 91, 92
Hab. 2:1-4,9-20 1 John 3:1-10 Luke 15:1-10
Saturday, 90, 93 / 117, 118
Hab. 3:1-10,16-18 1 John 3:11-18 Luke 15:1-2,11232

The Daily Office Revised 99

WEEK OF 27 PENTECOST (OR SECOND BEFORE ADVENT)

Monday, 96, 97 / 98, 99, [100]
Mal. 1:1, 6-14   2 Tim. 1:1-14   Matt. 17:1-13
Tuesday, 105:1-22 / 105:23-45
Mal. 2:1-9   2 Tim. 1:15-2:13   Matt. 17:14-21
Wednesday, 119:129-152 / 102
Mal. 2:10-16   2 Tim. 2:14-26   Matt. 17:22-27
Thursday, 106:1-18 / 106:19-48
Mal. 3:1-12   2 Tim. 3   Matt. 18:1-9
Friday, 103 / 107:1-31
Mal. 3:13-18   2 Tim. 4:1-8   Matt. 18:10-20
Saturday, 107:32-42, 108:1-6(7-13) / 134, 135
Mal. 4   2 Tim. 4:9-22   Matt. 18:21-35

LAST WEEK AFTER PENTECOST

Monday, 101, 109:1-4(5-19)20-30 / [120], 121, 122, 123
Zech. 9:9-16   1 Peter 1:1-12   Matt. 19:1-12
Tuesday, 124, 125, 126, [127] / 128, 129, 130
Zech. 10   1 Peter 1:13-25   Matt. 19:13-22
Wednesday, 119:153-176 / 131, 132, [133]
Zech. 12:1-10   1 Peter 2:1-10   Matt. 19:23-30
Thursday, 136, 137:1-6(7-9) / 138, 139:1-17(18-23)
Zech. 13   1 Peter 2:11-25   Matt. 20:1-16
Friday, 145 / 140:1-8(9-11)12-13, 141, 142
Zech. 14:1-11   1 Peter 3:13-4:6   Matt. 20:17-28
Saturday, 143, 144 / 148, 149, 150
Zech. 14:12-20   1 Peter 4:7-19   Matt. 20:29-34

WEEK OF 27 PENTECOST (OR SECOND BEFORE ADVENT)

Monday, 96, 97 / 98, 99, [100]
Lev. 19:1-2, 9-18   1 John 3:19-4:6   Luke 16:1-9
Tuesday, 105:1-22 / 105:23-45
Lev. 19:26-37   1 John 4:7-21   Luke 16:10-17(18)
Wednesday, 119:129-152 / 102
Lev. 23:1-21   1 John 5:1-12   Luke 16:19-31
Thursday, 106:1-18 / 106:19-48
Lev. 25:1-17   1 John 5:13-21   Luke 17:1-10
Friday, 103 / 107:1-31
Lev. 26:1-20   2 John   Luke 17:11-19
Saturday, 107:32-42, 108:1-6(7-13) / 134, 135
Lev. 26:27-42   3 John   Luke 17:20-37

LAST WEEK AFTER PENTECOST

Monday, 101, 109:1-4(5-19)20-30 / [120], 121, 122, 123
Joel 3:1-2, 9-17   Gal. 6:1-10   Luke 18:1-8
Tuesday, 124, 125, 126, [127] / 128, 129, 130
Nahum 1:1-13   1 Cor. 3:10-23   Luke 18:31-43
Wednesday, 119:153-176 / 131, 132, [133]
Obadiah 15-21   Eph. 1:3-14   Luke 19:1-10
Thursday, 136, 137:1-6(7-9) / 138, 139:1-17(18-23)
Zeph. 3:1-13   Eph. 1:15-23   Luke 19:11-27
Friday, 145 / 140:1-8(9-11)12-13, 141, 142
Zeph. 3:14-20   Rom. 15:7-13   Luke 19:28-40
Saturday, 143, 144 / 148, 149, 150
Micah 7:11-20   Phil. 2:1-11   Luke 19:41-48

SUPPLEMENT TO PRAYER BOOK STUDIES 27: AN ORDER OF WORSHIP FOR THE EVENING

Prepared by the Standing Liturgical Commission
of the Episcopal Church

1973

Concerning the Service

This order provides a form of evening service or vespers for use, on suitable occasions, in the late afternoon or evening. It may be used as a complete rite, or as the introduction to some other service, or as the introduction to an evening meal or other activity. It is intended that singing always be included in this service. In its shorter form, it is appropriate also for use in private houses.

Any part or parts of this service may be led by lay persons, but when a priest or deacon is presiding he should read the Prayer for Light, and the Blessing or Dismissal at the end. If the Bishop is present, it is appropriate that he give the Blessing.

This order is not appropriate for use on Monday, Tuesday, or Wednesday in Holy Week, or on Good Friday. Easter Eve has its own form for the Lighting of the Paschal Candle.

For the Short Lesson at the beginning of the service, any one of the following is also appropriate, especially for the seasons suggested:

	Revelation 21:10, 22-24 (Easter)
Isaiah 60:19-20 (Advent)	Psalm 36:5-9 (Ascension)
John 1:1-5 (Christmas)	Joel 2:28-30 (Whitsunday)
Isaiah 60:1-3 (Epiphany)	Colossians 1:9, 11-14 (Saint's Days)
Isaiah 58:6-8 (Lent)	1 Peter 2:9 (Saint's Days)
John 8:35-36 (Lent)	Revelation 22:1, 4-5 (Saint's Days)

The Short Lessons may be read from any version of the Scriptures authorized for public worship in this Church.

Any of the prayers in contemporary language may be adapted to traditional language by changing the pertinent pronouns and the corresponding verbs.

Additional Directions and Suggestions are on page 107.

An Order of Worship for the Evening

The church is dark, or partially so, when the service is to begin

All stand, and the Minister greets the People with these words

Light and peace, in Jesus Christ our Lord.

People

Thanks be to God.

From Easter Day through the Day of Pentecost, he says instead

Alleluia! Christ is risen.

People

The Lord is risen indeed. Alleluia!

One of the following, or some other Short Lesson of Scripture appropriate to the occasion or to the Season, is then read

Jesus said, "You are the light of the world. A city built on a hill cannot be hid. No one lights a lamp to put it under a bucket, but on a lamp-stand where it gives light for everyone in the house. And you, like the lamp, must shed light among your fellow men, so that they may see the good you do, and give glory to your Father in heaven."
[Matthew 5:14-16]

It is not ourselves that we proclaim; we proclaim Christ Jesus as Lord, and ourselves as your servants, for Iesus' sake. For the same God who said, "Out of darkness let light shine," has caused his light to shine within us, to give the light of revelation—the revelation of the glory of God in the face of Jesus Christ.
[2 Corinthians 4:5-6]

This is the message we have heard from him and proclaim to you, that God is light and in him is no darkness at all. If we say we have fellowship with him while we walk in darkness, we lie and do not live according to the truth; but if we walk in the light, as he is in the light, we have fellowship with one another, and the blood of Jesus his Son cleanses us from all sin.
[1 John 1:5-7]

If I say, "Surely the darkness will cover me, and the light around me turn to night," darkness is not dark to you, O Lord; the night is as bright as the day; darkness and light to you are both alike.
[Ps 139:10-11]

The Minister then says the Prayer for Light, using one of the following or some other suitable prayer, and first saying

Let us pray.

O Lord God Almighty, as you have taught us to call the evening, the morning, and the noonday one day; and have made the sun to know its going down: Dispel the darkness of our hearts, that by your brightness we may know you to be the true God and eternal light, living and reigning for ever and ever. *Amen.*

Almighty God, we give you thanks for surrounding us, as daylight fades, with the brightness of the vesper light; and we implore you of your great mercy that, as you enfold us with the radiance of this light, so you would shine into our hearts the brightness of your Holy Spirit; through Jesus Christ our Lord. *Amen.*

Grant us, Lord, the lamp of charity which never fails, that it may burn in us and shed its light on those around us, and that by its brightness we may have a vision of that holy City, where dwells the true and never-failing Light, Jesus Christ our Lord. *Amen.*

Lighten our darkness, we beseech thee, O Lord; and by thy great mercy defend us from all perils and dangers of this night; for the love of thy only Son, our Savior, Jesus Christ. *Amen.*

The candles at the altar are now lighted, as are other candles and lamps as may be convenient

The Canticle on the following page is then sung

O GRACIOUS LIGHT (*Phos hilaron*)

O gracious light,
pure brightness of the everliving Father in heaven,
O Jesus Christ, holy and blessed!

Now as we come to the setting of the sun,
and our eyes behold the Vesper light,
we sing your praises, O God: Father, Son, and Holy Spirit.

You are worthy at all times to be praised by happy voices,
O Son of God, O Giver of life,
and to be glorified through all the worlds.

Metrical versions of this Canticle will be found in The Hymnal 1940, numbers 173 and 176. Other versions of it may also be used

This service then continues in any of the following ways

- *It may continue with Evening Prayer, beginning with the Psalms; or with some other Office.*
- *Or, it may continue with the celebration of the Holy Eucharist, beginning with the Proclamation of the Word of God.*
- *Or, it may be followed by a meal or other activity, in which case Phos hilaron may be followed by the Lord's Prayer and a Grace or Blessing.*
- *Or, it may continue as a complete rite with the following elements:*

SELECTION FROM THE PSALTER.

BIBLE READING. A sermon, homily, a reading from Christian literature, or a brief silence, may follow.

CANTICLE OR HYMN OF PRAISE.

PRAYERS, using a litany, or other suitable devotions, concluding with the Lord's Prayer.

BLESSING OR DISMISSAL, or both; and the Peace may be exchanged.

On Feasts or other days of special significance, the Collect of the Day, or one proper to the Season, may precede or follow the Lord's Prayer. On ordinary days, if desired, any of the following may be so used

Blessed are you, O Lord, the God of our fathers, creator of the changes of day and night,
  giving rest to the weary,
  renewing the strength of those who are spent,
  bestowing upon us occasions of song in the evening.
As you have protected us in the day that is past, so be with us in the coming night; keep us from every sin, every evil, and every fear; for you are our light and salvation, and the strength of our life. To you be glory for endless ages. *Amen.*

Almighty, everlasting God, let our prayer in your sight be as incense, the lifting up of our hands as the evening sacrifice. Give us grace to behold you, present in your Word and Sacraments, and to recognize you in the lives of those around us. Stir up in us the flame of that love which burned in the heart of your Son as he bore his Passion, and let it burn in us to eternal life and to the ages of ages. *Amen.*

Look down, O Lord, from your heavenly throne, and illumine the darkness of this night with your celestial brightness; and from the children of light banish the deeds of darkness; through Jesus Christ our Lord. *Amen.*

O God, who art the life of mortal men, the light of the faithful, the strength of those who labor, and the repose of the dead: We thank thee for the timely blessings of the day, and humbly beseech thy merciful protection all the night. Bring us, we pray thee, in safety to the morning hours; through him who died for us and rose again, thy Son, our Savior Jesus Christ. *Amen.*

The Minister may use the following or some other Blessing or Grace

The Lord bless us and keep us. *Amen.*
  The Lord make his face to shine upon us and be gracious to us. *Amen.*
  The Lord lift up his countenance upon us and give us peace. *Amen.*

In the preceding Blessing, a bishop or priest may substitute "you" for "us"!

A Dismissal may be used (adding Alleluia, alleluia in Easter Season)
The People respond

Thanks be to God.

In Easter Season, the People respond

Thanks be to God, alleluia, alleluia.

Additional Directions and Suggestions

The extended suggestions which follow are intended primarily to provide assistance to those planning and experimenting with this service during the period of trial use.

Before this service, there should be as little artificial light as possible in the church, and no electric lights should be used in the area about the altar. A musical prelude or processional is not appropriate.

When the Minister enters, one or two lighted candles may be carried before him, and used to illuminate the book for reading the opening Short Lesson and the Prayer for Light. From Easter Day through the Day of Pentecost, the Paschal Candle; if used, should be burning in its customary place before the People assemble; the Minister then goes to a place close by it to begin the service by its light.

It is intended that the Short Lesson will be read without announcement.

For the Prayer for Light, any of the following Collects is also appropriate (page references are to *Services for Trial Use*):

First Sunday of Advent (p. 473)
Fourth Sunday of Advent (p. 476)
Second Proper for Christmas Day (p. 478)
Eighth Sunday after Epiphany (p. 491)
Last Sunday after Epiphany (p. 492)
Tuesday in Easter Week (p. 529)

For the lighting of the candles at the altar and elsewhere, in Easter Season the flame may be taken from the Paschal Candle. At other times, the candle or candles carried in at the beginning of the service may be placed on the altar, and other candles may be lighted from them. During Advent, the lighting of an Advent Wreath may take place after the Prayer for Light. On special occasions, lighted candles may be distributed to members of the congregation An appropriate Psalm, Refrain, or Anthem may be sung during the candle lighting.

When this service is used in private houses, candles may be lighted at the dining table, or at some other convenient place.

The hymn *Phos hilaron* is normally used at this service. On occasion, some other suitable hymn may be used. The following from The Hymnal 1940 are appropriate: 6, 89, 163, 171, 474.

If incense is to be used, it is appropriate when the candles are lit and the Hymn is being sung.

The foregoing portions of this service may be used not only to introduce Evening Prayer or the Eucharist, but may also be used before other suitable services in the evening, such as a healing service, the Stations of the Cross, or the Blessing of a House.

If this service continues as a complete rite, it is desirable to select a Psalm, or portion of a Psalm, suitable for the evening or for the particular occasion. Suitable evening Psalms include: 8, 23, 27, 36, 84, 93, 113, 114, 117, 121, 134, 139, 141, 143. The Psalm verses may be sung by a cantor, with the congregation joining in a refrain or antiphon. The psalmody may, if desired, be followed by a period of silence, or a suitable Collect, or both.

The Biblical lesson which follows the psalmody may be taken from the lectionary of the Daily Office, or from the Eucharistic lectionary, or from the Proper for special occasions. When desired, more than one lesson may be read, with silence or singing between them.

One of the Gospel Canticles, *Magnificat* or *Nunc dimittis*, is traditional at an evening Office, but some other Canticle may be chosen instead.

Suitable prayers may be selected for the occasion, but it is recommended that a litany with a response which the congregation can sing be used. The forms of intercession beginning on pages 93, 100, 101, and 459 of *Services for Trial Use*, or other similar forms, are appropriate. Litanies suitable for special occasions will be found on pages 90 ff. of *Prayers, Thanksgivings, and Litanies* (*Prayer Book Studies* 25).

If an additional hymn is desired, it may be sung immediately before the Blessing or Dismissal.

When a meal is to follow, the blessing over food may serve as the conclusion of this form of service.

An Order of Worship for the Evening Commentary

The provision of services suitable for the evening has, from the earliest times, been a special concern of Christian liturgy. Although different cultures and different individuals may arrange their days differently, the change from sunlight to darkness, and from the business of the day to other kinds of activity in the evening, is a transition which has significance for the human spirit. The evening marks, for most people, the end of the working day, but it is not the point at which most people go to bed. Indeed, it is the time when many important activities take place. It is the time when families are together; when friends eat and drink and talk together; when people listen to the news and discuss the events of the day; when they read, hear music, or enjoy other entertainments. It is a time, too, when people sometimes enjoy being alone. The Church cannot assume (as some familiar evening hymns do) that immediately after supper everyone goes to sleep. The evening is a time of special significance for many aspects of human life. The recognition of the presence of Christ with his people in the evening, and the offering of the evening to his sanctifying power, is a serious liturgical task.

Although people today have increased leisure in some respects, the daily recitation of Evening Prayer in church is not widespread. The regular choral offering of the evening Office on Sundays and Feasts is carried out in only a few places. On the other hand, on certain particular occasions, services in the evening are highly important. Lenten services and observances of holy days during the week must take place in the evening, in most parishes, if a reasonably large congregation is to attend. Special church programs and the meetings of various organizations likewise occur from time to time in the evening. On such occasions, Evensong has been customary, but in many places today neither the traditional music nor the words are sufficiently familiar for satisfactory singing. The Holy Eucharist is increasingly celebrated in the evening. In some respects, this is a welcome development. On the other hand, one misses any specifically vesper themes in the usual eucharistic rite. In many cases, furthermore, an evening Eucharist is simply not appropriate when, for instance, most of the worshipers have already communicated earlier in the day.

Thus, there are a number of gaps in our present usage. In order to meet some of these needs, several traditional elements of Christian evening worship have been brought together here in a simple but flexible form which may either be used from time to time as a separate evening Office, or be used as a special Vesper introduction to the Eucharist or other services on occasions when it is desirable. Experience in recent years indicates that these additional options do satisfy a need in certain instances.

Historical background

The earliest organized Christian service of worship of which we have any description (Acts 20:7-11) was held after dark in a room in which "there were many lights." When the Christian liturgy began to develop in later generations, the earliest regular evening service of which we have record followed the Jewish model of a gathering about the dinner table, where the proceedings were introduced by the bringing in of a candle or lamp which was solemnly blessed. The prayer said by the officiating bishop or priest on these occasions was, in fact, an early form of the *Phos hilaron*, which has continued down the centuries to be sung as an evening hymn.[1] In the fourth century, St. Basil the Great spoke of the singing of this ancient anonymous hymn as one of the cherished traditions of the Christian Church.[2] Later on, with the development of the Daily Offices, the lamp-lighting ceremony was transferred from the dinner table to the church building, where it preceded a short evening service including chants, Bible readings, and prayers.

Such a service continues to be the core of Vespers in the Eastern Orthodox Churches, although the addition of litanies and other devotions at the beginning and end of the service make the outline now somewhat difficult to discern.[3] In Western Europe, this type of service was generally displaced by the predominance of the monastic practice of reciting short services, consisting mainly of Psalms, at intervals during the day. The monastic Vespers, which had little specific reference to the evening, thus displaced the older form of lamp-lighting service, known as the *lucernarium*, which had been used in cathedrals and parish churches, principally on Saturday evenings and the Eves of Feasts. The lamp-lighting type of Vespers, on the other hand, continued in the Mozarabic rite in Spain[4] and in the Ambrosian rite of Northern Italy.[5] It is this type of Vespers which is the historic basis for the kind of service here proposed. Meanwhile, the ancient practice of blessing a light in Christ's name did not altogether die out in the prevailing Western rite. On one occasion of the year, 1 Easter Eve, the Western Church preserved the extremely elaborate blessing of the Paschal Candle. The blessing of candles in the evening in homes has apparently continued here and there during Christian history. Prayers for this purpose appear, for instance, in classical English books of private devotion.[6] The lighting of the candles of the Advent Wreath is a modern adaptation of this ceremony, related to a specific season of the Church Year.

In recent years, the movement for liturgical renewal has both called attention to the theological significance of ancient forms and stimulated the effort to find adequate patterns of worship for today. In particular, many have felt that actions

---

1. *The Apostolic Tradition of Hippolytus*, B. S. Easton, trans. and ed., Archon Books, Hamden, Conn., 1962, pp. 58-59.

2. Quoted by D. R. Dendy, *The Use of Lights in Christian Worship*, Alcuin Club Collections No. XLI, S.P.C.K., London, 1959, p. 148. Although containing much other interesting material about the ecclesiastical use of candles, this volume has little other information about the ancient evening service. The passage from Basil will be found in his "Concerning the Holy Spirit," chapt. 29, para. 73, *Nicene and Post-Nicene Fathers*, vol. VIII, p. 46.

3. I. F. Hapgood, *Service Book of the Holy Orthodox-Catholic Apostolic Church*, third edit., Brooklyn, 1956, pp. 1-15.

4. W. C. Bishop, *The Mozarabic and Ambrosian Rites*, Alcuin Club Tracts XV, London, 1924, chapt. III.

5. *Ibid.*, chapt. IV.

6. *A Book of Christian Prayers*, London, 1578 ("Queen Elizabeth's Prayer Book"), reprinted in *Private Prayers*, W. K. Clay, ed., Parker Society, Oxford, 1851, p. 445; Lancelot Andrewes, *Preces Privatae* [longer editions], Evening Prayers, *Phos hilaron*.

and visual content must have a significant place in liturgy, as well as the predominating words and music. Monastic and academic communities have experimented with forms of Vespers which might express, in a more direct way, the experience of evening and the awareness of Christ's presence in the evening. The pattern of the *lucernarium* has accordingly been successfully revived, for instance, in the famous Protestant monastery of Taizé in France,[7] and at the University of Notre Dame in this country.[8] Similar services have also been used at various conferences and meetings. The present service is based upon such recent experience, as well as on traditional liturgical sources.

The present service

It will be useful to survey the proposed service in detail, beginning with the opening rubrics. Experience will indicate those occasions when such a service as this is most desirable. It does not seem appropriate, however, in the strongly penitential mood which should characterize Holy Week. An exception is made for Maundy Thursday, because many parishes have a meal on that evening more or less patterned on traditional Jewish models. Such a meal properly includes a blessing over candles. On Easter Eve, the Lighting of the Paschal Candle [*Services for Trial Use*, pp. 521-523) is the proper candle-lighting ceremony for that day, and it establishes the basic symbolism which underlies a Christian service of light at any other time as well.

The present service is arranged with a view to simplicity, flexibility, and a harmonious relationship with both *The Book of Common Prayer* and *Services for Trial Use*. It is intended that this service may be begun, if desired, in a dark, church. Preliminary responses, which a congregation would have to read from books, are therefore kept at a minimum. It is intended that the silent entrance of the ministers, the opening greeting and Short Lesson, and the Prayer for Light, last long enough so that the congregation may consciously experience silence and darkness before many lights are lit. The Short Lessons suggested in the text, and others cited in "Concerning the Service," are but some of the many possible choices. Similarly, other choices may suitably be made, if desired, for the Prayer for Light. Of those provided, the first is Mozarabic,[9] the second is Ambrosian,[10]

---

7. *The Taizé Office*, Faith Press, London, 1966, pp. 22-23, Lucernarion.

8. *Morning Praise and Evensong*, W. G. Storey, F. D. Quinn, O. P., and D. F. Wright, O. P., edd., Fides Press, Notre Dame, Ind., 1973. Much interesting material will be found in this volume. Further texts and good discussions occur in a special issue of the Journal of the Liturgical Conference, *Liturgy*, May 1973, vol. 18, no. 5.

9. Bishop, op. cit., p. 75. Oratio for the end of Vespers through the Year; *Breviarium Gothicum*, Migne's Patrologia Latina, vol. LXXXVI, col. 50 and 1012.

10. Oratio I at Vespers on Common Fridays of the Year, *Manuale Ambrosianum ex Codice Saec. XI*, M. Magistretti, ed., Milan, 1905, p. 442.

the third is Celtic,[11] and the last is Cranmer's beloved translation of an ancient Roman evening prayer[12]. It was not felt necessary to give every prayer in two forms in order to make it clear that the service may be either in traditional or contemporary English.

The Canticle *Phos hilaron* is in many ways the heart of this rite, and it ought not normally to be replaced by another hymn, but other possible alternatives are suggested.

As the rubrics indicate, all of the foregoing may serve simply as an introduction to Evening Prayer, either as in the Prayer Book or in *Services for Trial Use*, or to the Holy Eucharist. Similarly, it may be used to introduce other services in the evening.

If this service is used as a separate Office, the provision of optimum flexibility in the selection of Psalms, Lessons, Canticles, and Prayers is deliberately intended to provide opportunities for responsible selection of the most pertinent material, while clearly and consciously adhering to the basic traditional structure of Anglican Offices with their sequence of psalmody, Scripture, canticles, and prayers. If an evening service is being held on some day in Advent, for instance, it is usually helpful to choose a Lesson which has to do with Advent as a season. A Psalm and Canticle which the congregation can sing can be used. In the large number of parishes that have a service on a weekday evening in Lent, again, a suitable penitential Psalm and the same Canticle can be used week after week, so that the congregation can sing them with ease and pleasure. Similarly, the use of a litany with a familiar response provides for a responsible coverage of pertinent topics for intercession, and the responses can be easily sung.

The prayers given at the end of the service are also suggestive of the many possibilities available. The first is adapted from the evening prayers of Lancelot Andrewes,[13] the second from the evening office of Taizé,[14] the third is an ancient Western evening prayer also used at Compline (*Services for Trial Use*, p. 299), and the last, which also occurs in the American Prayer Book, is an ancient Mozarabic Collect translated by William Bright.[15]

Any of these four prayers is also appropriate for use, on occasion, as the Prayer for Light.

---

11. Adapted by G. M. Gallup from a prayer of St. Columbanus found in *The Parish Priest of the Town*, Lectures delivered in the Divinity School, Cambridge, by John Gott, D.D., Bishop of Truro, London, S.P.C.K., 1895, in the Appendix (III) entitled "A Town Curate's Prayer Desk," p. 257.

12. *Book of Common Prayer*, American edition of 1928, p. 31.

13. Lancelot Andrewes, *Preces Privatae*, various editions. This prayer occurs in several forms in the longer versions of the Evening Prayers.

14. *The Taizé Office*, p. 23.

15. W. Bright, *Ancient Collects*, eighth edition, Oxford, 1908, p. 11. It is the Capitula for Vespers of the Third Sunday after Pentecost, *Breviarium Gothicum*, Migne's Patrologia Latina, vol. LXXXVI, col. 705.

PRAYER BOOK STUDIES 28: DEDICATION AND CONSECRATION OF A CHURCH CELEBRATION OF A NEW MINISTRY

1973

PREFACE

In fulfillment of the mandate given to the Standing Liturgical Commission by the General Convention of 1967, reaffirmed by the Convention of 1970, to prepare a revision of The Book of Common Prayer, the Commission concentrated its attention, first of all, on those rites and materials in the Prayer Book which are most frequently used in the common worship of the Church.

The service of Holy Communion received the greatest attention, because in submitting the Plan for Prayer Book Revision to the General Convention of 1967, the Standing Liturgical Commission also submitted a revised text of the service entitled "The Liturgy of the Lord's Supper" (*Prayer Book Studies XVII*), published by the Church Pension Fund. Thus, trial use of materials prepared by the Commission began with the trial use of "The Liturgy of the Lord's Supper."

During the following triennium, the Commission produced revisions of the rites of Holy Baptism with the Laying-on of Hands, the Church Year, the Ordination of Bishops, Priests, and Deacons, the Holy Eucharist (a first revision of "The Liturgy of the Lord's Supper"), the Daily Office, the Psalter (Part I), incorporating a new rendering of the Psalms most frequently used in public worship, and the Pastoral Offices.[1]

The experience of trial use, resulting in numerous comments and suggestions by the Reader-Consultants of the Standing Liturgical Commission, the Chairmen of Diocesan Liturgical Commissions, and the Bishops and other clergy, and many members of the Church, were taken into account in preparing the remaining services and materials for presentation to the General Convention of 1973.

With the publication of the present Study all the materials of the 1928 Book of Common Prayer have been reviewed and revised. These new materials include "Prayers, Thanksgivings, and Litanies" (*Prayer Book Studies* 25), the complete Psalter, published under the title "The Prayer Book Psalter Revised", "A Catechism", "Holy Baptism together with A Form for the Affirmation of Baptismal Vows with the Laying-On of Hands by the Bishop also called Confirmation" (*Prayer Book Studies* 26), "The Daily Office Revised", including a new lectionary (*Prayer Book Studies* 27), and "The Dedication and Consecration of

---

[1]. All of the above were published as *Prayer Book Studies* 18 through 24 respectively, by The Church Hymnal Corporation, and after having been approved for trial use by the General Convention of 1970, all were reprinted in *Services for Trial Use*.

a Church" and "The Celebration of a New Ministry" (both published as *Prayer Book Studies* 28).[2]

The last two services are intended as revisions of the Prayer Book Offices for the Consecration of a Church and the Institution of Ministers. The Standing Liturgical Commission desires to place on record its appreciation of the work of members of the Drafting Committee which prepared these two rites and the accompanying introductions: the Rt. Rev. Frederick Belden, the Rt. Rev. E. Otis Charles, the Rt. Rev. A. Donald Davies, the Rev. William M. Hale, Mrs. William Sloan, and the Rev. Dr. H. Boone Porter, Jr., Chairman. The Commission also desires to place on record its appreciation of the assistance rendered by the Rev. Dr. Marion J. Hatchett, who provided much of the historical material.

— The Standing Liturgical Commission.

---

2. All of these were published by The Church Hymnal Corporation, 800 Second Avenue, New York, N.Y. 10017.

The Dedication and Consecration of a Church

Introduction

The eternal God is to be worshiped by his creatures at all times and in all places. Yet if people are to worship together, they must agree upon times and places to meet, and they soon discover that certain times and certain places are more convenient, more appropriate, and more conducive to worship than others. The Church Year reflects the effort of Christian people down through the centuries to specify the most significant times for worship. Similarly, the rites for dedicating church buildings reflect the efforts of Christian communities to designate suitable places for worship.

How does a new building become a real church, a place where a worshiping community can expect to meet its Lord, and be met by him? The answer to such a question has two parts. First, if we are to meet God there, the initiative rests with him. We must recognize his will and his purposes in appointing places for his worship, and we must pray that he will use such places for his glory and for our benefit. Secondly, there is a human factor. A building becomes a house of prayer by being prayed in. A basin becomes a font by being used for Baptism. A table becomes an altar by having the Eucharist habitually celebrated at it. Accordingly, a Christian community inaugurates a church by meeting there, worshiping there, and committing themselves to go on using that place for the ministry of God's Word and Sacraments.

This is what happens in the traditional Christian rites for the dedication of a church. Thanksgiving is first offered to God for his grace in making the construction or acquisition of the new church possible, and his continuing presence is solemnly invoked. Secondly, the liturgy, particularly the eucharistic liturgy, is performed with appropriate solemnity. So that the church will be defined as a meeting place for a congregation of the Holy Catholic Church, and not as the private chapel of a local group, it has, since early times, been recognized that the Bishop should officiate and that clergymen and lay persons from the neighborhood should assemble to celebrate the event. These elements are basic for the liturgy of setting apart and hallowing a church. In different periods of history, however, and in different parts of the Christian world, differing emphases and differing interpretations have been expressed.

The Development of the Ancient Rites

The earliest Christians gathered to worship in private homes or other secular buildings, and sometimes out of doors. Some buildings came to be regarded as houses of prayer because of their habitual use for that purpose. Christians also sometimes built chapels in cemeteries, or in places where saints had been martyred. When Constantine made Christianity a legitimate and publicly favored religion during the fourth century, huge churches were rapidly erected in the Roman basilican style, which has continued to influence ecclesiastical architecture. In some cases, secular public buildings were given to the Church and adapted for purposes of worship. In other cases, pagan temples were adapted to Christian use, as was, for instance, the Parthenon in Athens[1] or the Pantheon in Rome. In still other cases, temples were demolished and churches erected on their sites. Constantine and his mother Helena were interested in developing Jerusalem as a great Christian shrine, and vast Christian edifices were erected on the traditional sites of our Lord's death and resurrection. In many cities, the chapels of local martyrs were replaced by great churches with the altars situated over the saints' graves. Plainly, these new buildings did not automatically acquire the hallowed associations of prayer. Contemporary writings record that at least in some instances these new churches were dedicated with impressive public rites attended by many ecclesiastical and civic dignitaries. No doubt, the assembled prelates celebrated the Eucharist in a grand manner, but we know nothing of the details of the liturgies used on those occasions.

Such rites did develop, however, in Eastern and Western Christendom, and they gradually attained the full form found in medieval service books. These forms included, first of all, prayers and ceremonies to accompany the marking off of ground for the new building, the laying of the cornerstone, and other stages of construction. The final service for the actual dedication or consecration of the building was always led by the Bishop. Just as a person began his Christian life by being baptized in water and anointed with the oil of chrism, so a new church was generously sprinkled with holy water, and the altar and certain other places were anointed with chrism. Because of the large number of martyrs in the ancient Mediterranean world, many great churches were built over saints' graves. Later, when new churches were built, it was felt desirable to secure the earthly remains of some saint, perhaps only a few bones, to place under the altar, and the solemn bringing in of the saintly remains, the "translation of the relics" as it was called, became a major feature in medieval rites for consecrating a new church.

The Later Medieval Western and Eastern Rites

The fully developed Latin rite for hallowing a new church, as it appears in the medieval pontificals and has come down to modern times in Roman Catholic usage, is a most elaborate celebration.[2] When all the preliminaries have been completed and the building is ready for use, the Bishop comes with his clergy and the door is then opened for him. A litany is sung, and an interesting ceremony

---

1. On a sunny day in Athens, the knowing tourist can still discern the faint outlines of the painting of our Lord's Mother on the front of this most beautiful of buildings.

2. The most convenient description is still in L. Duchesne's, *Christian Worship, Its Origin and Evolution*, fifth edition, London, 1919, pp. 409-413.

called the "abecedarium" is performed. Ashes are strewed on the floor, and the Bishop traces with his staff the letters of the Greek alphabet in a diagonal line across the entire building. He then goes to the other side and traces the Latin alphabet in a transverse diagonal, so that the two lines of letters make a great St. Andrew's Cross spanning the middle of the building. No doubt, this originally, was regarded as the Greek Chi, or X, the first letter of the word, Christ. The use of the alphabets presumably reflects a period in the early Middle Ages when only the clergy was literate and all letters, were regarded as sacred runes. Presumably, the abecedarium was originally performed on the earth before the building was erected. The altar, walls, and floor are liberally sprinkled with holy water, and a long general consecratory prayer is said. The altar is anointed with chrism by the Bishop, as are certain other points around the church where "consecration crosses" are carved in the wall for him to anoint. The relics are, then "translated" with great solemnity and encased in a box sealed into the altar. Finally, the Mass is celebrated. Every stage of these procedures is accompanied by prayers, chants, the sprinkling of holy water, and incense. The rite is so complicated that in modern times it has apparently been rarely carried out in its full form.

The rites for this purpose in the ancient Mozarabic, Gallican, and Ambrosian Latin Liturgies have unfortunately not survived.[3] It may be mentioned that Christian literature generally speaks of both the dedication and consecration of churches. The two terms have somewhat different connotations, but they are normally used almost interchangeably to refer to the same rites.

The Greek Orthodox consecration of a church similarly begins after many preliminary ceremonies.[4] Inside the new church, the legs for the altar are set up and the slab for the top of it is prepared. When the Bishop comes, the slab is put into place and he completes the construction of the altar. He then kneels to recite a lengthy general prayer of consecration. The altar is washed with holy water, anointed with chrism, and vested. The church is then sprinkled with holy water, and anointed with chrism above the doors. With much ceremony, relics are then brought in and sealed in a box beneath the altar. The Daily Office is then sung, and the Divine Liturgy is celebrated. The Armenians, Copts, and other non-Chalcedonian Eastern Churches have comparable solemnities.

Biblical Basis for the Christian Rites

The prayers and chants, as well as the actual readings from the Bible, in all of these medieval rites, draw heavily on the many biblical passages pertaining to

---

3. No doubt some Gallican and Mozarabic materials are incorporated in the medieval Latin rite just described, but we have no texts recording these non-Roman rites for a church in their original forms. Surviving Ambrosian texts are but variants of the Roman.

4. For convenient text in English see I. F. Hapgood's *Service Book of the Holy Orthodox-Catholic Apostolic Church*, third edition, Brooklyn, 1956, pp. 479-511.

the Temple at Jerusalem and its dedication. The construction and dedication are described in 1 Kings 5-8, and this is expanded upon in 1 Chronicles 28-29 and 2 Chronicles 2-7. These texts, on which Christian liturgists have frequently relied, develop the theme that God is the possessor of all, yet man can, by God's own grace, give him gifts. Similarly, God is everywhere, and yet he condescends to be especially present and especially accessible in the place where he makes "his Name to dwell."

Other references to the Temple, its prefigurement in the tabernacle in the wilderness, and its later destruction and restoration, abound in the Old Testament and have been repeatedly referred to. Of particular interest is the rebuilding and rededication of the Temple in December of 165 B.C. by Judas Maccabeus after its desecration by the Seleucid Syrians, 1 Maccabees 4:52-59 and 2 Maccabees 10:1-8. The commemoration of this event became an annual observance. This is the Feast of the Dedication of the Temple mentioned in the New Testament, John 10:22, and still observed today as Chanukkah. This provided the prototype for the annual observance of feasts of dedication in Christian churches.

The New Testament not only provides references to the Temple at Jerusalem, but speaks of our Lord's earthly body as a temple, and of individual Christians and the corporate community of the Church as a spiritual temple in which God is present through his Holy Spirit — a temple of living stones founded on Christ the cornerstone. The heavenly Jerusalem described in Revelation and elsewhere is also seen as the type of the true Church, the Bride of Christ, of which a physical church building is the visible sign.

This wide range of imagery has made the liturgies for the consecration and dedication of churches to be among the richest in poetry and in literary embellishments. This rite has provided a unique dramatic focus for a broad sector of biblical teaching and piety. The service of consecration has thus not only served to hallow buildings where Christians have worshiped, but it has provided moments of great joy for celebrating the reality of the Church as the spiritual temple of the Living God, the foreshadowing of that heavenly Jerusalem where the followers of the Lord Jesus will behold him face to face.

Classical Anglican Rites of Consecration

In the Reformation period, it was intended that an English version of the pontifical, or book of bishop's services, be produced. In due course, Archbishop Cranmer did provide versions of the ordination rites for bishops, priests, and deacons; and the service of confirmation was already included in the Book of Common Prayer. Everything else in the pontifical, including the procedures for hallowing new churches and their furnishings, fell into limbo. In any case, that period was more given to destroying old churches than to building new ones.

A few consecrations occurred during the reign of Queen Elizabeth I, however, and became much more frequent in the seventeenth century. Although there was no consistency at first, the bishops seem to have quickly reached some consensus as to the general style and structure of the order to be used. This order, subsequently followed with some variation in different parts of the Anglican Communion, may properly be called the Anglican order for consecrating churches. It is quite distinct from the pre-Reformation order, and it remains as the most elaborate and original liturgical composition of the Church of England in the period following the Reformation.

The Anglican order emerges in embryonic form in rites used by William Barlow, successively Bishop of Rochester and of Lincoln, under James I.[5] First, the officiating bishop entered the new church or chapel alone and said a long prayer of consecration, inspired in part by King Solomon's prayer in 1 Kings 8. The congregation and clergy then entered, and Morning Prayer was recited with special psalms and lessons, followed by the Litany with a special prayer at the end. The Sermon came next — apparently not an unusual point for it in this period, although a violation of the rubrics of the Prayer Book. Then the Eucharist was celebrated by the Bishop with special propers. At the end, before the usual Blessing, there was a blessing or prayer for the benefactor and his family. In the absence of any other evidence, it is assumed that Barlow composed these prayers.

Although Barlow's order continued to be followed closely by several other bishops, a few years later the revered Bishop of Winchester, Lancelot Andrewes, undertook a substantial revision of the material. In its oldest known form, this is a most extraordinary rite.[6] First, there is a lengthy address by the donor to the Bishop and, with suitable psalm verses, the latter enters the church with the donor and attendants, and recites the consecration prayer. All restraint having been abandoned, this is now several pages in length. At the end, there are four paragraphs addressed respectively to the Father, the Son, the Holy Spirit, and the Blessed Trinity. Andrewes' liturgical skill is better displayed in the section which follows. Going to the font and laying his hand on it, the Bishop prays for the efficacious administration of Baptism. He proceeds similarly to say suitable prayers at the pulpit, lectern, the holy table, the rail where marriages were blessed, and the pavement beneath which bodies were interred. This arrangement, which Andrewes apparently invented, was soon to become characteristic of the Anglican formularies. The congregation then entered the church and Matins and Litany followed, each with special prayers (Barlow's after the Litany). Baptism, the Solemnization of Matrimony, or the Thanksgiving after Childbirth were performed, if persons desiring these rites were present. After the Sermon, the Eucharist began with special propers. Following the Nicene Creed, the Bishop said King

---

5. The standard source is J. Wickham Legg's *English Orders for Consecrating Churches in the Seventeenth Century*, London, 1911 (Henry Bradshaw Society, Vol. XLI). This provides the text of twenty-nine different services, together with scholarly notes and comments. The first three orders given are Barlow's.

6. Legg, No. IX.

Solomon's prayer, 1 Kings 8:27ff., and the Act of Consecration was read, a Latin document of several pages in length. The Bishop's chaplains proceeded with the liturgy, the Bishop himself officiating at the eucharistic consecration. As in Barlow's order, there is a special blessing of the founder and his family. After dinner, the Bishop and others returned for a lengthy blessing of the churchyard in conjunction with Evensong.

A copy of this order was owned by Archbishop Laud, and evidently by others. During the course of the seventeenth and eighteenth centuries, Andrewes' order was adapted in various ways, sometimes substituting Barlow's briefer prayers. Long declarations, in which the secular lord gives over feudal control of the building to the Church, are characteristic, and perhaps explain why so many of the surviving records have only to do with family chapels or churches in small rustic communities. Secondly, the effort to inaugurate the full use of the building is striking. Besides the Daily Offices, the Litany, Eucharist, and other services we have noticed, large numbers of people were sometimes confirmed, and on one occasion a corpse was ready to be buried in the newly hallowed churchyard.[7]

The seventeenth century also witnessed adaptations of the order for reconsecrating desecrated churches.[8] On some occasions, bishops were called upon to dedicate new furnishings in existing churches. As in other periods, suitable prayers were used, at least on some occasions, for laying cornerstones or other preliminary actions. Never, however, was any distinction made between the ceremony of dedicating and that of consecrating a church. Both terms are often found together and both verbs were used in the services. Thus Bishop Cosin's most elaborate arrangement is entitled, *The Form and Order of Dedication and Consecration of Churches and Chappells together with the Church Yards or Places of Burial According to the Use of the Church of England.*[9]

Following the restoration of Charles II in 1660, the Prayer Book was revised, and an effort was made to secure a recognized text of the order for consecrating churches. Bishop Cosin's effort to compile such a standard form was not accepted. In the Church of Ireland, on the other hand, a highly elaborate adaptation of Andrewes' order was accepted and regularly printed in certain editions of the Irish Prayer Book. It is a striking monument of the old high-churchmanship of the Church of Ireland.[10]

Efforts to secure a uniform rite were renewed in England in the next century. A rather simplified version of Andrewes' order was considered by the Convocation

---

7. Legg, p. 12

8. Legg, *Appendices.*

9. Legg, p. 237

10. F. R. Bolton, *The Caroline Tradition of the Church of Ireland*, London, 1958, pp. 298-319. This remarkable text is not included among Legg's English orders. Bolton argues, not quite successfully, that Jeremy Taylor was the author of it.

of Canterbury in 1712[11] and, with further modification, in 1715. Although never officially approved, the order of 1712 has been widely used, with local variation, in many English dioceses down to the present time. This form abandoned the perambulation of the Bishop to different parts of the church: instead, he simply stood in the chancel to say the prayers pertaining to the font, lectern, and other furnishings.

American Episcopal Usage

In colonial America, there were no bishops, and so the proper rites of consecration could not be performed. In at least some instances, however, the opening of new churches was marked by special services and the assembling of clerical and lay guests from the surrounding region. The consecration of churches was soon introduced by the new American bishops. Samuel Provoost of New York consecrated Trinity Church, Manhattan, in 1790, in an impressive ceremony at which George Washington was present. He used the form which Thomas Wilson, saintly eighteenth-century Bishop of Sodor and Man, had adapted from the English order of 1715.[12] On some other occasions, however, Provoost used an adaptation of the order of 1712.[13] Wilson's order was used in substance by Samuel Seabury, first Bishop of Connecticut, who made it a part of his duties to consecrate churches during his lengthy pastoral tours of New England.[14] As in seventeenth century England, not only the Eucharist, but Baptism and Confirmation, and sometimes Ordination or other rites, were administered by the Bishop on the same day.[15] It should be noted that the churches consecrated by Seabury were newly built; he did not undertake to consecrate churches which had long been in use. They were evidently deemed hallowed by the use which they had received.

In 1799, Provoost's adaptation of the English Convocation order of 1712 was adopted for inclusion in the American Book of Common Prayer. There it has since remained with little change, except that in 1892 the omission of the Eucharist was permitted — a departure from ancient and universal custom.

The English orders have generally envisaged a donor, or founder, who gave land, had the building erected, and gave it over to the Church at the time of consecration. In America, this has not usually been the case. In the middle of the nineteenth century, new churches were often financed by selling pews, much

---

11. Printed in Richard Burn's *Ecclesiastical Law*, third edition, London, 1775, Vol. I, pp. 301-308.

12. Thomas Wilson's *Works*, Vol. VIII, Library of Anglo-Catholic Theology, pp. 143-149.

13. Marion J. Hatchett, *The Making of the First American Prayer Book*, unpublished Th.D. dissertation, General Theological Seminary, New York, 1972, pp. 261-263.

14. Seabury's order is found in a volume of his manuscripts entitled *Occasional Prayers and Offices*, St. Mark's Library of the General Theological Seminary in New York.

15. Bishop Seabury's Journal B (1791-1795), *The Historiographer of the Episcopal Diocese of Connecticut*, No. 12, May, 1955, *passim*.

as real estate is sold, to people living within the parish area — a practice which left little place for the poor to sit in church. The securing of loans by mortgage evidently came to be adopted in due course. In 1868, the General Convention enacted a canon (now numbered Title II. Canon 7) requiring that the premises be debt free in order to be consecrated. In 1871, the canon was expanded with the provision that the building must be secure against alienation.[16] This latter provision was occasioned by a small schism occurring at that time. The Rev. Charles Edward Cheney, rector of a parish in Chicago, left this Church in order to join the newly organized Reformed Episcopal Church. He took his parish and its buildings with him, and it was feared that some other church buildings might be lost by a similar process.

The subsequent effect of this canon has been highly ironical. With increasing frequency churches were financed by mortgage loans. Since it was evident that the canon precluded these churches from being consecrated for many years (perhaps during the lifetime of those who had arranged for their construction), some other way was sought to solemnize them. This was done by the simple expedient of calling the inaugural service "the dedication." As we have seen, both in pre-Reformation and Anglican usage, to dedicate and to consecrate a church is one and the same thing. Since, however, the service in the American Prayer Book was entitled Consecration, and since the same term is used in American canon law, a service entitled Dedication was deemed to be extra-legal and was performed at any time and in any manner the participants desired.

Accordingly, it is now the common American Episcopal custom to mark the opening of a new church with a ceremony of dedication, usually presided over by the Bishop, in which the new church and its furnishings are solemnly blessed. From a liturgical point of view, this service accomplishes everything attributable to consecration. At a later date, however, perhaps decades later, a consecration service is held to celebrate the liquidation of all debts.

This arrangement has been officially recognized by the provision of well arranged services for a new church in *The Book of Offices*. In the most recent edition (1960), there is a preliminary service for groundbreaking, including a much simplified version of the abecedarium, and an impressive order for laying the cornerstone.[17] The service for dedicating the church is formally entitled The Opening of a Church. (The authors of the rite were too well informed to use the title Dedication which they knew to be synonymous with consecration.) This involves the formal entrance of the Bishop and the signing of the threshold, the blessing of the font and other furnishings and of the altar, the vesting of the altar, and the celebration of the Eucharist. This rite obviously renders the later consecration

---

16. E. A. White and J. A. Dykman, *Annotated Constitution and Canons*, second edition, Greenwich, Conn., 1954, Vol. I, pp. 427-431.

17. *The Book of Offices*, third edition, New York, 1960, pp. 44 ff.

largely redundant. The Opening of a Church provides much biblical and traditional material omitted in the Prayer Book order, and it is so arranged that it may simply serve as a supplement to the latter.

This curious duplication of dedication and consecration may perhaps be defended on the grounds that it encourages the liquidation of debts, and provides a safeguard against alienation. It is doubtful, however, if it has these effects. In many cases, the securing of long-term loans is very desirable, and the Church has no reason to withhold its solemnities from a congregation which has made wise financial arrangements. Irresponsible debts, of course, should not be encouraged, but the withholding of consecration does not usually appear to be a solution to this problem.

The Present American Prayer Book

The existing order in the Prayer Book of 1928 has proved unsatisfactory in other respects. It says both too little and too much.

The solemn inauguration of worship in the building, especially eucharistic worship, is not sufficiently integral to the rite. The perambulation by the Bishop for dedicating the furnishings, a most characteristic and expressive feature of Anglican rites, is omitted. The consecration of a church provides a unique opportunity to recognize and give thanks for the physical building, in its visible and tangible aspects, and for the beauty of fabrics, musical instruments, and other things within it. This opportunity should not be lost, as it is in the Prayer Book order.

On the other hand, the existing order emphasizes the separation of the building "from all unhallowed, worldly, and common use." Such an emphasis may be misleading, for Christian churches have often been used down through the centuries for educational, humanitarian, and social purposes. If part of the building is intended to serve worthy "common uses", there is no reason why this should not be recognized.

Before concluding this analysis of American Episcopal usage, it should be noted that since 1928 our Prayer Book has contained very suitable propers for the "Feast of the Dedication of a Church."[18] Similar propers are provided in *Services for Trial Use*, on page 621. Christian liturgical tradition is practically unanimous that such a feast is the anniversary of the consecration of the church building.[19] It is no doubt commonly used in the United States on the anniversary of the service when the church was opened, but the only dedication known or recognized by the Prayer Book is the consecration service, which is plainly called "the

---

18. *Book of Common Prayer*, p. 259-60.

19. E. g., *The Prayer Book Dictionary* of Harford, Stevenson, and Tyrer, London, 1913, p. 227, "DEDICATION FESTIVAL: The annual commemoration of the consecration of a church."

Dedication" in the Collect for the Eucharist at the time of consecration.[20] Where existing American churches were "dedicated" on one date and later consecrated on another, they had to choose which was more suitable for them to observe as an anniversary. In the future, with the unequivocal reunification of dedication and consecration in one service on one day, this question will no longer arise.

The Proposed Rite

The service here being proposed for trial use is intended to remove the ambiguity of the current American usage, and to return to the fuller and more classical Anglican concept of the rite, without the necessity of a service of several hours' duration. It is also intended to provide greater lay participation, to restore expressive visible actions, and to give greater opportunity for recognition of the aesthetic aspects of the building being hallowed. The full traditional Anglican title of the service has been restored. The verbs dedicate and consecrate both occur in the rubrics and prayers of the rite, together with such words as set apart and sanctify, to make it clear that the full and complete hallowing of the church and all of its furnishings is intended.

The preliminary procession, circling the entire building if possible, represents in dramatic terms the Church's action in taking occupancy of the new building. The marking of the threshold by the Bishop is a simple and meaningful ceremony adopted from the rite for "Opening a Church" in *The Book of Offices*. As in other Anglican and pre-Reformation orders, there is a general prayer of dedication. The trinitarian structure of this prayer is somewhat suggestive of the conclusion of Bishop Andrewes' much longer prayer. Since the building of a church today is not normally the work of a single donor or "founder", but represents the collective endeavor of the local laity, of their clergy, and of the diocese, it was felt appropriate for their representatives to have parts in the prayer.

The service then proceeds in accordance with classical Anglican custom, with the Bishop and his attendants moving from place to place throughout the church to dedicate the font, lectern, pulpit, and other principal furnishings. It will be noted, however, that in the seventeenth and eighteenth century rites, the furnishings of the church are all first dedicated in a lengthy service and then subsequently put to use in the recitation of Matins and the Litany, the administration of Baptism and Confirmation, and the celebration of the Eucharist. In this proposed rite, however, the utilization of each part follows its dedication. Substantially the same goal is thus achieved, but the entire rite is greatly shortened. It should be noted also, that in localities where the dedication of a church is a

---

20. The proper lessons for Morning and Evening Prayer at a Dedication, pp. xlii-xliii, are presumably for use if the daily offices are recited at the time of the consecration, although their use on other occasions, such as anniversaries, is not precluded.

community celebration for which activities during the greater part of the day are desired, this service, or group of services, can be extended, and the old Anglican custom of returning after dinner for Evensong may be followed.

As in other orders, the font is visited first, with its reminders of the beginning of the world, the beginning of the history of Israel, the beginning of our Lord's ministry, and the beginning of our own Christian life. In accord with old Anglican custom, the font is filled with water on this occasion, dramatically illustrating its function, whether a Baptism is to follow or not. The permitted abbreviation of the baptismal liturgy should encourage its use at this point. It is a happy occasion for this sacrament to be administered to one or more persons.

The successive dedications of lectern, pulpit, and organ (or other instrument), do not require special comment, except to note that the significance of these dedications can be given fuller visual expression by members of the congregation. Not only is the Bible placed on the lectern, for instance, but colored place-markers may be inserted, candles may be lit on each side of it, and a vase of flowers may be put at the foot of the lectern. At the time of the sermon or address, preliminary experimentation Has already indicated that it can be very helpful to allow several members of the congregation to speak.

Following the Intercessions, the Bishop's Collect recognizes that the entire church is to be a place of prayer. There is then a general dedicatory prayer relating to the large numbers of ornaments, furnishings, and implements in the church, which cannot be mentioned separately, but all of which contribute significantly to the whole.

This order restores the solemn blessing of the altar as a climatic point in the rite. The altar is recognized as the table where the Eucharist is celebrated and as the continuing visible sign of that history of salvation which the Eucharist recalls. It is recommended that the lights about the altar then be lit for the first time and the church bells be rung. If the burning of incense is desired, it may be used around the altar when it has been vested. It is to be noted that there is no separate dedication of altar cloths, candlesticks, or eucharistic vessels. This rite as a whole, including the general dedicatory prayer mentioned above, serves as a total blessing of all such equipment in the church.

For the celebration of the Eucharist members of the congregation bring forward the alms, bread, wine, and water. It is assumed that the Bishop will be the chief celebrant of the Eucharist. On this, as on other such occasions, it is fitting for him to invite the priest of the parish, and other priests, to stand with him at the altar. If there is a deacon available, he or she prepares the elements at the Offertory and fulfills the other duties of the order.

As it is a primary purpose of a church building to draw together a Christian community, a social gathering will normally be arranged following the Eucharist, and the congregation will, of course, wish to greet their Bishop, their guests, and one another.

Although the proposed service may, in principle, be used for consecrating any church which meets suitable standards for use, a special problem arises with buildings which have been long in use, but which have not been consecrated because they were not debt-free, or because of other factors. In some instances, the members of the congregation desire, and look forward to having, such a service. In such cases, it is suggested that a suitable occasion be chosen for the consecration of the church without undue further delay. In other instances, a church has been used for generations, and it is no longer fitting to speak of consecrating it, as though its previous use had been ineffective or unacceptable. Similarly, it is unsuitable to speak of dedicating or consecrating fonts, altars, organs, or other furnishings long in use. In such cases, it is suggested that prayers of thanksgiving be offered for what the church is and has been, and that its benefactors be commemorated. This may be done on an anniversary or other suitable occasion. Suggestions and directions for these and other possibilities are provided.

The suggestions at the conclusion of this service also provide for the increasing number of cases in which a church is shared with another congregation, or used for non-liturgical or non-churchly functions. In such cases, the service may be altered and adapted as necessary. It is felt to be important that the Church be prepared to bestow her blessing on congregations which are making use of their buildings in new and responsible ways for missionary witness, ecumenical cooperation, or human welfare. Similarly, parts of the rite may be used or adapted to dedicate chapels on secular property or within secular buildings. The blessing of a chapel in an airport, for instance, or on a ship, or within an office building, or in a national park, all provide welcome opportunities to plan distinctive services expressive of the concern of the Church for those who live and work in these settings.

The Dedication and Consecration of a Church

Concerning the Service

This service provides for the dedication and consecration of a complete church building and its furnishings. Portions of the service may be used, or adapted when necessary, for dedicating parts of a building or furnishings that have been built, altered, or renovated. Likewise, suitable parts of this rite may be used for dedicating a chapel or an oratory within another building. Provisions for adapting the rite to special circumstances are given on page 137.

This service may be used to dedicate and consecrate a church at any time after the building is ready for regular use as a place of worship. The service does not prohibit the use of the building for educational or social purposes, or other suitable activities.

The Bishop presides. The Rector or Priest-in-charge takes part as indicated. Neighboring clergymen should be invited to participate, and may be assigned appropriate parts of the service.

It is desirable that all members of the congregation, young and old, have some individual or collective part in the celebration, as well as the architect, builders, musicians, artists, benefactors, and friends.

For a church or chapel long in use, a special order is provided on page 138.

Additional Directions and Suggestions are on page 135.

The Dedication and Consecration of a Church

On the day appointed, the Clergy and People gather with the Bishop in a place apart from the church or chapel.

When all are ready, the Bishop says the following or similar words

Through the ages, Almighty God has moved his people to build houses of prayer and praise, and to set apart places for the ministry of his holy Word and Sacraments. With gratitude for the building *(rebuilding or adornment)* of *(name of church)*, we are now gathered to dedicate and consecrate it in God's Name.

Let us pray.

Almighty God, we thank you for making us in your image, to share in your creativity in the ordering of your world: Receive the works of our hands in this place for your worship, in remembrance of those whom we love, to the praise and glory of your Name, through Jesus Christ our Lord. Amen.

Necessary announcements may now be made.

As the procession approaches the door of the church, singing and instrumental music are appropriate.

Standing at the door of the church, the Bishop says

Let the door(s) be opened.

The door is opened. With the pastoral staff the Bishop marks the threshold with the sign of the cross, saying

**Peace be to this house,
and to all
who enter here:**

**in the Name of the Father,
and of the Son,
and of the Holy Spirit.
Amen.**

As the procession moves into the church, Psalm 122 or some other appropriate Psalm is sung. Hymns and Anthems may also be sung.

The congregation standing, the Bishop begins the Prayer for the Consecration of the Church.

Bishop: Our help is in the Name of the Lord:
People: The Maker of heaven and earth.
Bishop: Let us pray.

Everliving Father, watchful and caring, our source and our end, all that we are and all that we have is yours. Accept us now, as we dedicate this place to which we come to praise your Name, to ask your forgiveness, to know your healing power, to hear your Word, and to be nourished by the Body and Blood of your Son. Be present always to guide and to judge, to illumine and to bless your people.

A Warden or other representative of the congregation continues

Lord Jesus Christ, make this a temple of your presence and a house of prayer; be always near us when we seek you in this place. Draw us to you, when we come alone and when we come with others, to find comfort and wisdom, to be supported and strengthened, to rejoice and give thanks. May it be here, Lord Christ, that we are made one with you and with one another, so that our lives are sustained and sanctified for your service.

The Rector or Priest-in-charge continues

Holy Spirit, open our eyes, our ears, and our hearts, that we may grow closer to you through joy and through suffering. Be with us in the fullness of your power when new members are added to your household, when we leave childhood behind, when we are joined in marriage, and, at the last, when we are committed into the Father's hands.

The Bishop concludes

Now, O Father, Son, and Holy Spirit, sanctify this place:
People: For everything in the heaven and on earth is yours.
Bishop: Yours, O Lord, is the Kingdom,
People: And you are exalted as head over all. Amen.

The Bishop moves to the Font, lays his hand upon it, and says

We dedicate this Font in the Name of the Father, and of the Son, and of the Holy Spirit. *Amen.*
  Father, we thank you that through the waters of Baptism we die to sin and are made new in Christ. Grant through your Spirit that those baptized here may enjoy the liberty and splendor of the children of God. *Amen.*

If there are persons to be baptized, water is now poured into the Font, and the service continues with the shortened order for Holy Baptism given on page 35 of this book.

If no Baptism is to take place, water is now poured into the Font, and the Bishop says the following prayer

The Lord be with you.
And also with you.

Let us give thanks to the Lord our God.
It is right to give him thanks and praise.

We thank you, heavenly Father, for the gift of water. Over it the Holy Spirit moved in the beginning of creation. Through it you led the children of Israel out of their bondage in Egypt into the land of promise. In it your Son Jesus received the Baptism of John and was anointed by the Holy Spirit as the Messiah, the Christ who would lead us by his death, and resurrection from the bondage of sin into everlasting life.

We thank you, heavenly Father, for the water of Baptism. In this water we are buried with Christ in his death. By it we share in his resurrection. Through it we are renewed by the Holy Spirit. Therefore, in joyful obedience to your Son, and looking for his coming again as Lord of all the nations, we bring into his fellowship those who believe in him and come to him, baptizing them in the Name of the Father, and of the Son, and of the Holy Spirit.

Grant by the power of your Holy Spirit that those who here are cleansed from sin and born again may continue for ever in the risen life of Jesus Christ our Savior;

To him, to you, and to the Holy Spirit, be all honor and glory, now and for ever. *Amen.*

The Bishop proceeds to the Lectern. Laying his hand upon it, he says

We dedicate this Lectern in the Name of the Father, and of the Son, and of the Holy Spirit. *Amen.*

Father, your eternal Word speaks to us through the words of Holy Scripture. Here we read about your mighty acts and purposes in history, and about those whom you chose as the agents of your will. Inspired by the revelation of your Son, we seek your present purposes. Give us ears to hear and hearts to obey. *Amen.*

The Bishop goes to the Pulpit and, laying his hand upon it, says

We dedicate this Pulpit in the Name of the Father, and of the Son, and of the Holy Spirit. *Amen.*

Father, in every age you have spoken through the voices of prophets, pastors, and, teachers. Purify the lives and the lips of those who speak here, that only your Word may be proclaimed, and your Word only may be heard. *Amen.*

If one Reading Stand serves both for Lectern and for Pulpit, the two preceding prayers are said there.

At the Ministry of the Word

Three Lessons are read. Lay persons read the Old Testament Lesson and the Epistle. The Deacon (or a priest) reads the Gospel. Selections may ordinarily be made from the following list; but on a Major Feast, Sunday, or Patronal Feast, selections may be made from the Proper of the Day.

Old Testament:	1 Kings 8:22-23, 27b-30
	2 Samuel 6:12-15, 17-19
Suggested Psalm:	84, or 48
Epistle:	Revelation 21:2-7
	1 Corinthians 3:1-11, 16-17
	1 Peter 2:1-9

When an instrument of music is to be dedicated, after the Epistle the Bishop proceeds to an appropriate place and says

We dedicate this *(name of instrument)* in the Name of the Father, and of the Son, and of the Holy Spirit. *Amen.*

Father, your people worship you with many voices and sounds, in times of joy and sorrow. Move us to express the wonder, the power, and the glory of your creation in the music we make and the songs we sing. *Amen.*

Instrumental music is now played, or a Hymn or Anthem sung.

All then stand for the Gospel, which may be one of the following

	Matthew 5:13-16
Gospel:	Luke 2:22-32
	John 2:13-22

The Sermon or Address

Additional Pastoral Offices may follow.

If the Apostles' Creed has not already been said, the Nicene Creed is now said or sung.

The Deacon or a member of the congregation leads the Intercessions.

After a period of silence, the Bishop concludes the Intercessions with the following prayers

Almighty God, in your hands you hold all things and dispose all seasons. Accept our prayers and intercessions offered in this place today and in the days to come; through Jesus Christ, our Mediator and Advocate. *Amen.*

We give you thanks, O God, for the gifts of your people and for the work of many hands which have beautified this place and furnished it for the celebration of your holy mysteries. Accept and bless all we have done, and grant that in these earthly things we may behold the order and beauty of things heavenly, through Jesus Christ our Lord. *Amen.*

Let us now pray for the setting apart of the Altar.

The Bishop goes to the Table, lays his hand upon it, and says

Hear us, Lord. Sanctify now this table dedicated to you. Let it be a sign to us of the heavenly altar where your saints and angels praise you for ever. Accept here the continual recalling of the sacrifice of your Son. Grant that all who eat and drink at this holy table may be fed and refreshed by his flesh and blood, receive forgiveness of sins, be united with one another, and strengthened for service.

Extending his arms, the Bishop continues

We praise you that for us and for our salvation, you sent your Son Jesus Christ to be born among us, that through him we might become your sons and daughters;

Blessed be your Name, Lord God

We praise you for the fullness of his life and for his death upon the cross, through which he offered himself as a perfect sacrifice;

Blessed be your Name, Lord God

We praise you for raising him from the dead, and for exalting him to be our great High Priest;

Blessed be your Name, Lord God

We praise you for sending your Holy Spirit to make us holy, and to unite us in your holy Church;

Blessed be your Name: Father, Son, and Holy Spirit, now and for endless ages. Amen.

Bells may now be rung and music played. Members of the congregation vest the altar, place the vessels on it, and light the candles.

The Peace

The Bishop then says

The Peace of the Lord be always with you. And also with you.

Then the Bishop and other Clergy and the People greet one another.

At the Celebration of the Eucharist

The Bishop, or the Priest appointed by him as chief celebrant, says the Offertory Sentence.

A Psalm, Hymn, or Anthem may be sung.

When the elements have been prepared and all are ready, the chief celebrant proceeds with the Great Thanksgiving, saying

The Lord be with you.
And also with you.
Lift up your hearts, etc.

The Proper Preface may be

Through Jesus Christ our great High Priest: in whom we are built up as living stones of a holy temple, that we might offer before you a sacrifice of praise and prayer which is holy and pleasing in your sight.

After Communion

After the Communion, one of the usual post-communion prayers follows, or the Litany of Thanksgiving on page 38 omitting the concluding Doxology.

The Bishop then gives his blessing; and a deacon or priest may dismiss the people, now or later. (See Additional Directions, page 36.)

Additional Directions and Suggestions

The complete form of the service for the Dedication and Consecration of a Church is to be used at the opening of a church or chapel. Whenever possible, this service should take place on the feast, or in the season, of the Saint, the doctrine, or the event in our Lord's life, for which the church or chapel is named. This service does not require that the premises be debt free or owned.

When the Clergy and People assemble before the service, they may gather out of doors, in the parish house, in a former or neighboring place of worship, or in some other building. When convenient, the procession may go around the building(s) to be dedicated and then go to the principal door. Hymns or Psalms may be used in procession. The use of portable musical instruments is suitable. If there is an organ, it is appropriate that it remain silent until dedicated. When the weather is inclement, or other circumstances make it necessary, the congregation may assemble inside the church; but the Bishop, other Clergy, and attendants, will enter in procession through the principal door.

When a new church is being consecrated, it is desirable that portable furnishings, decorations, and gifts be carried into the building in the procession. Each member of the congregation may carry a Prayer Book, Hymnal, candle, flower, or other ornament or utensil. Such things as the deed for the property and the blueprint of the building(s), the keys, and tools used in its construction may also be carried by appropriate persons. It is unwise to burn the original deed or mortgage papers.

The cross signed on the threshold by the Bishop may be marked in lasting form (incised, painted, inlaid). In place of a pastoral staff, the foot of a processional cross may be used for the signing.

At the dedication of the Font, children or other lay persons are to be assigned the task of pouring the water. If Holy Baptism is not to be administered, the Bishop may bless the oil of Chrism, as in the office of Holy Baptism, for subsequent use in this church. If Baptism is to be administered, the following order will suffice on this occasion:

> The Gospel (from the baptismal service)
> The Presentation and Renunciations
> The Affirmations (omitting the Litany)
> The Blessing of the Water (and Chrism if desired)
> The Administration
> The Prayer over the newly baptized and the Signing
> The Reception

As the furnishings in the Church are dedicated, they may be decorated by members of the congregation with flowers, candles, hangings, or other ornaments.

Selected verses of Psalms and Hymns, or instrumental music, may be used as the ministers move from one part of the church to another.

At the dedication of the Lectern, the Bible is brought forward and put into place by a donor, or a lay reader, or another suitable person.

It is the prerogative of the Deacon, if one is present, to read the Gospel.

If there is an Address, instead of a Sermon, it is suitable that a Warden or other lay persons outline the plans of the congregation for witness to the Gospel. The Bishop may respond, indicating the place of this congregation within the life of the Diocese.

The Sermon or Address may be followed by an appropriate Pastoral Office such as Thanksgiving for the Birth of a Child, Commitment to Christian Service, or Blessing of Oil for the Sick.

Intercessions may be chosen from *Services for Trial Use,* or from "Prayers, Thanksgivings, and Litanies" (*Prayer Book Studies* 25); or some other form may be composed for the occasion, having due regard for the distinctive nature of the community, and with commemoration of benefactors, donors, artists, artisans, and others.

For, the covering and decoration of the Altar, it is suitable that the donors of these furnishings, or other lay persons, bring them forward and put them in place. If incense is to be used, it is appropriate at this time.

When the Bishop is the chief celebrant of the Holy Eucharist, the priests of the congregation and other priests should stand near him at the Altar for the consecration of the elements and the breaking of the Bread.

Instead of the Proper Preface suggested, that of the season may be used, or one appropriate to the name of the church.

At the conclusion of the service, the congregation and guests may move to a suitable place to share a meal, after which a deacon (or a priest) may say the Dismissal.

For the Dedication of Churches and Chapels in Special Cases

If the place of public worship is also to serve as a school, or parish hall, or some other suitable purpose, the service may be adapted to the circumstances.

If the church is also to be used for regular worship by other Christian bodies, it is appropriate that their representatives take part, in the service, and that the service be adapted.

Suitable portions of this service may be used by the Bishop, or by a priest with the Bishop's permission, for dedicating a private chapel or oratory.

For the Dedication of Furnishings, or Parts of a Church or Chapel

Relevant portions of the service for the Dedication and Consecration of a Church may be used by the Bishop or a priest for blessing alterations, additions, or new furnishings in a church or chapel. In each such case, the suitable prayer may be said, or adapted to the circumstances; and prayers and Bible readings related to the particular occasion may be selected. When possible, the areas or furnishings should be put into use at this time. Thus, it is desirable that the administration of

Holy Baptism should follow the blessing of a new font or baptistry. The blessing of an Altar should always be done by the Bishop and should always be followed by the celebration of the Holy Eucharist.

For a Church or Chapel Long in Use

When buildings have been used for public worship for an extended period of time without having been consecrated, the service may provide an opportunity for the congregation to reaffirm its commitment to its mission and ministry, and it will be particularly appropriate when a congregation attains recognition as a parish. The following order may, be used.

   I. Procession
  II. Signing of threshold
 III. Litany of Thanksgiving for a Church (next page)
  IV. Te Deum
   V. Ministry of Word with Sermon or Address
  VI. Intercession, including commemoration of benefactors
 VII. The Peace
VIII. The Eucharist beginning with the Offertory

A Litany of Thanksgiving for a Church

The Bishop says

Let us thank God whom we worship here in the beauty of holiness.
    Eternal God, the heaven of heavens cannot contain you, much less the walls of temples made with hands. Graciously receive our thanks for this place and accept the work of our hands, offered to your honor and glory.

For the Church universal, of which these visible buildings are the symbol:

We thank you, Lord.

For your presence whenever two or three have gathered together in your Name:

We thank you, Lord.

For this place where we may be still and know that you are God:

We thank you, Lord.

For the knowledge of your will and the grace to perform it:

We thank you, Lord.

For the fulfilling of our desires and petitions as you see best for us:

We thank you, Lord.

For the pardon of our sins when we have fallen short of your glory:

We thank you, Lord.

For the blessing of our vows and the crowning of our years with your goodness:

We thank you, Lord.

For the faith of those who have gone before us and for our encouragement by their perseverance:

We thank you, Lord.

For the fellowship of all your Saints (and especially for N. our patron):

We thank you, Lord.

After a brief silence, the Bishop concludes with the following Doxology:

Bishop: Yours, O Lord, is the greatness, the power, the glory, the victory, and the majesty:
People: For everything in the heaven and on earth is yours.
Bishop: Yours, O Lord, is the Kingdom,
People: And you are exalted as head over all. Amen.

This Litany may also be used on the anniversary of the Dedication or Consecration of a church, or on other suitable occasions.

The Celebration of a New Ministry

Introduction

The basic and original rite for conferring pastoral responsibilities on clergymen is ordination. In ancient times, a bishop, priest, or deacon was usually ordained in order to serve permanently in a particular diocesan or parochial position, and no further ceremonies of installation or induction were required. This has generally continued to be the case in most Eastern Orthodox communities. A new situation arose in Western Europe during the Middle Ages, however, when it became customary to ordain large numbers of young priests for assistant positions, with the understanding that they would seek "preferment", as it was called, to beneficed positions in subsequent years.

The English Practice of Institution and Induction

It was in this context that the traditional English procedures for the institution of ministers originated. Feudal landowners were desirous of securing priests acceptable and loyal to themselves to serve as rectors or vicars of parishes within their lands. The bishops, on the other hand, naturally wished to see parishes held by priests who would be obedient and loyal to their diocesan. After generations of conflict, a balanced procedure was finally achieved. The lay lord would select the priest for a benefice and present him for it. The new appointee would then go to the bishop and swear canonical obedience to him in front of witnesses.[1] The bishop then declared him admitted and instituted into his office, and gave him letters of institution and a mandate to the archdeacon or some other official of the Church to induct him into the possession of the premises and perquisites of his new parish. Institution was thus not a religious ceremony in any sense, but a feudal legal action at the residence of the bishop, or wherever a priest might be able to arrange to meet him. The induction was carried out by the archdeacon or some other cleric, often the priest of a nearby parish. The inductors went with the new priest to the latter's church, gave him the key, and put him into possession of the church, the rectory or vicarage, and the glebe lands.[2]

All of this continued through the Reformation and, indeed, in England down to modern times. Spiritual interpretations began to be attached to induction, however. A famous set of directions by the saintly and influential seventeenth-century bishop, Lancelot Andrewes,[3] prescribes that the inductor is to meet the new priest in the porch of the church, it being locked and empty. The inductor is to read the bishop's mandate for induction, and give the key to the new incumbent, stating that he is giving him the "real, actual, and corporal possession of this Parish, together with all and singular the tithes, rights, and commodities of and belonging to the same." The new incumbent then unlocks the door, enters the church alone, prays, touches the altar, and rings the church bell. He then writes a signed statement in Latin on the back of the mandate, affirming that he has carried out these acts.[4] This completed the induction by which a priest acquired possession of the benefice in freehold for the rest of his life.

---

1. W. K. Lowther Clarke and C. Harris, *Liturgy and Worship*, London, 1947, pp. 714 ff.

2. Institution and induction are sometimes differentiated by the theory that institution conferred power over the "spiritualities" of the parish, whereas induction conferred power over the "temporalities" of the parish (i.e., the property and the income from rented real estate).

3. Andrewes's *Minor Works*, Library of Anglo-Catholic Theology, p. 164.

4. "The neighbour minister, that inducts you, let him read in the Church Porch (the Church being empty and the door locked) *the Mandate ad Inductionem, verbatim.*

"That done, let him give you hold of the ring or key, and say,

"By virtue hereof, I, C.D., give you, I.N., real, actual and corporal possession of this Parish, together with all and singular the tithes, rights, and commodities of and belonging to the same.

American Offices of Institution and Induction

It remained for the Church in North America, where few of the old feudal customs had any force, to translate institution and induction into a liturgical ceremony of spiritual rather than purely legal significance. A form of service was compiled in Connecticut in 1799[5] and subsequently adopted in New York in 1802.[6] In 1804, an office for inducting ministers was accepted for inclusion in the American Book of Common Prayer. At that time, the service was so arranged that it might be used for assistant ministers as well as rectors, and for congregations that were not parishes as well as those that were.[7] At the same time, a Canon was enacted that clergy must be so inducted to have tenure as incumbents and in order to have a vote in the choice of a bishop.[8] This Canon was later repealed.

Subsequently, proper election by a vestry and approval by the bishop have had the legal force of instituting a priest in the American Church. "A Minister is settled, for all purposes here or elsewhere mentioned in these Canons, who has been engaged permanently, or for any time not less than one year, by any Parish ..." (Title III. Canon 22, Sec. 4). The liturgical office is thus optional and, in some periods and in some dioceses, it has been rarely used.

In 1808, the name of the service was changed to "An Office of Institution of Ministers." This terminology, like the Canon quoted above, reflects the tendency in that era to use the word Minister to mean incumbent or rector. The word Institution is misleading, and the original title, Induction, is more accurate. In the 1928 Prayer Book, the service provides a form for a Letter of Institution, but the actual rite is based upon the old ceremony of induction, which includes giving the keys to the new incumbent and the prayer he says for himself at the altar (perhaps reflecting the old requirement that he touch the altar).

Although the purpose of this office is devotional and edifying rather than legal, the tradition has been maintained that it may be used only for incumbents of parishes. Assistant ministers are usually given little if any liturgical recognition when they take up their, work. The same has been true of vicars of missions,

---

"Then unlock the door, and go into the Church alone, and lock or bolt the door, and execute these particulars, which you shall write on the back side of your mandate, vis.: — *Accepi clavem, intravi solus, oravi, tetigi sacra, pulsavi campanas, In nomine Patris, Filii, et S. St. Amen. Per me, I.N.* (Then endorsed by C.D.)" *op cit.* Quoted in *Liturgy and Worship*, p. 717.

5. *An Office of Induction, Adopted by the Bishop and Clergy of the Diocese of Connecticut, in Convocation, at Derby, Nov. 20, 1799,* by the Reverend William Smith, D.D., Rector of St. Paul's Church, Norwalk, New Haven, Conn., n.d.

6. Marion J. Hatchett, *The Making of the First American Prayer Book,* unpublished Th.D. dissertation, General Theological Seminary, New York, 1972, p. 267.

7. Hatchett, p. 268.

8. White, E. A., and Dykman, J.A., *Annotated Constitution and Canons,* Vol. II,. p. 199; Seabury Press, Greenwich, Conn., 1952.

although their spiritual duties may be no different from those of rectors. Archdeacons, deans, and various other dignitaries are often installed with rites composed for the occasion. American imagination has also been stimulated, in recent years, by services of institution or of induction that have been compiled in England and in other parts of the Anglican Communion.[9] These are often very elaborate rites. In a manner reminiscent of classical Anglican orders for consecrating churches, the institutor and the new incumbent go to different parts of the parish church for appropriate exhortations and prayers. Thus, for example, at the font the new rector is charged to administer Baptism faithfully; at the lectern, to read the Scriptures diligently.

In all such services, as in the new proposed form, the fundamental purpose is to articulate and express, in terms of specific people in specific places, those responsibilities and powers which were conferred in a broad and comprehensive way by ordination. There was also clearly a secondary motive. The rites of ordination in the Book of Common Prayer have been somewhat austere, and were felt by many to be unduly restrained both in verbal and ceremonial references to the liturgical and sacramental duties. Consequently, the orders for institution or induction compiled during the past two centuries have reflected a desire to augment and enrich the view of the priesthood expressed in the Prayer Book.[10]

The Service Now Proposed

The service now being proposed for trial use within the Episcopal Church reflects the American situation. Its force is moral and spiritual, rather than legal. This being the case, we have returned to the position taken in the American Church in 1804. There is no reason to limit the use of the service to rectors. It may be used, with adaptations where necessary, for vicars of missions, assistants in parishes, chaplains of institutions, canons of cathedrals, and auxiliary or non-stipendiary clergy who spend part of their time in secular work. Nor is it limited to priests. A deacon's ministry may be so inaugurated. So, too, may the work of a Church Army Officer, or a lay vicar of a mission. It would not seem suitable, however, for temporary positions, or for positions which do not involve a significant measure of pastoral responsibility. (Other forms are available for admission to office of church wardens, lay leaders, and other such officials.)[11] Whatever the nature of the position, it is important for the bishop to state it clearly, either through the Letter of Institution or some other less formal statement. The ceremonial delivery to a new rector of the keys of the church, associated in the Prayer Book with

---

9. *Liturgy and Worship*, pp. 720-721.

10. Thus in the American Book of Common Prayer we find such phrases as "sacerdotal Function", "our Presbyters", and "Apostolic Succession." Note also "Altar" and "Eucharist" in the rubrics.

11. *The Book of Offices*, third edition, New York, 1960, pp. 29-40, and *Services for Trial Use*, New York, 1971, p. 327 (A Form of Commitment to Christian Service).

the institution, has been retained as an optional feature, following the reading of the Letter of Institution.

Services approved for trial use in 1970 provide rites of ordination with sufficient expression of the sacerdotal aspects of the ministry. It is not, therefore, deemed advisable for the celebration of a new ministry to appear to supplement the forms for ordination. Indeed, it is only misleading for a service of institution or induction to rival the solemnity of ordination.

The present service is deliberately less formal and less fixed in manner than the ordination liturgy. The latter must be a service of the utmost dignity, and it must be evident to everyone that it confers holy orders that will be recognized throughout the Church. The service for beginning a pastoral ministry, on the other hand, is intended to be localized in character. Indeed, it has no other function. It provides an opportunity for the members of a particular congregation to celebrate a significant event in the life of their own church in the way that means most to them. Accordingly, the rubrics allow a large measure of flexibility. Preliminary experience has demonstrated that parishioners can make effective use of this opportunity to plan a satisfying liturgical celebration; it can express and articulate their hopes and aspirations, submitting them to Almighty God for his guidance and sanctification.

The most distinctive portion of this service is the delivery of symbolic objects to the new minister with charges to fulfill various aspects of his ministry. This may be done in a traditional manner, or in a more spontaneous and contemporary style. Water, for instance, may be given to him in a cruet from the sacristy, or in a portable baptismal font, or in a ewer; or he may be led to a permanent font which is filled for this ceremony. The bread may be customary altar bread, or bread specially baked by a parishioner for this occasion, or a large and conspicuous loaf of ordinary bread. He may be presented with a stole long used in that church, or a new one given to him or to the church on this occasion.

In any case, however, when members of the congregation give a priest such things as a stole or eucharistic vessels, it should be understood that they are not conferring on him the right or the power to administer the sacraments. His sacerdotal authority was permanently conferred on him by the bishop at ordination. The giving of these objects should not appear to be a supplement to ordination, nor a ceremony of investiture. Rather, these articles and substances should be visible and recognizable signs of the pastoral, fraternal, and ecclesial relationship that should exist between ministers and people. These things belong in the setting of that community in which the Bible is always a reminder of the mighty acts of God, the stole of authority is always a yoke of service, and bread — any kind of bread — is always evocative of that Living Bread which has come down from heaven.

It is anticipated that this service will normally conclude with the Eucharist, since the service as a whole is intended to express the bond between minister and people. The bond they have with one another must be based on the relationship all have with God. The Eucharist expresses most directly our place in the family of God, as members of the Body of Christ, within the fellowship of the Holy Spirit. It will be noted that the rubrics at the end permit the use of any of the eucharistic prayers currently authorized for use in the Episcopal Church.

Following the post-communion prayer, a form of the priest's prayer for himself — a formulary unique to American Prayer Books — has been provided for optional use by newly inducted rectors, vicars, or other priests having similar canonical charge.

Although this service may be adapted to a wide variety of ministries of priests, deacons, and lay ministers, it is not intended as the model for the installation of a bishop in a new jurisdiction. Dioceses usually devote considerable time to planning their own arrangement of such a service.

Celebration of a New Ministry

Letter of Institution

N., Presbyter of the Church of God, you have been called to work together with your Bishop and fellow-Presbyters as a pastor, priest, and teacher, and to take your share in the councils of the Church.

Now, in accordance with the Canons, you have been selected to serve God in _____ Church (of) _____.

This letter is a sign that you are fully empowered and authorized to exercise this ministry, accepting its privileges and responsibilities as a priest of this diocese, in communion with your Bishop.

Having committed yourself to this work, do not forget the trust of those who have chosen you. Care alike for young and old, strong and weak, rich and poor. By your words and in your life, proclaim the Gospel. Love and serve Christ's people. Nourish them and strengthen them to glorify God in this life, and in the life to come.

May the Lord who has given you the will to do these things, give you the grace and power to perform them.

Given under my hand and seal, in the city of ____ on the ___ day of ___, 19 __ and in the ___ year of my consecration.

Concerning the Service

This order is for use when a priest is being instituted and inducted as the rector of a parish. It may also be used for the installation of deans and canons of cathedrals, or the inauguration of the ministry of clergy to other diocesan or parochial positions, including vicars of missions and assistant ministers. Alterations in this service may be made according to the circumstances.

The chief minister at this service is normally the Bishop, but, if necessary, he may appoint a priest to act for him. When the Bishop is present, he is the chief celebrant of the Holy Eucharist. In the Bishop's absence, the priest being inducted into the new ministry is the chief celebrant.

If the new minister is a deacon, it is his or her prerogative to read the Gospel, prepare the elements at the Offertory, and assist the Bishop or priest who is officiating at the altar.

Other priests, if any, who serve in the same congregation also stand with the chief celebrant at the altar, and deacons assist according to their order. Lay persons from the congregation read the Old Testament lesson and the Epistle and perform other actions as indicated in the rubrics. Other clergy of the diocese participate in this celebration as an expression of the collegiality of the ministry in which they share.

A letter of Institution may be read aloud, and presented by the Bishop to the new minister immediately before the Litany. The text of the Letter may be adapted to the nature of the new ministry.

Additional suggestions and directions are given on page 61.

Celebration Of A New Ministry

A Psalm, Hymn, or Anthem may be sung during the entrance of the Ministers.

The Bishop begins the service, saying

Blessed by God, Father, Son, and Holy Spirit.
And blessed be his Kingdom, now and for ever. Amen.

From Easter Day through the Day of Pentecost, in place of the above, he says

Alleluia! Christ is risen.
The Lord is risen indeed. Alleluia!

There is one Body and one Spirit;
There is one hope in God's call to us.
One Lord, one Faith, one Baptism;
One God and Father of all.

The Institution

The Wardens, standing before the Bishop with the new Minister, say these or similar words:

Father in God, we have come together today to welcome *N.N.*, who has been chosen to serve as *Rector* of *(Name of Church)*. We believe that he is well qualified, and that he has been prayerfully and lawfully selected. Do you concur in this choice?

Bishop: I do.

A person appointed reads the Letter of Institution; or else the purpose of the new ministry is stated.

> *If the new Minister is the Rector of the Parish, a Warden may now present to him the keys of the church, saying*
>
> In the name of this congregation I present to you the keys of this church.

The Bishop, standing, says

As we offer our prayers to God for all his people, let us ask him especially to bless this congregation and *N.*, their *Rector.*

> *The Litany for the Ministry or other appropriate Litany is led by the person appointed. At the end of the Litany the Bishop, standing, says the following or some other Collect, first saying*

The Lord be with you.
And also with you.
Let us pray.

Everliving God, strengthen and sustain N., that with patience and understanding he may love and care for your people. Pour forth your blessing upon them, that together they may follow Jesus Christ and grow into the fullness of his manhood, who lives and reigns with you and the Holy Spirit, one God, for ever and ever. Amen.

The Ministry of the Word

> *The people sit. One or two lessons are announced and read (See Additional Directions and Suggestions).*
>
> *A Psalm, Hymn, Anthem, or silence, follows each Lesson.*
>
> *Lesson:*   Joshua 1:7-9, or Numbers 11:16-17, 24-25
> *Suggested Psalms:* 43, or 132:1-9, or 146
>   133 and 134 (especially suitable for use in the evening)
> *Epistle:*   Romans 12:1-18, or Ephesians 4:7, 11-16
>
> *Then, all standing, the Deacon (or a priest) reads the Gospel.*

          John 15:9-17
Gospel: Luke 10:1-2
          John 14:11-15

The Sermon
The Nicene Creed

We believe in one God,
the Father, the Almighty,
maker of heaven and earth,
of all that is seen and unseen.

We believe in one Lord, Jesus Christ,
the only Son of God,
eternally begotten of the Father,
God from God, Light from Light,
true God from true God,
begotten, not made, one in Being with the Father.
Through him all things were made.
For us men and for our salvation
he came down from heaven:
by the power of the Holy Spirit
he was born of the Virgin Mary, and became man.
For our sake he was crucified under Pontius Pilate;
he, suffered, died, and was buried.
On the third day he rose again
in fulfilment of the Scriptures;
he ascended into heaven
and is seated at the right hand of the Father.
He will come again in glory to judge the living and the dead,
and his kingdom will have no end.

We believe in the Holy Spirit, the Lord, the giver of life,
who proceeds from the Father.
With the Father and the Son he is worshiped and glorified.
He has spoken through the Prophets.
We believe in one holy catholic and apostolic Church.
We acknowledge one baptism for the forgiveness of sins.
We look for the resurrection of the dead,
and the life of the world to come. Amen.

The Induction

Representatives of the congregation and of the clergy of the Diocese stand before the Bishop with the new Minister. According to the nature of the new ministry, any of the presentations that follow may be added to, omitted, or adapted.

The Bishop addresses the new Minister, saying

N., do you in the presence of this congregation commit yourself to this new trust and responsibility?

New Minister: I do.

Bishop: Accept this ministry which is mine and yours.

The Bishop then addresses the congregation, saying

Will you who witness this new beginning support and uphold N. in this ministry?
People: We will.

A representative of the congregation presents a Bible, saying

Be among us as one who proclaims the Word.
People: AMEN!

Another representative of the congregation may present a book of prayers or other symbol, saying

Be among us as a man of prayer.
People: AMEN!

Another representative of the congregation may present a stole or other symbol, saying

Be among us as a pastor and priest.
People: AMEN!

Another representative of the congregation may present olive oil or some other symbol saying

Be among us as a healer and reconciler.
People: AMEN!

Another representative of the congregation presents water, saying

Be among us to baptize in the Name of Christ.

People: AMEN!

> *Other representatives of the congregation present bread and wine, saying*

Be among us to break the Bread and bless the Cup.
People: AMEN!

> *The Bishop then presents the new Minister to the congregation, saying*

Greet your new Rector.

> *The congregation may respond with applause or other acclamations. A doxology may be sung.*
>
> *The Bishop greets the new Minister.*
>
> *The new Minister then says to the people*

The peace of the Lord be always with you.

People: And also with you.

> *He may then greet his family and the congregation. The Bishop and clergy may also greet the family and congregation.*

At the Celebration of the Eucharist

> *The new minister says the Offertory Sentence, and the offerings of the congregation are received. A Hymn, Psalm, or Anthem may be sung.*
>
> *The Bishop, or in his absence the Priest beginning the new ministry, standing at the Lord's Table as chief celebrant and joined by the other clergy, proceeds with the Great Thanksgiving of the Eucharist.*
>
> *Except on major feasts of our Lord, the Preface may be that for Apostles and Ordinations.*

After Communion

> *At the Induction of a Priest or Deacon, in place of the usual post-communion prayer, the Bishop leads the people in the following, but if the new Minister is a layman the usual post-communion prayer is used.*

Almighty Father, we thank you for feeding us with the holy food of the Body and Blood of your Son, and for uniting us through him in the fellowship of your. Holy Spirit. We thank you for raising up among us faithful servants for the ministry of your Word and Sacraments. We pray that N. may be to us an effective example in word and action, in love and, patience, and in holiness of life. Grant that we, with him, may serve you now, and always rejoice in your glory; through Jesus Christ your Son, our Lord, who lives and reigns with you and the Holy Spirit, one God, now and for ever. Amen.

If the new Minister is a Priest being given a pastoral charge, he, kneeling alone at the Altar, may say the following prayer for himself:

O Lord my God, I am not worthy to have you come under my roof; yet you have called your servant to stand in your House, and to serve at your Altar. To you and to your service I devote myself, body, soul, and spirit. Fill my memory with the record of your mighty works; enlighten my understanding with the light of your Holy Spirit; and may all the desires of my heart and will center in what you would have me do. Make me an instrument of your salvation for the people entrusted to my care, and grant that I may faithfully administer your holy Sacraments, and by my life and teaching set forth your true and living Word. Be ever with me in carrying out the duties of my ministry. In prayer, quicken my devotion; in praises, heighten my love and gratitude; in preaching, give me readiness of thought and expression; and grant that by the clearness and brightness of your holy Word, all mankind may be drawn to your blessed kingdom. All this I ask for the sake of your Son, our Savior Jesus Christ. *Amen.*

If the new Minister is a Priest, the Bishop then asks him to bless the people.

If the new Minister is a Deacon, he or she dismisses the assembly.
The people respond: Thanks be to God.

In Easter Season, add "Alleluia, alleluia", *both to the Dismissal and the response.*

Additional Directions and Suggestions

The Institution, the Ministry of the Word, and the Induction should occur at the entrance of the chancel or some other place where the Bishop and other ministers can be clearly seen and heard by the people. It is desirable that a seat for the Bishop be provided facing the people.

The Letter of Institution is appropriate for the institution of a rector of a parish, the dean of a cathedral, and others having similar tenure of office. Its wording may be altered by the Bishop when circumstances require. In other cases, the Bishop may state briefly in his own words the nature of the office and the authority being conferred.

The new minister is normally presented to the Bishop by the Wardens of the parish, but additional, or other, persons may do this when circumstances make it suitable.

The Litany may be sung or said standing or kneeling, but the Bishop always stands for the Salutation and Collect at the end of it. The Collect of the Day, or a Collect of the season, may be used instead, or another prayer suitable to the circumstances.

Before the Gospel, there may be one or two readings from Scripture. Any of the readings, including the Gospel, may be selected from the Proper of the Day, or from the passages cited in the service. Other passages suitable to the circumstances may be selected. Appropriate selections may be found in the service for the Ordination of a Deacon or in the eucharistic lessons for Special Occasions.

The Sermon may be preached by the Bishop, the new minister, or some other person; or an Address may be made regarding the work of the congregation and of the new minister. Representatives of the congregation, or of the community, or other persons present, may speak in response to such an Address.

For the Great Thanksgiving, any of the eucharistic prayers authorized for use in this Church may be used at this service. It is appropriate that other priests join the chief celebrant in the breaking of the consecrated Bread, and that priests and deacons who are present assist in the distribution of the Elements to the people.

The Priest's prayer for himself, which follows the post-communion prayer, is appropriate only for rectors of parishes, vicars of missions, hospital chaplains, and other priests having similar canonical charge.

PRAYER BOOK STUDIES 29: INTRODUCING THE PROPOSED BOOK

A Study of the Significance of the Proposed Book of Common Prayer for the Doctrine, Discipline, and Worship of the Episcopal Church

By Charles P. Price
for the Standing Liturgical Commission

1976

The following abbreviations are used throughout this study:

AS   Authorized Services, 1973.
BCP   Book of Common Prayer. Unless otherwise noted, this abbreviation designates the American Book of Common Prayer of 1928.
DPB   Draft Proposed Book. The Report and recommenda- tions of the Standing Liturgical Commission to the General Convention of 1976 on Prayer Book revision.
ICET   International Consultation on English Texts.
LLS   Liturgy of the Lord's Supper, 1967. PBS 17.
PBS   Prayer Book Studies, numbered from 1 through 28, a series of revisions of Prayer Book services proposed by the Standing Liturgical Commission for study by the Church.
PrBCP   The Proposed Book of Common Prayer. The subject of this study.
SLC   The Standing Liturgical Commission.
STU   Services for Trial Use, 1970.

I. Perspectives on the Proposed Book

In 1973, the Louisville General Convention by resolution requested the Standing Liturgical Commission to present for consideration at the next Convention a draft of a proposed revision of the Book of Common Prayer. In compliance with that request, the Commission has, during the past triennium, reviewed and revised its prior studies, brought unfinished work to completion, and presented the Draft Proposed Book of Common Prayer (DPB) to the General Convention of 1976. The General Convention adopted DPB, with amendments, by impressive majorities: in the House of Deputies by more than 95% in the clerical order and 80% in the lay order; in the House of Bishops by near unanimity. By a separate resolution, the Convention authorized the alternative use of The Proposed Book of Common Prayer (PrBCP) during the triennium 1976-1979, to acquaint the Church with its contents and to accustom it to its use. If the Proposed Book is accepted without change by the General Convention of 1979, it will become the established Book of Common Prayer for The Episcopal Church.

PrBCP represents the focus of a number of different developments in the life of our Church, of the Anglican Communion, and of other Churches throughout the world.

In one perspective, PrBCP is the culmination of a process which began in 1928, when the present BCP was authorized by General Convention, and the Standing Liturgical Commission was established. At that time, it was realized that the forces which produced that revision, as well as its predecessor, the Book of 1892, were still operative. As Edward Lambe Parsons, one of the chief architects of the 1928 revision, said, "further change is inevitable." The factors recognized by the end of the nineteenth century as requiring liturgical revision were two: the insights of the Catholic revival, which aimed at the recapture of some of the liturgical material jettisoned during the sixteenth century Reformation; and the needs of a society whose characteristics were shaped by industry and technology, rather than by agriculture. The pace of life increased. It was widely felt that worship had to become more varied and more intense, rather than uniform and leisurely. "Enrichment" and "flexibility" were watchwords for these two prayer book revisions. The Book of 1892 represented a few small steps in these directions: seasonal opening sentences, the permission to omit the penitential beginning of Evening (not Morning!) Prayer, and the addition of the Feast of the Transfiguration. The Book of 1928 embodied more advance: e.g., the several ways to shorten and vary the Daily Offices, the addition of invitatories, the flexible treatment of the Decalogue and the Exhortations of the Eucharist, the alterations and additions to the Visitation of the Sick (making it possible to suggest that not all illness was of divine visitation), the addition of many new occasional prayers.

A complete review of the 1928 BCP was undertaken by the Standing Liturgical Commission between 1950 and 1963. It resulted in the first series of Prayer

Book Studies (PBS 1-16). They were not authorized for trial use. It might be a valid generalization to say that the trends perceptible in 1892 and 1928 continued and intensified. Much careful and thoughtful work went into these Studies. Nevertheless, the changes envisioned were small, of the order of magnitude represented in PrBCP by Rite I Daily Offices and Eucharist. In particular, Elizabethan English was preserved throughout. Prayer Book Study 16, Lesser Feasts and Fasts, was authorized for optional use (the Constitution having been amended to permit trial use). It simply recommended an enrichment of the Calendar and required no change in regular services.

Prayer Book Study 17 was *The Liturgy of the Lord's Supper*, 1967 (LLS). It did make a change in language. It moved toward a contemporary use of words, although God was still addressed as "thou", in the style of the Revised Standard Version of the Bible. It introduced an Old Testament lesson and psalm into the service of the Word; and the order of the subsequent parts of the service was conformed to the recommendations of the Lambeth Conference of 1958. LLS was authorized for trial use, and through this modest but finely worked revision, the principle of authorized trial use became familiar to the Church.

An examination of PrBCP from the closer perspective of the '50's and '60's reveals other significant factors at work. The influence of these forces, in themselves not new, added to the older ones already mentioned, goes a long way toward explaining the more thoroughgoing revisions proposed after 1967. These added new forces are (1) the liturgical movement; (2) the ecumenical movement, with its roots in the twentieth-century understanding of the mission of the Church; and (3) the revival of Biblical theology.

It would not be appropriate to go into great detail about any of these. As far as the liturgical movement is concerned, it is pertinent for our purposes to observe that Roman Catholic scholars after World War I began to push behind the Middle Ages, seeking earlier forms of the liturgy. Partly because of new manuscript discoveries and partly because of the theological work of the Benedictine monks at Maria Laach, it came to be widely held that the liturgy in the early Church frequently grasped and expressed basic Christian faith more plainly and adequately for the twentieth century than later medieval forms of the liturgy. Insights of the liturgical movement were introduced into the Church of England by such scholars as A. G. Hebert and Dom Gregory Dix; and to the American Episcopal Church by William Palmer Ladd, Theodore O. Wedel, Burton Scott Easton, Massey H. Shepherd, among others.

At the same time, Protestant Biblical theologians like Hans Lietzmann and Oscar Cullmann began to understand the importance of liturgical documents of these same early centuries as embodying the formulation of New Testament faith in the Hellenistic world. This convergence of interest in the early Christian centuries from both Catholic and Protestant sides has been significant for the liturgical life of the contemporary Church. On the one hand, it has provided a common meeting ground for Protestants, Anglicans, and Roman Catholics in ecumenical conversations. The agreement reached by delegates to the Faith and Order Commission and Roman Catholic observers is remarkable. (See *One Baptism, One Eucharist, and a Mutually Recognized Ministry*, Faith and Order Paper No. 73, World Council of Churches, Geneva, 1974.) On the other hand, the spare simplicity of this earlier liturgical style and its modest non-triumphalist tone have a good deal to commend it to modern liturgical practice in our increasingly secularized and pluralistic Western society.

For all these and perhaps other reasons, most of the Churches of Western Christianity are currently involved in liturgical reform aimed at the renewal of faith and at providing a way to worship which is at once more ancient in its roots and more ecumenical in its outreach than currently used major liturgies are. Roman Catholics accomplished the first major change in centuries at the Second Vatican Council, 1962-1965. These same influences were brought to bear on the productions of our Liturgical Commission after 1968. Beginning in that year, with the publication of Prayer Book Study 18, *Holy Baptism*, a new series of Studies was issued (Nos. 18-28), much more thoroughgoing than the first series. Language was modernized; although, of course, Rite I services retain the older literary style. Other more radical changes have been proposed for a variety of reasons to be made clear later in this Study. A much greater wealth of material, both ancient and modern, has been supplied. All of these Studies were authorized for trial use in STU 1970, or shortly thereafter. Some were revised again in AS 1973, and in subsequent interim publications.

From the perspective of 1973, PrBCP is a thorough reworking of these liturgical texts: the *Liturgy of the Lord's Supper*, 1967; *Services for Trial Use*, 1970; and *Authorized Services 1973*. All of this material has been carefully reviewed and extensively revised in the light of the innumerable comments received from concerned individuals, parishes, diocesan liturgical commissions, and scholars of this and other Churches. We believe that it is safe to say that no previous revision of a Prayer Book in any of the Churches of the Anglican Communion has been accompanied by a comparable effort to consult the Church at large. As a result, we believe that PrBCP will more adequately meet the needs of the Church today than STU or AS would. The details of this last stage of revision will emerge when the contents of PrBCP are examined.

From an overall Anglican perspective, PrBCP is still recognizably an Anglican Book of Common Prayer. It belongs to a familiar genus, whose archetypal member, the Book of 1549, set a style of worship which this new Book is intended to maintain and enhance. The elements of continuity are obvious and pervasive, and scarcely need to be underscored. The table of contents is virtually identical with that of BCP and its predecessors. The creeds professed are the same. (For a discussion of the changes in the text of the creeds, see page 170.) The services provided for regular worship are the same — Daily Morning and Evening Prayer, and the Holy Eucharist. The basic contents and structure of these services are the same. The ordained ministers required are the same. In Rite I there is large scale verbal identity. Even in Rite II many BCP phrases have remained intact.

Thus PrBCP should be seen as the latest in a series of Anglican Prayer Books, 1549, 1552, 1559, 1603, 1637, 1662, 1789, 1892, 1928. In each case there were changes; sometimes, as in 1552, there were major ones. In each case there was recognizable continuity. Anglican Prayer Books presume continuity in change. The authors of the Preface to the American Prayer Book of 1789, who made some far-reaching changes in the English Book of 1662, wrote:

"While these alterations and amendments [regarding prayers for Civil Rulers] were in review before the Convention, they could not but, with gratitude to God, embrace the happy occasion which was offered to them (uninfluenced and unrestrained by any worldly authority whatsoever) to take a further review of the Public Service, and to establish such other alterations and amendments therein as might be deemed expedient . . . In which it will also appear that this Church is far from intending to depart from the Church of England in any essential point of doctrine, discipline or worship; or further than local circumstances require."

It is in the spirit of this Preface, which appears as the Preface to PrBCP also, that this revision has been undertaken. For the reasons already adduced, the changes are of a greater magnitude than those made in any earlier revision. We believe that the times call for them. Furthermore, a revision of this nature is indicated in order to remain in any kind of liturgical community with other Anglican Churches, all of which are moving in the same direction as that taken by PrBCP. Although changes proposed here are great, we believe that they do not depart at any *essential* point from the doctrine, discipline, or worship of our forebears.

II. Limits and Guidelines of Judgment

In seeking to establish the essential continuity of PrBCP with its predecessors, we must consider the features of the new proposals in some detail. At the beginning of such a survey, however, it is necessary to acknowledge the difficulty involved in making precise theological judgments about liturgical material, and also to set forth some criteria which may inform such judgments as can be made.

Limits

What a liturgy communicates about doctrine is not easily or quickly determined. A liturgy does not yield its meaning simply to a close reading of a text like PrBCP. Biblical tradition as made explicit in the appointed scriptural readings must be taken into account. Moreover, not all parts of a prayer book are used with equal frequency. Not all frequently used parts make the same impact. Simply to have the right words is far from insuring the communication of evangelical truth. So much depends upon which words in the new rites will etch themselves on the minds and hearts of worshipers, as have BCP phrases like "whose service is perfect freedom," or "unto whom all hearts are open, all desires known, and from whom no secrets are hid," and countless others. Until there has been longer and more widespread use of PrBCP, this dimension of theological judgment must elude us.

The task is complicated by the difficulty of applying theological standards directly to liturgical texts at all. For example, Anglican Prayer Books from the very beginning have been used by people of quite different theological outlooks. Both Evangelicals and Catholics have found it possible to read the Prayer of Consecration at the Eucharist, especially in the English version of 1662, in ways compatible with their respective theologies. It is simply impossible to state *the* theology of existing Anglican Prayer Books; and it is equally impossible to state *the* theology of the PrBCP.

This continuing difficulty of interpreting liturgical texts theologically is further compounded by a salient feature of the new proposals—their intentional comprehensiveness. In recognition of the fact that our Church today embraces a truly catholic variety of styles of worship, these new texts supply enough material to enable congregations within a wide spectrum of theological belief and liturgical practice to conduct worship soundly. The best resources available to contemporary liturgical scholarship have now been brought within the covers of a single Book.

Criteria for Judgment

Within the limits imposed by the foregoing considerations, the essential qualities of PrBCP with respect to doctrine, discipline, and worship can be judged by the following criteria which have guided the SLC.

1. The most obvious norm for judgment has been the 1928 American Book of Common Prayer, and behind it the long tradition of American and English Books.

2. Another norm is adequacy to the worshiping needs of contemporary American Episcopal congregations and individuals. Many parts of BCP have fallen into disuse. Some of the provisions for the sick, for example, are at best clumsy; and phrases in the Communion of the Sick suggest that all illness is the result of divine wrath. The Thanksgiving for Women after Childbirth stresses pain and peril too exclusively. Family Prayer, though eloquent, presupposes a more leisurely pace of life. More suitable material had to be found.

3. Another set of criteria which influenced the making of PrBCP is provided by the pre-Reformation liturgical tradition. This is a rich tradition, and the residual hostility to it which resulted from its misuse or distorted use in the late

Middle Ages has largely disappeared. It seems possible and desirable to enrich our worship by providing some of this ancient material in a revised form. In this category belong the provision for imposition of ashes on Ash Wednesday, the procession with palms on Palm Sunday, the Great Vigil of Easter, and in general, the whole section in PrBCP entitled Proper Liturgies for Special Days. The forms for the reconciliation of a Penitent, adapted from this pre-Reformation tradition, meet widespread pastoral needs. The new rites of Christian initiation, which seek to restore the practice of the undivided Church, seem to answer present practical and theological problems (see pp. 190-196).

4. None of the above criteria has been taken as ultimate. To make the 1928 Prayer Book a norm from which deviation is unthinkable would make revision of any kind impossible or, at best, trivial. Relevance to existing needs, important as it is, can never be a *final* norm for worship. The value of tradition, though great, is also not ultimate. Both must be brought under the demands of the Gospel as recorded in Scripture. Scripture, of course, provides no ready-made liturgies; and widely different practices are believed to be grounded in Scripture by those who worship in different traditions. Yet the Church must certainly be assured that everything which a worshiper is required to hear, say, and do, can be plausibly justified by an appeal to Scripture; and that nothing in liturgical provisions, either required or optional, contradicts Scriptural teaching. In its best judgment, SLC believes that PrBCP is in conformity with this Scriptural norm—in what it adopts from previous Prayer Books, in what it has devised for the world it confronts, and in what it has taken over from earlier liturgical traditions.

III. Survey of the Contents

The title of PrBCP on the title page conforms to that of The Book of Common Prayer of 1928, with the exception of the necessary qualifying phrase, "Proposed." The alternative name of the Church, "The Episcopal Church", adopted by the General Convention of 1964 (Preamble to the Constitution), is used, rather than the longer name. The decision to use the shorter designation of the Church originated in the House of Bishops as a recognition that the Prayer Book of this Church is used not only in the United States of America, but also in many independent nations, in which the fuller designation of the Church is an embarrassment. Otherwise the title page is word-for-word the same.

PrBCP also contains all the items listed in the BCP Table of Contents. The order of some of the parts has been altered, and there are a number of new entries. The Ratification (of the 1789 Book) and the Preface to the 1789 Book appear in PrBCP as in BCP. These items have appeared in every American version of BCP and establish the continuity of PrBCP with the American Anglican tradition. As in BCP, there follow two pages of rubrics, Concerning the Service of the Church, and The Calendar of the Church Year. Both have been considerably modified, as will appear later. Lectionaries, and the tables for finding Easter and other Holy Days have been moved to the end of the Book. It is believed that in that place they will be less obtrusive and equally easy to find when wanted.

The liturgical texts begin with the Daily Office in both PrBCP and BCP. This is a convenient order, one with which the Church is familiar, and one which serves to emphasize that continuity with earlier Anglican Books which SLC wished to preserve.

Morning and Evening Prayer appear in both Rite I (traditional language) and Rite II (contemporary language). In addition to Morning and Evening Prayer, a form for Noonday Prayer, a new Order of Worship for the Evening, and Compline, are provided in contemporary language. Brief forms for individual and family devotions, which have proved welcome in trial use, conclude this section.

The section of Prayers and Thanksgivings which follows Evening Prayer in BCP has been moved to a place after the Psalter in PrBCP. The collection in PrBCP, in fact, combines two sections of prayers in BCP, the section following Evening Prayer and the section following Family Prayer. It was felt that these prayers would be easier to find following a major section of the Book, like the Psalter, than following the Daily Office. Since they are used not only in connection with the Offices but on a variety of other occasions as well, convenience justifies the move.

The Great Litany follows next, as in BCP.

After the Litany in PrBCP come the Collects in both traditional and contemporary language. In this location they are midway between the Daily Office and the Eucharist, in both of which they are used. Texts of proper lessons have not been printed.

There are two reasons for not printing out the proper lessons. One is connected with the fact that in conjunction with a number of other Western Churches—Roman Catholic, Anglican, Lutheran, Reformed, and Methodist—we have elected to work out a new common lectionary for main Sunday services. This Lectionary includes an Old Testament lesson in addition to an Epistle and Gospel, and runs through a three-year cycle instead of a one-year cycle. On the assumption that the Old Testament lesson might take no more space than the Collect for the Day, it would still take three times as many pages to print lessons for PrBCP as to print Collects, Epistles, and Gospels in BCP. What takes 180 pages in BCP would require adding 540 pages to PrBCP, increasing its present size by 50%. (For a further discussion of the Lectionary see page 224.) However, this new Lectionary seems to be a desirable ecumenical and enriching feature of PrBCP.

The second reason for not printing the text of the proper lessons is that to do so would involve choosing one translation among the nine now authorized, giving the chosen one an arbitrary preference.

A new section follows the Collects, Proper Liturgies for Special Days. These are the special liturgies for Ash Wednesday, Palm Sunday, Maundy Thursday, Good Friday, Holy Saturday, and the Great Vigil of Easter—one of the most striking enrichments of PrBCP, as already noted. Since on these occasions the special liturgies usually come before eucharistic celebrations, it seems logical and convenient to print them before the text of the Eucharist. This placement also reminds us of a theological point of importance: that the death and resurrection of our Lord, celebrated in these liturgies, is the basis for the two great sacraments which follow in the Book, Baptism and Eucharist.

The Eucharist is presented in Rite I and Rite II forms. Each is preceded by a Penitential Order. The Order for Celebrating the Holy Eucharist is retained from trial use as an experiment which has proved successful.

The Pastoral Offices follow the Eucharist, as in BCP. Baptism has been moved forward, as indicated. The following offices are common to the two Books: Confirmation, Celebration and Blessing of a Marriage, Thanksgiving for the Birth or Adoption of a Child (Thanksgiving after Childbirth), Ministration to the Sick, and Burial of the Dead. The following offices have been added: Commitment to Christian Service, Blessing of a Civil Marriage, An Order for Marriage, Reconciliation of a Penitent, Ministration at the Time of Death, and An Order for Burial. The Burial Service itself occurs in both Rite I and Rite II versions.

Episcopal Services come next, before the Psalter, instead of after it as in BCP. These are the services which require a bishop as celebrant. They include ordination services for Bishop, Priest, and Deacon; a Litany for Ordinations; the Celebration of a New Ministry, replacing BCP's Institution of Ministers into Parishes or Churches, as being more widely applicable than the latter; and a service for the Consecration of a Church or Chapel.

The Psalter follows; and after the Psalter, a section of Prayers and Thanksgivings, as mentioned. There is a completely new Catechism; and where BCP has only the Thirty-Nine Articles, PrBCP contains a section of five historical documents: the Chalcedonian Definition of the Union of the Divine and Human Natures in the Person of Christ, the Athanasian Creed, the Preface to the First Book of Common Prayer (1549), the Articles of Religion (The Thirty-Nine Articles), and the Chicago-Lambeth Quadrilateral.

Tables of Holy Days, the "Main Service" Lectionary, and the Daily Office Lectionary conclude the Book.

IV. General Observations

Use of Contemporary Language

One of the most striking features of PrBCP, marking a sharp departure from BCP, is its use of contemporary language in Rite II services and throughout the rest of the Book. No aspect of trial use has occasioned more comment than the effort to find adequate contemporary liturgical language. What appears in PrBCP are texts revised and refined in the light of these comments and suggestions. We continue to believe that it is important to be able to use contemporary language for worship.

The reason for this conviction can be stated briefly. It is shared by those engaged in liturgical revision in every Western Church: namely, that in a religion centered in the Word made flesh, liturgy should be rooted in the language of the people. Such language will necessarily differ from that of the Book of Common Prayer in a number of significant respects. Perhaps the most obvious change, the one which has generated the most discussion during trial use, is the substitution of "you" for "thou" and the other alterations which this shift entails.

In the 16th century it was a sign of intimacy to address any person as "thou," whether God or human being. A perusal of any good English dictionary will disclose this fact. In Cranmer's day, the use of "thou" paralleled the present day French and Spanish use of "tu" or the German "du". In French, Spanish, and German to this day, the language of love and religion employs the familiar forms of second person pronoun. In English, however, the non-religious use of "thou" has virtually disappeared. Even in love poetry it begins to sound quaint.

Consequently "thou" in its religious use has acquired a sense of distance, of awe and mystery, which it did not originally have and was not intended to have. It is almost certainly true that the relation to God which Cranmer expressed in his sixteenth-century Prayer Books can be expressed today only by saying "you." There are ways to convey the sense of awe and wonder so necessary in worship without saying "thou."

Many other changes have been found necessary, of course, to make language contemporary. Third person singular verb endings and in some cases the whole form (hath, doth) had to be changed. But in fact, one quickly discovers that one is dealing not simply with forms of *words* but with forms of *thought*. Word *order* must frequently be altered. The lovely phrase from the All Saints' Preface, for example, ". . .receive the crown of glory that fadeth not away," is not contemporary English. One would neither say it nor write it in 1976. The rhythms and most of the sounds are preserved as nearly as possible in PrBCP's Rite II, ". . .receive the crown of glory that never fades away."

Sentences often have to be shortened. One might compare, for example, the BCP Preface to the Ordinal (p. 529) with that of PrBCP (p. 510). Only one sentence in the PrBCP version runs over four lines. In the shorter BCP Preface, one sentence is five lines long, and two are six. The exhortation in the BCP Solemnization of Matrimony consists of three sentences, one eleven lines long. The exhortation in PrBCP's Celebration and Blessing of a Marriage, which is somewhat longer, contains only one sentence as long as six lines.

Sometimes it has seemed desirable to invert the order of ideas, the result of a basic change in attitudes. It is instructive in this regard to compare the BCP

Exhortation to Communion (p. 85) with that in PrBCP (p. 316). The BCP Exhortation begins with a summons to self-examination and penitence, under the threat of judgment. It continues with a moving call to thanksgiving because of Christ's self-giving death. It ends with a reminder that Christ instituted the sacraments as "pledges of his love and a continual remembrance of his death." To twentieth century hearers, however, the logical place to begin seems to be with the institution of the sacrament. PrBCP then makes the point that sacraments are a reminder of God's love for us, in creation as well as in the redemption of the world by Christ. It *ends* with a call to self-examination. To modern ears, that seems the more persuasive order.

A quite different kind of linguistic change has been made in the generic terms which refer to the human race. BCP almost invariably uses "man" or "men." One thinks of such well-known phrases as "Who for us *men* and for our salvation," "O God, who hast made of one blood all nations of *men*," or "Blessed is the *man* that hath not walked in the counsel of the ungodly." In response to a widespread, though admittedly not universal, sense that the word "man" in many such instances is ambiguous, and can be taken to designate males only instead of including females as well, SLC has undertaken a careful review of all generic references, and has sought to eliminate ambiguity wherever possible. In the parallels to the BCP instances cited, for example, PrBCP reads, "For us and for our salvation," "O God, you have made of one blood all the peoples of the earth," and "Happy are they who have not walked in the counsel of the wicked."

In making alterations as a result of this consideration, each case has been considered on its own merit. Not every generic "man" or "brother" has been eliminated (*cf.* the fifth offertory sentence on p. 376), and no single rule for making the change has been employed. The generic "man" has been less systematically removed from Rite I, to preserve its traditional character better. But it is hoped that many ambiguities have been clarified. (See also the discussion of generic references in the Psalter on p. 110.)

These changes do not require the language of liturgy to be crude, irreverent, or ugly. The SLC is convinced that it is just as possible by sensitive nuance to convey reverence and dignity in the presence of God by means of twentieth century words and style as by sixteenth century words and style. To the best of its ability, the Commission has sought just such a vehicle for worship. What is offered in PrBCP has emerged out of a conversation with the whole Church during the past nine years.

Variety and Flexibility

A second striking general feature of PrBCP is its attempt to supply more variety for the worship of the Episcopal Church. Successive Prayer Book revisions since 1892 have introduced more variety, because life in the United States has become increasingly complex and the membership of this Church has become increasingly diverse.

It would be tedious to list all the new degrees of flexibility which have been introduced into PrBCP. They will emerge on inspection. To consider just Morning Prayer, by way of example, the Jubilate has been set as an alternative to the Venite, and the use of the Easter Canticle (formerly permitted for Easter Week only) has been extended optionally throughout the Easter Season. Lessons are on a two-year cycle instead of a one-year cycle. The selection of canticles after the lessons is richer, Evening Prayer canticles having been made available for morning, and Morning for evening. New canticles have been included in Rite II and are available also for Rite I. The optional use of the Collect of the Day and a more extensive set of fixed Collects permits much greater variation than in BCP; and in place of the fixed intercessions one is directed to choose from among any of the authorized prayers and thanksgivings.

Rubrics have been designed to provide essential information and describe essential action without imposing a straight-jacket. Oil may or may not be used in connection with the laying on of hands at Baptism. Ashes may or may not be imposed in the course of the Ash Wednesday liturgy. The rubric regarding posture during the prayer of consecration at the Eucharist reads, "The people kneel or stand." A congregation is assured considerable latitude in setting its own liturgical use, although necessary guidelines have been established.

Further flexibility is provided by the presence of both traditional and contemporary language versions of the Daily Offices, Eucharist, and Burial Service. It is hoped that the presence of Rite I in PrBCP will accomplish several objectives.

First, as someone has said, Rite I connects us to our Anglican past and Rite II connects us to our Anglican and ecumenical present and future. The forms of Rite I establish a link to our Anglican heritage which is unmistakable. The Commission wished to affirm it in the most positive way.

Secondly, and as part of the foregoing, we trust that having Rite I Daily Offices and Eucharist in the form in which they appear in PrBCP will make it possible for congregations to worship comfortably within permissible limits, even if they do not wish to make many changes in what they are presently doing. To a far greater extent than the material previously provided for trial use, PrBCP makes possible a Rite I reading of Morning Prayer or a Rite I celebration of the Eucharist almost identical to that of BCP.

Thirdly, we think that a slightly different use of Rite I services, paying attention to different rubrical permissions, will make it possible to introduce a congregation gradually to some of the changes in the ordering of the parts of the service and to some of the variety and flexibility which the Commission believes to be important additions to our ways of worship.

Fourthly, and perhaps most importantly, Rite I may offer an irreplaceable alternative to Rite II. Just because 16th century language no longer represents customary usage, it has acquired an aura of mystery. To some, it has come to express most perfectly the numinous majesty of God. Even if contemporary language services should gain widespread use, it is expected that Rite I will not simply disappear. Both styles should be available. It is hoped that congregations of this Church will become familiar with both and learn to use each for its own value.

PrBCP also contains Orders for celebrating Eucharist, Marriage, and Burial. These Orders are outlines of major parts of the services, together with brief descriptions of what should occur in each part. In the case of the Eucharist, the crucial sections of two prayers of consecration are written out; in the case of Marriage, the vows to be exchanged are stipulated. Otherwise, those planning the service have been left free to create a liturgy appropriate for a special occasion for which none of the other provisions is suitable. Ethnic or local custom and various cultural traditions can be thus incorporated. Such occasions are sometimes, though by no means always, times of less formality than that implied by the other texts. In any case, PrBCP recognizes that it is in fact impossible to provide suitably and adequately for every conceivable occasion, and that there are times when maximum freedom will permit a better liturgical response than detailed prescription.

Maximum Participation

Another general difference between PrBCP and BCP is the principle, enunciated, and as far as possible actualized, in PrBCP, that all worshipers should be actively involved in corporate worship. In particular, leadership in the liturgy should be widely shared. The emphasis on the liturgical ministry of the laity is strong in these services. SLC intends this liturgical ministry to express the central role of the ministry of the laity in the world, but not to be a substitute for it. A similar remark should be made for each of the orders. (See also the discussion of Christian Community, page 176). As we read in the directions, Concerning the Service of the Church,

> "In all services, the entire Christian assembly participates in such a way that the members of each order within the Church, lay persons, bishops, priests, and deacons, fulfill the functions proper to their respective orders, as set forth in the rubrical directions for each service" (PrBCP, p.13).

This principle has been tested and validated during trial use. The Commission believes it to be an important feature of the new services. Thus, each service has a rubric at the beginning, indicating what parts of the service are appropriate for each order. At a Marriage, for example, it is specified that a bishop or priest should preside, that a deacon may deliver the charge, ask for the Declaration of Consent, read the Gospel, and perform other assisting functions, but may be the celebrant only under specified conditions. Lay persons are encouraged to read the Old Testament lesson and the Epistle.

Place of the Eucharist

Another feature of PrBCP which marks it as different from BCP is the explicit moving of the Holy Communion to a more prominent place among the services of the Church. In BCP we read in the introductory rubrics,

> "The Order for Holy Communion, the Order for Morning Prayer, the Order for Evening Prayer, and the Litany, as set forth in this Book are the regular services appointed for Public Worship . . ." (BCP, p. vii).

In PrBCP the corresponding rubric runs,

> "The Holy Eucharist, the principal act of Christian worship on the Lord's Day and other major Feasts, and Daily Morning and Evening Prayer, as set forth in this Book, are the regular services appointed for public worship in this Church" (PrBCP, p. 13).

The continuity is obvious, the change in emphasis significant.

Baptisms, Confirmations, Marriages, Burials, as well as all the Episcopal Services, are arranged to fit naturally into a Eucharistic celebration. All the necessary directions are given *in situ* for making the combination. In no instance is the Eucharist required where it was not required before; but its appropriateness and availability are more apparent than before.

Several points should be made about this new emphasis on the Eucharist. For one thing, it is *scriptural*. Our Lord instituted the Supper for his remembrance and he made himself known "in the breaking of bread."

For another thing it is *ecumenical*. Eucharist is the principal Sunday celebration of Orthodox and Roman Catholic alike. A recent statement prepared by the Faith and Order Commission of the World Council of Churches expresses a widespread Protestant conviction that

> "as the eucharist is the new liturgical service Christ has given to the Church, it seems normal that it should be celebrated every Sunday or once a week" (*One Baptism, One Eucharist, and a Mutually Recognized Ministry*, p. 27).

The fact that the eucharistic service itself constitutes a summary and focus of essential Christian faith scarcely needs to be labored. The inclusion of an Old Testament lesson and psalmody in the eucharistic propers both broadens and sharpens our understanding of salvation history. Moreover, Western culture today seems open to sacraments in a way that has not been true for centuries. It has been said that the printing press provided cultural resonance for the Reformation emphasis on the Word. Television may provide cultural resonance for communication by means of visual and enacted symbols.

For all these reasons the move to center worship in the Eucharist seems timely. In the past, frequent celebrations of Holy Communion have led to attendance without reception. In reaction against late medieval practice, the sacramental devotion of Reformation Churches emphasized intensity rather than frequency of observance. Quarterly celebrations became the rule. Within Anglicanism, there has been a steady return to more frequent celebrations, however: monthly, as a result of the evangelical revival, weekly as a result of the Oxford movement. Today, most of our parishes have at least an early celebration every Sunday. PrBCP does not make any requirements about the frequency of eucharistic celebrations. But the current wave of eucharistic piety, fostered by the liturgical movement, is not tending to non-communicating participation. We believe that this new interest in the Eucharist will continue to enrich the life of the Church, and that it will be encouraged by the provisions which PrBCP makes.

International Consultation on English Texts

The International Consultation on English Texts was a group of twenty-five scholars from Roman Catholic, Anglican, Presbyterian, Lutheran, Baptist, Methodist, and Congregational Churches. Nations whose chief language is English were represented: England, Ireland, Scotland, Wales, Canada, Australia, South Africa, and the United States. At a time when all these Churches in all these countries were producing modern language liturgies, a score of new translations of the Lord's Prayer, Creeds, and other common texts could have been produced. The result would have been confusion compounded.

The Consultation was convened to produce agreed versions of a number of liturgical texts which could be used by everyone in an ecumenical age. The Consultation met from 1969 to 1975. Three members of our Commission sat on it at various times: Dr. Massey Shepherd and Canon Charles Guilbert, representing the Episcopal Church, and Dr. Charles W. F. Smith, representing the Consultation on Church Union. Texts upon which agreement was reached appear in a publication entitled *Prayers We Have in Common*, published by Fortress Press in 1970 and revised in 1971, and in a second still further revised edition in 1975. The texts in PrBCP which are the work of the Consultation are the Lord's Prayer, the Apostles' Creed, the Nicene Creed, Kyrie, Gloria in excelsis, Sursum corda, Sanctus and Benedictus, Agnus Dei, Gloria Patri, Te Deum, Benedictus, and Magnificat. These texts have been common to English-speaking Churches in the past because of the influence of the King James Bible and earlier Books of Common Prayer. To have reached such a broad ecumenical consensus on new versions of these texts today is an achievement of the first magnitude.

STU and AS used the version of ICET texts issued prior to 1971. The Second Revised Edition of *Prayers We Have in Common* (1975) is the basis of the PrBCP texts. A number of changes were adopted in 1975, of which the most significant are these:

The Lord's Prayer

- After a great deal of discussion within the Consultation, "hallowed be your Name" replaces "holy be your Name." *Prayers We Have in Common* (1975) remarks: "No absolute and exclusive decision on this line of the prayer can be fairly made. Ideally the translation should allow the whole breadth of interpretation whether doxological or petitionary for the action of God and/or man. 'Hallowed be your Name' is probably the translation which keeps most of the options open. Though the word *hallowed* has an archaic ring, it has not entirely passed out of currency, and no really satisfactory synonym for it is at hand."
- "Do not bring us to the test" has become "Save us from the time of trial." There is probably no completely satisfactory way to translate this line either, with its description of the final woes prior to the establishment of God's kingdom. The present version seems somewhat less open to misunderstanding than its predecessor. A similar attitude towards God's coming judgment is expressed in the verse, "if those days had not been shortened, no human being would be saved; but for the sake of the elect, those days will be shortened."(Matt. 24:22).

The Nicene Creed

- In the earlier ICET version of the Nicene Creed, the phrase "all that is seen and unseen" did not seem to many the equivalent of "all things visible and invisible." The latter is taken to denote an objective state, the former a subjective limitation. The present form, "all that is, seen and unseen," attributes to God the creation of everything—and that is the heart of the matter.
- "Of one Being with the Father" now replaces "one in Being with the Father." "In speech," notes *Prayers We Have in Common* (1975), "the noun *Being* is easily confused with the gerund *being*, which would give a different emphasis."
- In the earlier ICET Nicene Creed, the line "he was born of the Virgin Mary and became man" apparently ignored the Biblical teaching that God was active in the Incarnation from the moment of conception. The present, "he became incarnate from the Virgin Mary and was made man," more adequately renders the sense of the original creedal text.
- The new phrase, "suffered death" is closer in meaning to the Greek text than either "suffered" (BCP) or "suffered, died" of the earlier ICET version. (See Additional Note on page 175.)

PrBCP has departed from ICET translations in only a handful of instances. It supplies a different version of the Nunc dimittis which seems far superior. The use of the Nunc dimittis on ecumenical occasions is so infrequent that this discrepancy will not be found disturbing. Also, for purely stylistic reasons, SLC altered the line of the ICET Te Deum in the 1975 version from "you did not spurn the Virgin's womb" to "you did not shun the Virgin's womb."

PrBCP has also exercised an option left open by the Consultation for decision by Churches which elect to use these texts: In the Nicene Creed, PrBCP has elected to drop the word *men* from the line, "who for us men and for our salvation." As a generic term, it adds nothing to the sense of the line and a number of critics have felt that the word excludes women from Christ's saving work. PrBCP reads "For *us* and for our salvation."

Theological Emphases

PrBCP seeks to express the fulness of the Christian faith, as has every earlier Anglican Prayer Book. Each, however, has laid emphasis on certain aspects of Christian doctrine, and each has been led to certain expressions of Christian truth, because of the particular grasp of faith characteristic of the age in which each Book appeared and because of the needs of that time. PrBCP is no exception to this rule. Certain aspects of Christian doctrine receive a stress somewhat different from that in BCP and previous Books.

Creation

The doctrine of creation is a case in point. A positive doctrine of creation and a strong statement of the relation between God and his world have always been important parts of Anglican public worship. These affirmations were expressed mainly in one service, Daily Morning Prayer, notably in the canticles (Venite, Benedicite, Jubilate). Since, however, Morning Prayer was the best known office of the Church, and since it always formed the first part of the Sunday morning service (which until 1892, by rubric, continued with the Litany and Ante-Communion or Communion), this emphasis on creation was extremely conspicuous. God's control over both natural and human affairs was likewise formerly recited every Sunday in the Litany.

This doctrinal emphasis has been obscured in modern times, however, with the customary dismemberment of the Anglican Sunday morning service into *either* the Office *or* the Eucharist; and even further obscured in America with the widespread use of the Benedictus es and the disuse of the Benedicite at Morning Prayer.

PrBCP brings the doctrine of creation to new expression in several different ways for several different reasons. As far as Morning Prayer itself is concerned, the Benedicite is still present, and it is hoped that its new arrangement will encourage more frequent use of that canticle. In several of the new canticles the themes of creation and God's control of the world are prominent: A Song of Penitence, for example, with the phrase, "You made the heavens and the earth/with all their vast array;" A Song to the Lamb has the line, "For you created everything that is."

As far as the Eucharist is concerned, care has been taken in all the new Eucharistic Prayers (Prayers of Consecration) to recognize God's work in creation. This element has been added as a result of recent liturgical scholarship, for it is now known that thanksgiving for the created order was a feature of the Jewish *Berakah*, the prayer which probably underlies Christian eucharistic prayers. Praise to God for his gift in creation was a feature of most of the earliest eucharistic prayers. It disappeared, however, in the Western tradition. PrBCP has restored it. Creation language has been provided for Rite I in Eucharistic Prayer II ("for that thou didst create heaven and earth"). In Rite II, Prayer C contains an extended and moving section on creation, and less detailed mention appears in A, B, and D. The first Proper Preface of the Lord's Day focuses centrally on creation.

For different reasons, creation is mentioned much more frequently than heretofore in the Prayers of the People. Because of our new concern for the environment, an "ecological clause" has been added to the Prayer for the Whole State of Christ's Church and the World in Rite I; and there are explicit petitions in alternative Forms I, IV, V, and VI. In this connection, the greatly enlarged collection of prayers and thanksgivings for the Natural Order, in Prayers and Thanksgivings, should be noted (PrBCP, pp. 827-828, 840).

In the new order for Holy Baptism also one notices a much more positive attitude toward creation than in the old—especially in the Thanksgiving over Water; and the new Order of Worship for Evening celebrates the blessings of creation, especially light. In still other services, physical things are used more frequently than in BCP. Provision is made for the use of ashes, palms, the Paschal candle. The Great Vigil of Easter celebrates the redemption of the whole created order in a remarkably dramatic way.

Redemption

Redemption is a "buying back" of the world, presumably from Satan, who in the New Testament was understood to hold the world in his power (Matt. 4:9, 1 John 5:19). The language of being "sold" into captivity and rescued again from this-worldly enemies constitutes the so-called Deuteronomic framework for the history of Israel (*cf.* Judges 2:11-23). To speak of redemption in Christian worship is to confess that by Christ's life and death, his people have been "bought back" from their ultimate enemies.

In terms of the explicit mention of redemption and the number of instances in which Jesus is called Redeemer or Savior, BCP and PrBCP are nearly the same. There is no doubt in either book that Jesus is worshiped as Lord because of what God accomplished through him for the redemption of the world. Neither Book has an obvious advantage over the other.

The remarkable feature of PrBCP in this respect, however, is its use, particularly in the Eucharistic Prayers, of a wider range of language to describe this saving work. The BCP Prayer of Consecration speaks of Christ's death as a "sacrifice, oblation, and satisfaction," and of his work as "our redemption." In other places in BCP, to be sure, other descriptions appear: victory and deliverance in the Lenten Collects, for example.

To think of Christ's death as a *sacrifice* and *oblation* is to confess that his death accomplished what the Old Testament sacrificial system did not accomplish—reconciliation and restoration of communion between God and his creation.

To think of Christ's death as a *satisfaction* evokes a theory of atonement in which God is conceived as a stern judge who demands justice. The works of humanity do not satisfy his demands. They are unrighteous (Rom. 1:18). Christ's death did satisfy this demand. He is our righteousness, and on the strength of his perfect life and innocent death, wrath is averted. "He is the propitiation for our sins." This theory of the atonement dominated Christian theology and liturgy in the late Middle Ages and during the 16th century Reformation. It is not now very appealing, although it does emphasize the seriousness of sin and the reality of God's wrath. It should not be the sole expression of God's reconciling work, but it is appropriate that it should appear as a sub-theme (*cf.* Rite I, Eucharistic Prayer I; Evening Prayer Rite I, Collect for Peace; Collects for Friday in Easter Week, Proper 22, Proper 26, Great Vigil of Easter).

Sacrifice, oblation, and satisfaction are only three of the numerous ways in which God's act in Christ is described in the New Testament. In fact, *satisfaction* is not used in the New Testament in this connection. But God's act is described there as victory, freedom, ransom, salvation, deliverance, new creation, justification, forgiveness, reconciliation. And the new Eucharistic Prayers make use of a notably larger supply of images:

A: "reconcile us to you"
"perfect sacrifice for the whole world"
B. "Savior and Redeemer of the World"
"delivered us from evil" (victory)
"made us worthy to stand before you"
(justification and reconciliation)
"in his sacrifice"
C. "to open for us the way of freedom and peace"
"he reconciled us"
"we are healed"
"we who have been redeemed by him,
and made a new people . . ."

D. "destroyed death" (victory)
"made the whole creation new"
"sanctification"
"redemption"
"salvation"

Forgiveness or remission of sins is mentioned in every prayer, as part of the institution narrative.

In the Proper Prefaces, which in PrBCP are more numerous and used more frequently than in BCP, the motifs of victory and triumph sound forth clearly. (Advent, Lent, Easter, second alternative for the Lord's Day.)

It seems a reasonable conclusion that there is a richer expression of the atoning work of Christ in PrBCP than in BCP.

Sin and Penitence

The tone of all the English Books and the first American Book was deeply penitential. All the opening sentences at the Daily Offices were of a penitential character; the General Confession was always required. The Eucharist opened with a mandatory rehearsal of the Ten Commandments. They served as an examination of conscience, with their response, "Lord, have mercy upon us, and incline our hearts to keep this law." The Communion service of American Books hovered continually around a sense of the worshipers' unworthiness ("And although we are unworthy, through our manifold sins, to offer unto thee any sacrifice," "we are not worthy so much as to gather up the crumbs under thy table"). The tone of the resulting liturgies corresponded to a deep-seated need of late medieval and post-medieval psyches. There seems to be little doubt, however, that the language strikes many serious Christians of the twentieth century as exaggerated. There never seems to be a chance to express the unfettered joy at deliverance which Christ's death and resurrection accomplished.

Successive American revisions of BCP have tended to mitigate this tone of unrelieved penitence and unworthiness. Non-penitential opening sentences were added to the Daily Offices in 1892, and in 1928 most of the traditional penitential sentences were dropped. The use of the General Confession at the Daily Offices has become optional, and the rubrical direction in BCP requiring the use of the Ten Commandments with the Communion service at least once a month is widely disregarded.

Trial use carried this mitigation much further. Some critics felt that the process had gone too far. Confession at the Eucharist became optional in LLS. It was restored as a norm in STU. The form provided for General Confession in the Second Service, however, included no explicit expression of repentence and sorrow for sin. Without trying to restore all the expressions of penitence characteristic of BCP, some added emphasis has been made in PrBCP. A striking option for Morning

Prayer is the new canticle, A Song of Penitence, which provides a moving expression of repentance especially suitable for Lent. An alternative opening dialogue of a penitential nature has been provided in the Eucharist for use in Lent and on other penitential occasions. The language of the Rite II General Confession has been altered. It now includes the line, "We are truly sorry and we humbly repent."

We should also note the presence for the first time in an English or American Prayer Book of a form for the Reconciliation of a Penitent. It deals seriously and pastorally with the sins of individuals.

These provisions will in no sense minimize sin; rather, their effect is to deal soberly with sin, both as it troubles individual consciences and as it affects the life of a congregation and society as a whole. It is hoped that PrBCP will be found to permit also the expression of Christian joy in the confidence of God's full and free pardon through Jesus Christ.

Christian Hope

Christian worship that is faithful to its biblical foundations and to its own history should be consciously oriented to the future as well as to the past. We proclaim the Lord's death "until he comes." We pray, "thy Kingdom come." The fullness of God's kingdom is in the future, though in worship we encounter it as present.

This understanding of Christian hope, realized by anticipation in the community at worship, is one of the striking recoveries of the liturgical movement. Its expression in BCP was perhaps not adequate, although the Lord's Prayer always spoke of it, and the BCP Prayer of Consecration contains the phrase, ". . . command us to continue a perpetual memory of that his precious death and sacrifice *until his coming again.*" Nevertheless, it would be fair to say that BCP Eucharist is primarily oriented toward the past.

PrBCP, like STU and AS, makes an effort to introduce a more prominent future thrust. There is a greater emphasis on our Lord's coming in the four Advent Collects. The three Sundays before Advent sound an unmistakable eschatological note. The Benedictus qui venit has been added after the Sanctus in the Eucharist, optionally in Rite I, necessarily in Rite II. The eschatological note is virtually shouted in the congregational acclamations in Prayer A ("Christ will come again"), Prayer B ("We await his coming in glory"), and Prayer C ("We celebrate his death and resurrection, As we await the day of his coming.") The anamnesis of Prayer D ends on this future "recollection": "Recalling Christ's death and his descent among the dead, proclaiming his resurrection and ascension to your right hand, *awaiting his coming in glory.*" This emphasis appears also in Morning Prayer, with the new suffrage, "In you, Lord, is our hope," and its response, "And we shall never hope in vain." The last question of the Catechism (PrBCP, p. 862) runs, "What then is our assurance as Christians?" Its answer is, "Our assurance as Christians is that nothing, not even death, shall separate us from the love of God which is in Christ Jesus our Lord. Amen."

Christian Community

It has been said that as assurance of immortality was the acute spiritual need of the early Church, and assurance of forgiveness the acute need in sixteenth century Europe, community is the acute need in our time. Some critics of STU and AS have felt that the accent on the "horizontal" dimension of worship has threatened to supplant the "vertical."

A careful reading of the text of PrBCP will not reveal any effort to diminish or dilute the focus in worship on the presence of the transcendent God. But at least three features of PrBCP do attempt to assert the strength and the character of the Christian community in the face of this contemporary search for it. They supplement but do not replace our worship of the Holy One.

The first of these features is the Exchange of the Peace. As a verbal greeting exchanged between celebrant and congregation, it is now required at every Eucharist, whether Rite I or Rite II. No action is specified. But in the course of trial use, many congregations have found that this moment provides a significant time for mutual greeting and recognition, an expression of the fact that Christianity is not simply a matter of an individual's private relation to God. Indeed, one basic Christian experience is of God's relation to his whole people, and the uniting of his people in bonds of love. The growth in popularity of the Peace is one of the most noteworthy features of the liturgical life of our Church during the past few years.

A second feature expressive of the character of the Christian community at worship is the careful specification at the beginning of each service of the particular roles which lay persons, deacons, priests, and bishops should play. For worship is the work of the whole People of God, not a performance by one or two persons. This feature of PrBCP has already been discussed on page 167.

The third feature which stresses community is the Eucharist itself. We have already called attention to the new centrality of this service. But we should also note that to a degree not present in BCP it is thought of as a common meal of the people of God ("The gifts of God for the people of God," PrBCP, pp. 338, 364). The new stress on this original character of the Eucharist probably more than any other aspect of it accounts for its increasing use.

Additional Note on the Nicene Creed

Line 27 of the Nicene Creed in the ICEText, reads as follows: "who proceeds from the Father [and the Son].

The words in brackets (the so-called *filioque*) were a Western addition to the Creed. They were put in brackets as indicating that some Churches might include them and other Churches might not.

SLC, beginning with LLS, in 1967, recommended that the words be omitted, on the grounds that they were not part of the text approved by the ecumenical

Councils of Nicaea (325), Constantinople (381), and Chalcedon (451). The General Convention, however, decided to retain the words. They have also been retained by other Churches of the Anglican Communion.

V. Analysis of the Contents

We must now examine specific provisions of PrBCP. We shall consider them in the order in which they appear in the Book.

The Church Year (The Calendar)

Although the Church Year provided by PrBCP is in many respects like the Church Year of BCP, there are some variations worth noting. For the most part they represent Anglican and ecumenical agreements.

Seven days are designated as principal feasts which take precedence over any other day or observance: Easter, Ascension, Pentecost, Trinity, All Saints' Day, Christmas, and Epiphany. This is a much shorter list than that provided in BCP (p. li).[i]

In PrBCP, Sundays, as feasts of the Lord Jesus Christ, have precedence over any other celebration except three: the Holy Name (formerly Circumcision), the Presentation, the Transfiguration. These three are also feasts of the Lord, and they are of dominant importance. As a result of trial use, this nearly absolute precedence of Sundays has been softened. Permission is now given to celebrate a major Saint's Day on Sundays after Epiphany, except the first and the last, and on Sundays after Pentecost, except the first and the last. The new emphasis on Sunday as the weekly remembrance of the resurrection of our Lord is a theological point of importance.

In PrBCP, the pre-Lenten Sundays, Quinquagesima, Sexagesima, and Septuagesima have been eliminated, and Epiphany season extended to include as many as nine Sundays. Propers for the whole season are chosen to make it a celebration of the revelation of Christ to the world, from the Baptism of Christ on the First Sunday after Epiphany to the Transfiguration on the last. (The Transfiguration is also, of course, observed on August 6.) Liturgical celebration of revelation, as well as incarnation, resurrection, and redemption, is now built into the calendar.

---

[i] [Ed. note: Page li of the 1928 BCP lists fourteen entries for Holy Days having "precedence of any other Sunday or Holy Day." They are 1) the Sundays in Advent, 2) Christmas Day, 3) The Epiphany, 4) Septuagesima Sunday, 5) Sexagesima Sunday, 6) Quiquagesima Sunday, 7) Ash Wednesday, 8) The Sundays in Lent, 9) All the days of Holy Week, 10) Easter Day and the following seven days, 11) Rogation Sunday, 12) The Ascension Day and the Sunday after Ascension Day, 13) Whitsunday and the six following days, 14) Trinity Sunday]

Lent has also been put into clearer focus. There is no longer a "Passiontide" extending from the Fifth Sunday. Palm Sunday, the day on which the Passion Gospel is read, is the "Sunday of the Passion," as in earlier Anglican usage.

The centrality of the resurrection to the Christian faith has dictated the restoration of the great season of Easter, lasting in the ancient Church for fifty days and reaching its completion and climax on the feast of Pentecost. Therefore several changes have been made in the BCP calendar from Easter to Pentecost. Sundays are no longer designated "after Easter," as though Easter were only of one day's duration, but "of Easter." In BCP, the Fifth Sunday after Easter was commonly called Rogation Sunday. In order not to interrupt the succession of the great fifty days, this name has been dropped as a title. Its substance, however, has been retained in the propers of the day, the Sixth Sunday of Easter. For the same reason, BCP's Sunday after Ascension Day has been renamed the Seventh Sunday of Easter.

(There is no change, of course, in the observance of Ascension Day itself.) Thus, the resurrection and ascension of Christ, and the coming of the Holy Spirit on Pentecost, have become once more a "unitive feast."

In PrBCP, Sundays are reckoned "after Pentecost" instead of "after Trinity." This practice conforms to ecumenical custom; and by frequent repetition of the name Pentecost, emphasis will be laid upon a Christian's life in the Spirit rather than upon a summary doctrine, the Trinity. By the device, new to PrBCP, of adjusting the length of the Pentecost season by dropping Sundays at the beginning rather than at the end, an invariable pre-Advent emphasis has been secured. The propers of the three Sundays before Advent herald the coming of God's kingdom and register a clear eschatological theme.

The Proper Prefaces for the Lord's Day articulate the significance of every Sunday as a feast of creation, redemption, and new life in the Spirit.

The days of Lent, especially Ash Wednesday and Good Friday, and all other Fridays of the year (except for Fridays in the Christmas and Easter seasons), are described as days to be observed "by special acts of discipline and self-denial" (PrBCP, p. 17). In BCP, Ash Wednesday and Good Friday are listed as fasts; and the forty days of Lent, the Ember days, and all the Fridays in the year, except Christmas Day, and the Epiphany, or any Friday which may intervene between these Feasts, are described as "other days of fasting, on which the Church requires such a measure of abstinence as is more especially suited to extraordinary acts and exercises of devotion" (BCP, p. li). The gain in clarity and consistency is considerable.

Seven "red-letter" days have been added to the calendar: The Confession of St. Peter on January 18; St. Joseph on March 19; the Visitation on May 31; St. Mary Magdalene on July 22; St. Mary the Virgin on August 15; Holy Cross Day on September 14; and St. James of Jerusalem, the Brother of our Lord, on

October 23. In addition, June 29 has been restored as St. Peter and St. Paul's Day instead of St. Peter's Day alone. In general, these days extend the BCP principle of commemorating New Testament saints.

A large number of "black-letter" days appear for the first time in the calendar of an American Book. Their observance is optional. Propers are to be found in *Lesser Feasts and Fasts* (revised edition, 1973). Black-letter days have been included in the calendar of English Prayer Books since 1561; and an American calendar of lesser feasts has been authorized for optional use since 1964.

The distinction between red-letter days and black-letter days is comparable to the distinction between canonical scripture and other works in which believers sense the Spirit of God to be moving. The canonical writings preserve what was believed to be eye-witness testimony to the life, death, and resurrection of the Lord. Any subsequent writing, no matter how inspired and inspiring, is dependent on that witness. Similarly, red-letter saints are New Testament saints who saw the Lord. When the apostles determined to elect someone as Judas' successor among the Twelve, they required that such a person be "one of the men who have accompanied us all the time that the Lord Jesus went in and out among us, beginning from the baptism of John until the day he was taken from us" (Acts 1:22-23). Subsequent persons, no matter how heroic their witness or saintly their lives, are dependent on the witness of that first generation. Both the presence of these black-letter days and their very different status have precedent in Anglican tradition.

Morning and Evening Prayer

Separation of the Offices

In both the forms authorized for trial use (STU and AS), Morning and Evening Prayer were printed as one service, with only certain items indicated as belonging especially to the morning or to the evening. The title in AS, "Morning and Evening Prayer," did not indicate that the office was intended for daily use, though such was the intention, as the Lectionary showed.

PrBCP reverts to the traditional Anglican practice of printing the two services separately, and entitles them *Daily* Morning Prayer and *Daily* Evening Prayer. This arrangement more adequately expresses the expectation that each day should be sanctified by prayers at its beginning and at its end. A continuity of prayer, morning and evening, is thereby established, not only with the rest of Anglicanism, but with an ancient Christian custom rooted in the devotional practice of the Jews. It also suggests a rule of life which, during the four hundred years of Anglican history, most clergy and many lay persons have found strengthening. With the new richness of the offices in PrBCP, they will constitute an even greater devotional resource.

Emphasis on the Seasons

Heightened emphasis on the seasons of the Church Year was one mark of the changes introduced in 1928. This trend continues in PrBCP. The list of seasonal opening sentences has been lengthened, and put at the beginning of the list of opening sentences, before the general sentences, rather than after them, as in 1928. All the BCP general sentences and most of the seasonal ones, however, are included in PrBCP, as well as some new ones. The provision of STU and AS that opening sentences should be read responsively has been dropped as a result of trial use.

Antiphons for use with the Venite, another way of marking the seasons, made their appearance in 1928. In PrBCP they appear more prominently, more of them are provided, and the fuller directions provided in Additional Directions should encourage their wider use. The recitation of the Easter Canticle, Christ our Passover, now permitted throughout Easter Season, is a further seasonal variant.

Lessons

Until the 1928 BCP, the reading of two lessons at both Morning and Evening Prayer was required. In 1928 only one lesson was required at Evening Prayer, although two were of course permitted. This provision is a mark of flexibility, allowing for a shorter service if desired. In PrBCP, the same permission to have but one lesson is applied to Morning Prayer also, as an obvious extension of the same principle. (For a discussion of the Lectionaries, see pages 224-225.)

Canticles

In line with the principle of enrichment, a number of new canticles have been provided in Rite II, and they are available for use in Rite I as well. Some are already familiar from AS. Three are new to PrBCP: The Song of Moses (Exod. 15:1-6, 11-13, 17-18), the Third Song of Isaiah (Isa. 60:1-3, 11a, 14c, 18-19), A Song of Penitence (Prayer of Manasseh 1-2, 4, 6-7, 11-15). In line with the principle of flexibility, any canticle may be used at either Morning Prayer or Evening Prayer.

In Rite I, only BCP canticles have been supplied, with BCP texts. The psalm canticles at Evening Prayer, which were rarely used, have been dropped.

Collects

The set Collects at both offices have been given a treatment rather different from that of either BCP or AS, to provide for several circumstances. There are now two groups of Collects. The Officiant is to read at least one from each group. Since the first group contains the Collect of the Day and the BCP office Collects in addition to others, one may so select these prayers as to reproduce what was required in BCP. But one may also choose to mark Sundays, Fridays, and

Saturdays, pointing to their significance in the paschal mystery. One may also mark the time of day—morning or evening. Other choices are also available. The required addition of one prayer from the second group, having to do with the ministry or mission of the Church, is a welcome emphasis not found in BCP. From a theological point of view, this second group of Collects constitutes the most significant difference between the BCP and the PrBCP versions of the Daily Offices. The Collects in this new group serve as a healthy balance to the ones adopted from BCP, which pray for preservation and protection only.

Intercessions

No intercessions are printed after the office Collects. The rubric instead indicates that "authorized intercessions and thanksgivings may follow." This provision is similar to the rubric in BCP at the end of the fixed Collects; and the custom of using intercessions different from those printed at the end of the office is in fact almost universal. In any case, all the intercessions printed after the Collects in BCP appear in the collection of Prayers and Thanksgivings in PrBCP.

Conclusion of the Office

Both Morning and Evening Prayer conclude optionally with the General Thanksgiving and the Prayer of St. Chrysostom, as in BCP. In addition to the one familiar "grace" of BCP (2 Cor. 13:14), two new concluding sentences from Scripture have been supplied. Of the three, one is to be chosen.

New Offices

There are new offices for Noonday and Compline. These additions are useful for certain special occasions. With Morning and Evening Prayer, they also provide the possibility of a fourtime-a-day rule of life, if that should be desired.

The Order of Worship for the Evening is based on pre-monastic forms of Vespers. Authorized since 1973 but not printed in AS, it offers the possibility of greater variety in the evening. This order may be used with Evening Prayer, instead of it, or together with some other service occurring in the evening.

Daily Devotions for Individuals and Families, in the Morning, at Noon, in the Early Evening, and at Close of Day, conclude this section. Their structure and content parallel the traditional forms of the Daily Office. Trial use has proved them to be welcome and popular substitutes for BCP's Family Prayer.

The Great Litany

The Great Litany appears after the Daily Offices, in traditional language only. It is a conservative revision of the Litany of BCP, called now the Great Litany to distinguish it from the many other prayers in litany form which PrBCP contains.

It is felt that in neither scope nor style does this great prayer lend itself to modernization. Several of the petitions have been reworked, and a number reordered, all in the interests of clarity and realism. There are new petitions for each of us in our several callings, to work for the common good; for the lonely and infirm; and for those whose homes are broken or torn by strife.

The Supplication designed for times of war, national anxiety, or disaster has been separated from the main body of the Litany and put at the end, for the sake of convenience.

Collects

There are 158 Collects for the Church Year. Of these, 70 are to be found in both BCP and AS; 52 are in AS only, 10 in BCP only, and 26 are new to PrBCP. What can be said about these changes?

Proper Collects are in four groups: Sundays of the Church Year, Holy Days, the Common of Saints, and Various Occasions. The latter two groups were not distinguished by title in BCP, although there was one proper Collect, Epistle, and Gospel for A Saint's Day, as well as propers for the Ember Days, Rogation Days, At a Marriage, and At a Burial. The Common of Saints and propers for Various (Special) Occasions did appear in STU in approximately their PrBCP form.

The BCP Collects for the major days are retained. (1 Advent, Christmas, Epiphany, Ash Wednesday, Palm Sunday, Easter, Ascension, Pentecost, Trinity). For some of these days, however, new Collects have been added in addition to the old. Easter and Christmas have been given three Collects each, Ascension Day and Pentecost two each.

Thirty-one BCP Collects have not been included in PrBCP. Most of them fall into three groups.

A large group of BCP Collects were not included because they repeat a theme already sufficiently represented: the defence and preservation of the Church. These are the BCP Collects for 3 Epiphany,[ii] 4 Epiphany,[iii] 5 Epiphany,[iv] Sexagesima,[v] 3 Lent,[vi] 5 Lent,[vii] 2 Trinity,[viii] 3 Trinity,[ix] 15 Trinity,[x] 18 Trinity.[xi] There is no desire to eliminate this emphasis, but it is adequately

---

[ii] BCP 3 Epiphany: ALMIGHTY and everlasting God, mercifully look upon our infirmities, and in all our dangers and necessities stretch forth thy right hand to help and defend us; through Jesus Christ our Lord. Amen.

[iii] BCP 4 Epiphany: O GOD, who knowest us to be set in the midst of so many and great dangers, that by reason of the frailty of our nature we cannot always stand upright; Grant to us such strength and protection, as may support us in all dangers, and carry us through all temptations; through Jesus Christ our Lord. Amen.

[iv] BCP 5 Epiphany: O LORD, we beseech thee to keep thy Church and household continually in thy true religion; that they who do lean only upon the hope of thy heavenly grace may evermore be defended by thy mighty power; through Jesus Christ our Lord. Amen.

and eloquently voiced in the PrBCP Collects for 4 Epiphany,[xii] 3 Lent,[xiii] Proper 2,[xiv] Proper 3,[xv] Proper 4,[xvi] Proper 13,[xvii] Proper 24.[xviii]

---

[v] BCP Sexagesima: O LORD God, who seest that we put not our trust in any thing that we do; Mercifully grant that by thy power we may be defended against all adversity; through Jesus Christ our Lord. Amen.

[vi] BCP 3 Lent: WE beseech thee, Almighty God, look upon the hearty desires of thy humble servants, and stretch forth the right hand of thy Majesty, to be our defence against all our enemies; through Jesus Christ our Lord. Amen.

[vii] BCP 5 Lent: WE beseech thee, Almighty God, mercifully to look upon thy people; that by thy great goodness they may be governed and preserved evermore, both in body and soul; through Jesus Christ our Lord. Amen.

[viii] BCP 2 Trinity: O LORD, who never failest to help and govern those whom thou dost bring up in thy stedfast fear and love; Keep us, we beseech thee, under the protection of thy good providence, and make us to have a perpetual fear and love of thy holy Name; through Jesus Christ our Lord. Amen.

[ix] BCP 3 Trinity: O LORD, we beseech thee mercifully to hear us; and grant that we, to whom thou hast given an hearty desire to pray, may, by thy mighty aid, be defended and comforted in all dangers and adversities; through Jesus Christ our Lord. Amen.

[x] BCP 15 Trinity: KEEP, we beseech thee, O Lord, thy Church with thy perpetual mercy; and, because the frailty of man without thee cannot but fall, keep us ever by thy help from all things hurtful, and lead us to all things profitable to our salvation; through Jesus Christ our Lord. Amen.

[xi] BCP 18 Trinity: LORD, we beseech thee, grant thy people grace to withstand the temptations of the world, the flesh, and the devil; and with pure hearts and minds to follow thee, the only God; through Jesus Christ our Lord. Amen.

[xii] PrBCP 4 Epiphany: Almighty and everlasting God, you govern all things both in heaven and on earth: Mercifully hear the supplications of your people, and in our time grant us your peace; through Jesus Christ our Lord, who lives and reigns with you and the Holy Spirit, one God, for ever and ever. Amen.

[xiii] PrBCP 3 Lent: Almighty God, you know that we have no power in ourselves to help ourselves: Keep us both outwardly in our bodies and inwardly in our souls, that we may be defended from all adversities which may happen to the body, and from all evil thoughts which may assault and hurt the soul; through Jesus Christ our Lord, who lives and reigns with you and the Holy Spirit, one God, for ever and ever. Amen.

[xiv] PrBCP Proper 2: Almighty and merciful God, in your goodness keep us, we pray, from all things that may hurt us, that we, being ready both in mind and body, may accomplish with free hearts those things which belong to your purpose; through Jesus Christ our Lord, who lives and reigns with you and the Holy Spirit, one God, now and for ever. Amen.

[xv] PrBCP Proper 3: Grant, O Lord, that the course of this world may be peaceably governed by your providence; and that your Church may joyfully serve you in confidence and serenity; through Jesus Christ our Lord, who lives and reigns with you and the Holy Spirit, one God, for ever and ever. Amen.

[xvi] PrBCP Proper 4: O God, your never-failing providence sets in order all things both in heaven and earth: Put away from us, we entreat you, all hurtful things, and give us those things which are profitable for us; through Jesus Christ our Lord, who lives and reigns with you and the Holy Spirit, one God, for ever and ever. Amen.

[xvii] PrBCP Proper 13: Let your continual mercy, O Lord, cleanse and defend your Church; and, because it cannot continue in safety without your help, protect and govern it always by your goodness; through Jesus Christ our Lord, who lives and reigns with you and the Holy Spirit, one God, for ever and ever. Amen.

The Collects for some of the Saints' Days have been replaced in order to point up the particular character of the saint more sharply. This factor accounts for the new Collects for St. Mark,[xix] St. Barnabas,[xx] and St. James.[xxi]

The third group of omitted Collects contain those which seem to express at best questionable theology. In this group belong the Collect for Holy Innocents,[xxii] with its searing phrase, "madest infants to glorify thee by their deaths," and its prayer to make us innocent. The prayer which replaces it[xxiii] is a prayer for the "innocent victims of evil tyrants." It seems more appropriate for our age.

[xviii] PrBCP Proper 24: Almighty and everlasting God, in Christ you have revealed your glory among the nations: Preserve the works of your mercy, that your Church throughout the world may persevere with steadfast faith in the confession of your Name; through Jesus Christ our Lord, who lives and reigns with you and the Holy Spirit, one God, for ever and ever. Amen.

[xix] The 1928 BCP collect (O ALMIGHTY God, who hast instructed thy holy Church with the heavenly doctrine of thy Evangelist Saint Mark; Give us grace that, being not like children carried away with every blast of vain doctrine, we may be established in the truth of thy holy Gospel; through Jesus Christ our Lord. Amen.) was replaced with this collect (Almighty God, by the hand of Mark the evangelist you have given to your Church the Gospel of Jesus Christ the Son of God: We thank you for this witness, and pray that we may be firmly grounded in its truth; through Jesus Christ our Lord, who lives and reigns with you and the Holy Spirit, one God, for ever and ever. Amen.)

[xx] The 1928 BCP collect (O LORD God Almighty, who didst endue thy holy Apostle Barnabas with singular gifts of the Holy Ghost; Leave us not, we beseech thee, destitute of thy manifold gifts, nor yet of grace to use them alway to thy honour and glory; through Jesus Christ our Lord. Amen.) was replaced with this collect (Grant, O God, that we may follow the example of your faithful servant Barnabas, who, seeking not his own renown but the well-being of your Church, gave generously of his life and substance for the relief of the poor and the spread of the Gospel; through Jesus Christ our Lord, who lives and reigns with you and the Holy Spirit, one God, for ever and ever. Amen.)

[xxi] The 1928 BCP collect (GRANT, O merciful God, that, as thine holy Apostle Saint James, leaving his father and all that he had, without delay was obedient unto the calling of thy Son Jesus Christ, and followed him; so we, forsaking all worldly and carnal affections, may be evermore ready to follow thy holy commandments; through the same Jesus Christ our Lord. Amen.) was replaced with this collect (O gracious God, we remember before you today your servant and apostle James, first among the Twelve to suffer martyrdom for the Name of Jesus Christ; and we pray that you will pour out upon the leaders of your Church that spirit of self-denying service by which alone they may have true authority among your people; through Jesus Christ our Lord, who lives and reigns with you and the Holy Spirit, one God, now and for ever. Amen.)

[xxii] BCP Holy Innocents: O ALMIGHTY God, who out of the mouths of babes and sucklings hast ordained strength, and madest infants to glorify thee by their deaths; Mortify and kill all vices in us, and so strengthen us by thy grace, that by the innocency of our lives, and constancy of our faith even unto death, we may glorify thy holy Name; through Jesus Christ our Lord. Amen.

[xxiii] PrBCP Holy Innocents: We remember today, O God, the slaughter of the holy innocents of Bethlehem by King Herod. Receive, we pray, into the arms of your mercy all innocent victims; and by your great might frustrate the designs of evil tyrants and establish your rule of justice, love, and peace; through Jesus Christ our Lord, who lives and reigns with you, in the unity of the Holy Spirit, one God, for ever and ever. Amen.

The old Collect for the Circumcision,[xxiv] with its implicitly dualistic "being mortified from all worldly and carnal lusts," has been replaced by a Collect more appropriate to the new title of the day, The Holy Name.[xxv] The phrase in the BCP Collect for the First Sunday in Lent,[xxvi] "flesh being subdued to the Spirit," although not necessarily dualistic, lends itself to misunderstanding. Similarly, the Collect for Easter Eve,[xxvii] with its "continual mortifying our corrupt affections," has become a prayer for participating in the resurrection.

In view of the opinion sometimes expressed that the Collects of AS weakened the Prayer Book's strong Augustinian understanding of human sinfulness, it should be remarked that human sinfulness is vividly acknowledged in PrBCP Collects for 3 Advent,[xxviii] 5 Epiphany,[xxix] 6 Epiphany,[xxx] Ash Wednesday,[xxxi]

[xxiv] BCP Circumcision: ALMIGHTY God, who madest thy blessed Son to be circumcised, and obedient to the law for man; Grant us the true circumcision of the Spirit; that, our hearts, and all our members, being mortified from all worldly and carnal lusts, we may in all things obey thy blessed will; through the same thy Son Jesus Christ our Lord. Amen.

[xxv] PrBCP Holy Name: Eternal Father, you gave to your incarnate Son the holy name of Jesus to be the sign of our salvation: Plant in every heart, we pray, the love of him who is the Savior of the world, our Lord Jesus Christ; who lives and reigns with you and the Holy Spirit, one God, in glory everlasting. Amen.

[xxvi] The 1928 BCP collect (O LORD, who for our sake didst fast forty days and forty nights; Give us grace to use such abstinence, that, our flesh being subdued to the Spirit we may ever obey thy godly motions in righteousness, and true holiness, to thy honour and glory, who livest and reignest with the Father and the Holy Ghost, one God, world without end. Amen.) was replaced with this collect (Almighty God, whose blessed Son was led by the Spirit to be tempted by Satan; Come quickly to help us who are assaulted by many temptations; and, as you know the weaknesses of each of us, let each one find you mighty to save; through Jesus Christ your Son our Lord, who lives and reigns with you and the Holy Spirit, one God, now and for ever. Amen.)

[xxvii] The 1928 BCP collect (GRANT, O Lord, that as we are baptized into the death of thy blessed Son, our Saviour Jesus Christ, so by continual mortifying our corrupt affections we may be buried with him; and that through the grave, and gate of death, we may pass to our joyful resurrection; for his merits, who died, and was buried, and rose again for us, the same thy Son Jesus Christ our Lord. Amen.) was replaced with this collect (O God, Creator of heaven and earth: Grant that, as the crucified body of your dear Son was laid in the tomb and rested on this holy Sabbath, so we may await with him the coming of the third day, and rise with him to newness of life; who now lives and reigns with you and the Holy Spirit, one God, for ever and ever. Amen.)

[xxviii] PrBCP 3 Advent: Stir up your power, O Lord, and with great might come among us; and, because we are sorely hindered by our sins, let your bountiful grace and mercy speedily help and deliver us; through Jesus Christ our Lord, to whom, with you and the Holy Spirit, be honor and glory, now and for ever. Amen.

[xxix] PrBCP 5 Epiphany: Set us free, O God, from the bondage of our sins, and give us the liberty of that abundant life which you have made known to us in your Son our Savior Jesus Christ; who lives and reigns with you, in the unity of the Holy Spirit, one God, now and for ever. Amen.

[xxx] PrBCP 6 Epiphany: O God, the strength of all who put their trust in you: Mercifully accept our prayers; and because in our weakness we can do nothing good without you, give us the help of your grace, that in keeping your commandments we may please you both in will and deed; through Jesus Christ our Lord, who lives and reigns with you and the Holy Spirit, one God, for ever and ever. Amen.

[xxxi] PrBCP Ash Wednesday: Almighty and everlasting God, you hate nothing you have made and forgive the sins of all who are penitent: Create and make in us new and contrite hearts, that we,

1 Lent,[xxxii] 2 Lent,[xxxiii] 3 Lent,[xxxiv] 5 Lent,[xxxv] Good Friday,[xxxvi] Easter (1),[xxxvii] Friday in Easter Week,[xxxviii] Saturday in Easter Week,[xxxix] Propers 1,[xl] 11,[xli] 13,[xlii] 15,[xliii] 19,[xliv] 22,[xlv] 29.[xlvi]

---

worthily lamenting our sins and acknowledging our wretchedness, may obtain of you, the God of all mercy, perfect remission and forgiveness; through Jesus Christ our Lord, who lives and reigns with you and the Holy Spirit, one God, for ever and ever. Amen.

[xxxii] PrBCP 1 Lent: Almighty God, whose blessed Son was led by the Spirit to be tempted by Satan; Come quickly to help us who are assaulted by many temptations; and, as you know the weaknesses of each of us, let each one find you mighty to save; through Jesus Christ your Son our Lord, who lives and reigns with you and the Holy Spirit, one God, now and for ever. Amen.

[xxxiii] PrBCP 2 Lent: O God, whose glory it is always to have mercy: Be gracious to all who have gone astray from your ways, and bring them again with penitent hearts and steadfast faith to embrace and hold fast the unchangeable truth of your Word, Jesus Christ your Son; who with you and the Holy Spirit lives and reigns, one God, for ever and ever. Amen.

[xxxiv] PrBCP 3 Lent: Almighty God, you know that we have no power in ourselves to help ourselves: Keep us both outwardly in our bodies and inwardly in our souls, that we may be defended from all adversities which may happen to the body, and from all evil thoughts which may assault and hurt the soul; through Jesus Christ our Lord, who lives and reigns with you and the Holy Spirit, one God, for ever and ever. Amen.

[xxxv] PrBCP 5 Lent: Almighty God, you alone can bring into order the unruly wills and affections of sinners: Grant your people grace to love what you command and desire what you promise; that, among the swift and varied changes of the world, our hearts may surely there be fixed where true joys are to be found; through Jesus Christ our Lord, who lives and reigns with you and the Holy Spirit, one God, now and for ever. Amen.

[xxxvi] PrBCP Good Friday: Almighty God, we pray you graciously to behold this your family, for whom our Lord Jesus Christ was willing to be betrayed, and given into the hands of sinners, and to suffer death upon the cross; who now lives and reigns with you and the Holy Spirit, one God, for ever and ever. Amen.

[xxxvii] PrBCP Easter (1): O God, who for our redemption gave your only-begotten Son to the death of the cross, and by his glorious resurrection delivered us from the power of our enemy: Grant us so to die daily to sin, that we may evermore live with him in the joy of his resurrection; through Jesus Christ your Son our Lord, who lives and reigns with you and the Holy Spirit, one God, now and for ever. Amen.

[xxxviii] PrBCP Friday in Easter Week: Almighty Father, who gave your only Son to die for our sins and to rise for our justification: Give us grace so to put away the leaven of malice and wickedness, that we may always serve you in pureness of living and truth; through Jesus Christ your Son our Lord, who lives and reigns with you and the Holy Spirit, one God, now and for ever. Amen.

[xxxix] PrBCP Saturday in Easter Week: We thank you, heavenly Father, that you have delivered us from the dominion of sin and death and brought us into the kingdom of your Son; and we pray that, as by his death he has recalled us to life, so by his love he may raise us to eternal joys; who lives and reigns with you, in the unity of the Holy Spirit, one God, now and forever. Amen.

[xl] PrBCP Proper 1: Remember, O Lord, what you have wrought in us and not what we deserve; and, as you have called us to your service, make us worthy of our calling; through Jesus Christ our Lord, who lives and reigns with you and the Holy Spirit, one God, now and for ever. Amen.

[xli] PrBCP Proper 11: Almighty God, the fountain of all wisdom, you know our necessities before we ask and our ignorance in asking: Have compassion on our weakness, and mercifully give us those things which for our unworthiness we dare not, and for our blindness we cannot ask; through the worthiness of your Son Jesus Christ our Lord, who lives and reigns with you and the Holy Spirit, one God, now and for ever. Amen.

A few BCP Collects omitted from AS have been restored to PrBCP: 2 Epiphany is PrBCP's Epiphany;[xlvii] Sunday after Ascension Day is PrBCP's Seventh Sunday of Easter,[xlviii] 2 Trinity is PrBCP's Proper 2,[xlix] 8 Trinity is PrBCP's Proper 4,[l] 13 Trinity is PrBCP's Proper 26.[li] BCP Collects for a few Saints' Days and other occasions have also been restored. There is no particular theological trend in this restoration; in the extensive reworking of the propers, these Collects were felt to be more appropriate.

[xlii] PrBCP Proper 13: Let your continual mercy, O Lord, cleanse and defend your Church; and, because it cannot continue in safety without your help, protect and govern it always by your goodness; through Jesus Christ our Lord, who lives and reigns with you and the Holy Spirit, one God, for ever and ever. Amen.

[xliii] PrBCP Proper 15: Almighty God, you have given your only Son to be for us a sacrifice for sin, and also an example of godly life: Give us grace to receive thankfully the fruits of this redeeming work, and to follow daily in the blessed steps of his most holy life; through Jesus Christ your Son our Lord, who lives and reigns with you and the Holy Spirit, one God, now and for ever. Amen.

[xliv] PrBCP Proper 19: O God, because without you we are not able to please you, mercifully grant that your Holy Spirit may in all things direct and rule our hearts; through Jesus Christ our Lord, who lives and reigns with you and the Holy Spirit, one God, now and for ever. Amen.

[xlv] PrBCP Proper 22: Almighty and everlasting God, you are always more ready to hear than we to pray, and to give more than we either desire or deserve: Pour upon us the abundance of your mercy, forgiving us those things of which our conscience is afraid, and giving us those good things for which we are not worthy to ask, except through the merits and mediation of Jesus Christ our Savior; who lives and reigns with you and the Holy Spirit, one God, for ever and ever. Amen.

[xlvi] PrBCP Proper 29: Almighty and everlasting God, whose will it is to restore all things in your well-beloved Son, the King of kings and Lord of lords: Mercifully grant that the peoples of the earth, divided and enslaved by sin, may be freed and brought together under his most gracious rule; who lives and reigns with you and the Holy Spirit, one God, now and for ever. Amen.

[xlvii] PrBCP 4 Epiphany: Almighty and everlasting God, you govern all things both in heaven and on earth: Mercifully hear the supplications of your people, and in our time grant us your peace; through Jesus Christ our Lord, who lives and reigns with you and the Holy Spirit, one God, for ever and ever. Amen.

[xlviii] PrBCP 7 Easter: O God, the King of glory, you have exalted your only Son Jesus Christ with great triumph to your kingdom in heaven: Do not leave us comfortless, but send us your Holy Spirit to strengthen us, and exalt us to that place where our Savior Christ has gone before; who lives and reigns with you and the Holy Spirit, one God, in glory everlasting. Amen.

[xlix] PrBCP Proper 2: Almighty and merciful God, in your goodness keep us, we pray, from all things that may hurt us, that we, being ready both in mind and body, may accomplish with free hearts those things which belong to your purpose; through Jesus Christ our Lord, who lives and reigns with you and the Holy Spirit, one God, now and for ever. Amen.

[l] PrBCP Proper 4: O God, your never-failing providence sets in order all things both in heaven and earth: Put away from us, we entreat you, all hurtful things, and give us those things which are profitable for us; through Jesus Christ our Lord, who lives and reigns with you and the Holy Spirit, one God, for ever and ever. Amen.

[li] PrBCP Proper 26: Almighty and merciful God, it is only by your gift that your faithful people offer you true and laudable service: Grant that we may run without stumbling to obtain your heavenly promises; through Jesus Christ our Lord, who lives and reigns with you and the Holy Spirit, one God, now and for ever. Amen.

Of the twenty-six new Collects in PrBCP, by far the largest group occurs in the Common of Saints. Most of these have appeared already in *Lesser Feasts and Fasts*. Perhaps the most striking new prayers are the Collect for Independence Day[lii] and the first Collect for Pentecost.[liii] The opening of the Independence Day Collect, "in whose Name the founders of this country won liberty for themselves and us, and lit the torch of freedom for nations then unborn," celebrates the world-wide significance of the American Revolution. The first Collect for Pentecost, "Shed abroad this gift throughout the world by the preaching of the Gospel," introduces for the first time in an Anglican Prayer Book a missionary theme into the available Pentecost Collects!

Thus the Collects of PrBCP do represent some significant changes in emphasis from those of BCP; but no significant theological notes have been suppressed, much repetition has been avoided, and a number of welcome new themes have been represented.

Proper Liturgies for Special Days

One of the most striking features of the PrBCP is the section entitled Proper Liturgies for Special Days: Ash Wednesday, Palm Sunday, Maundy Thursday, Good Friday, Holy Saturday, and the Great Vigil of Easter. Much of this material appeared in STU, but there the various services were distributed throughout the rest of the propers for the Christian Year, at their Calendar places. Here this special material is gathered in one place. It has been considerably amplified and thoroughly revised.

The Paschal Mystery

The resulting section makes obvious one of the most important emphases of the new proposal, *the paschal mystery*. The phrase "paschal mystery" refers to the death and resurrection of Christ, but the reference contains some special and powerful connotations. The word *paschal*, for example, reminds us that the New Testament word for Passover (Hebrew *pesach*) is *pascha*. The death of Jesus occurred at the time of the Jewish Passover, as is well known; and the Cross of Christ was already

---

[lii] PrBCP Independence Day: Lord God Almighty, in whose Name the founders of this country won liberty for themselves and us, and lit the torch of freedom for nations then unborn: Grant that we and all the people of this land may have grace to maintain our liberties in righteousness and peace through Jesus Christ our Lord, who lives and reigns with you and the Holy Spirit, one God, now and for ever. Amen.

[liii] PrBCP Pentecost: Almighty God, on this day you opened the way of eternal life to every race and nation by the promised gift of your Holy Spirit: Shed abroad this gift throughout the world by the preaching of the Gospel, that it may reach to the ends of the earth; through Jesus Christ our Lord, who lives and reigns with you, in the unity of the Holy Spirit, one God, for ever and ever. Amen.

interpreted by St. Paul as the fulfillment of the Passover sacrifice. Thus the death of Christ has come to be understood in the Church, from New Testament times on, as the culmination or fulfillment of God's mighty acts to save his creation. God acted to rescue his people from Pharaoh's army at the Red Sea. God acted to rescue his people from sin and death through the death and resurrection of Christ. Communion with God, which the Jewish people expected through participation in the Passover sacrifices, was fully realized through sacramental participation in the death and resurrection of the Incarnate Son.

The word *mystery* conveys this sense of the community's participation in the life of its risen Lord, who is known to be present in the gatherings of the Church for worship. The chief means of this participation have, from the beginning, been the hearing of the Word of God and the representation of Christ's death and resurrection in the sacraments of Baptism and Eucharist (*cf.* Luke 24:31-35, Rom. 6:3-11, John 20:19-29, 21:9-14, etc.).

Nowhere in PrBCP does the centrality of the paschal mystery, the death and resurrection of Christ made present and available for the participation of the worshiping community, become more apparent than in these Proper Liturgies for the chief days of Lent, especially Holy Week.

To illustrate how the paschal mystery is focused in these proper liturgies, one need only recall the solemn reading of the passion narrative on Palm Sunday (p. 271), the commemoration of the institution of the Supper on Maundy Thursday (pp. 274-5), the rehearsal of the history of God's saving acts in the Good Friday devotions. Most especially the paschal mystery is focused in the Old Testament readings provided for the Great Vigil of Easter, which begin at the Creation and end with the great visions of the gathering and the renewal of the people of God in Ezekiel and Zephaniah. Easter baptisms follow, and issue in the first eucharistic celebration of Easter Day.

Use of Pre-Reformation Material

All of these services have analogues in medieval or more ancient traditions. Thus, these Proper Liturgies in PrBCP represent one of the clearest attempts to enrich the liturgical practices of our Church by utilizing material long discarded. We recognize that these new provisions may be variously greeted. Some will welcome them, as legitimating their present custom. Others may regard them with suspicion or disapproval. It is important to observe, therefore, that the use of none of these Proper Liturgies is required. To be more precise, nothing is required in this material which is theologically different from BCP provisions. Thus, in the Ash Wednesday Liturgy, we find the proper Collect and lessons, and a reworked Penitential Office including the 51st Psalm and rather more specific prayers of penitence than BCP's Penitential Office. The imposition of ashes is optional, and it is worth noting that whereas the traditional prayer over the ashes was "to bless and make holy these ashes," the DPB form is "that these ashes may be to us a sign of our mortality and penitence," a form more congruent to the considerable reticence of Anglican Prayer Books regarding the blessing of material objects.

Similarly, the Palm Sunday liturgy gives thanks to God for Christ's redeeming acts of love, and prays that "these branches may be for us signs of his victory."

The restoration of the optional Maundy Thursday foot-washing, the Good Friday Solemn Collects and devotions, and the Exsultet and the lessons of the Great Vigil of Easter, are valuable enrichments which are being widely and gladly used. All the Proper Liturgies are sensitive Anglican adaptations of important traditional liturgical substance.

Holy Baptism and Confirmation

Review of Initiatory Rites Proposed Since 1968

The services of Holy Baptism and Confirmation in PrBCP are, with only minor changes, the version of these services published and authorized for trial use in Spring 1975, under the title *Holy Baptism and a Form for Confirmation, for Reception, and for the Reaffirmation of Baptismal Vows*.

These services in PrBCP represent the end product of a development which began in 1968, with the publication of Prayer Book Studies 18, *Holy Baptism with the Laying on of Hands*. It will be useful to survey the forces which shaped that proposal, and to trace the development which has led to the present form of the rite.

For a number of years prior to 1968, considerable discontent had been voiced throughout the American Episcopal Church, and indeed throughout the Anglican Communion, about rites of initiation. Two separate strands of criticism can be discovered, although they interacted. One criticism was pastoral. Something in the practice of Baptism and Confirmation was not working. The number of baptisms began to drop and the number of confirmands who became inactive after only a few years was commonly put at 50%. (*Confirmation Crisis*, Seabury Press, 1968, pp. 9-10.) The other criticism was theological. Liturgical studies revealed more clearly than had been realized before that Baptism and Confirmation were, at the beginning of the Christian movement, part of one unified rite. When they were separated, the interpretation of each, and particularly of Confirmation, became difficult and muddy. It should be noted here that PBS 1 (1958) had already moved to restore the unity of the initiation rite. The appearance of *Confirmation Crisis* in 1968, and of its English counterpart (*Crisis for Confirmation*, by Michael Perry, SCM Press, 1967) the previous year, mark an attempt to bring this criticism of contemporary practice of Confirmation to greater public consciousness.

It was to these forces, although not, of course, to these particular publications, that the provisions of PBS 18 sought to respond. This service of Baptism with the Laying on of Hands represented a sharp break with traditional Anglican practice. Confirmation was abandoned as a separate rite. A sealing with the Holy Spirit by the laying on of hands, with or without Chrism, followed directly upon the administration of water baptism. The whole was set within a celebration of the Eucharist, although provision was made to perform the initiatory rite separately if desired. The bishop was envisioned as the chief minister at this service, but a priest could act in his absence.

In this service, the unity of Baptism, sealing with the Spirit, and first Communion, was restored, as together forming the initiatory rite. The identity of the bishop as the normative celebrant was emphasized, although it was anticipated that, should the Church adopt the new rite, priests would be authorized to perform it, as in Eastern Orthodox practice. In fact, it might be said that PBS 18 proposed to institute the Eastern, rather than the Western, rites of initiation. And despite a number of changes in detail, these major new features are retained in PrBCP, as far as Holy Baptism is concerned.

But the decision to drop Confirmation as a separate rite proved impossible to sustain. To the question, "When do adults baptized as infants commit themselves to Christ?" the answer given by PBS 18 was, "By the answering of the questions asked of the whole congregation at every service of Baptism." Each baptismal liturgy was thought to provide for the renewal of baptismal vows by each member of the congregation, in addition to celebrating the initiation of new members.

The discussion which ensued after the publication of PBS 18 made it clear that a special rite in which an adult could make an individual act of mature commitment by reaffirming baptismal vows served an essential function in the Church. The psychological and pedagogical value of the BCP service of Confirmation could not be overlooked. In PBS 26, authorized by the General Convention of 1973 at Louisville, Holy Baptism continued to combine water baptism with a prayer for the sevenfold gifts of the Spirit and a sealing formula; but a new service of Confirmation was added, by which an adult could reaffirm baptismal vows, and receive the laying on of hands by a bishop. This service was in no sense a completion of baptism; moreover, it was no longer conceived as a once-and-for-all act. It could be repeated on any occasion in a person's life when a solemn prayer for the gifts of the Spirit would be appropriate.

The major difference between the PBS 26 version of the Confirmation rite and that of PrBCP lies in DPB's more precise specification of the term *confirmation*, and in providing clearly differentiated formulae for the three separate circumstances under which the service would be appropriate. The term *confirmation* is now reserved for the first time a person who grows to maturity under the discipline of the Episcopal Church makes a commitment to Christ by a formal reaffirmation of baptismal vows in the presence of the bishop. It is recognized that those who grow up in other Churches may formally and individually reaffirm their baptismal vows in some other way.

Although this first reaffirmation of the Baptismal Covenant cannot by definition be repeated, so that Confirmation, or its equivalent in other Churches, is once and for all, there are other crucial times when it seems appropriate that a person should be able to receive the strengthening gifts of the Spirit through a special rite. One such occasion is when a person joins the Episcopal Church, having been baptized in another denomination and having already made a mature reaffirmation of baptismal vows according to its requirements. It is thought to be psychologically, liturgically, and spiritually sound to offer such a person an opportunity to express this new commitment to the Episcopal Church before the bishop, for in Episcopal polity the bishop represents the whole Church. These new members should be able also to receive the gifts of the Spirit to establish them in their new relationship to the Church. No more than Confirmation is this act, called in PrBCP Reception, to be considered as a completion of Baptism, but as a liturgical expression of a new commitment undertaken with solemn prayer.

Similarly, if a person enters a new phase of his or her life with Christ, or has fallen away from active participation in the life of the Church for a time and becomes active again, it is appropriate for such a person to reaffirm baptismal vows and to receive gifts of the Spirit for this renewed relationship to the Church. This action, called in PrBCP Reaffirmation, is not a completion of baptism either, but a liturgical expression of a renewed commitment undertaken with solemn prayer.

Special Issues

Agreed Positions

In the course of discussion leading to the PrBCP rite, the SLC and the Theological and Prayer Book Committees of the House of Bishops met together and reached agreement on the following positions. They are fundamental to understanding the PrBCP services. They were published in the introduction to PBS 26.

Concerning Baptism.

1. There is one, and only one, unrepeatable act of Christian initiation, which makes a person a member of the Body of Christ.
2. The essential element of Christian initiation is baptism by water and Spirit, in the Name of the Holy Trinity, in response to repentance and faith.
3. Christian initiation is normatively administered in a liturgical rite that also includes the laying on of hands, consignation (with or without Chrism), prayer for the gift of the Holy Spirit, reception by the Christian community, joining the eucharistic fellowship, and commissioning for the Christian mission. When the bishop is present, it is expected that he will preside at the rite.

Concerning a Post-Baptismal Affirmation of Vows

1. An act and occasion for (more or less) mature personal acceptance of promises and affirmations made on one's behalf in infancy is pastorally and spiritually desirable.

2. Such an act and occasion must be voluntary, but it should be strongly encouraged as a normal component of Christian nurture, and not merely made available.
3. It is both appropriate and pastorally desirable that the affirmation should be received by a bishop as representing the diocese and the world-wide Church, and that the bishop should recall the applicants to their Christian mission, and, by a laying on of hands transmit his blessing, with a prayer for the strengthening graces.
4. The rite embodying such affirmations should in no sense be understood as being a "completion of Holy Baptism," nor as being a condition precedent to the Holy Communion, nor as conveying a special status of Church membership.
5. The occasion of the affirming of baptismal vows and obligations that were made by godparents on one's behalf in infancy is a significant and unrepeatable event. It is one's "Confirmation Day."
6. The rite itself, however, is suitable, and should be available for other occasions in the lives of Christian people. For example, (1) when a person who has been baptized in some other fellowship of Christians wishes to become a member of the Episcopal Church, it is desirable and appropriate that this person be presented to the bishop as representing the world-wide episcopate, and that the new relationship be blessed with the laying on of hands and a recommissioning to Christian service, and (2) when a person whose practice of the Christian life has become perfunctory, or has completely lapsed, awakes again to the call of Christ and desires to signalize his response publicly, and to receive a strengthening gift of the Spirit for renewal.

A careful perusal of PrBCP services of Holy Baptism and Confirmation will show that they embody these principles.

The Reunification of the Rite

The reunification of two parts of the initiatory rite, water baptism in the Name of the Trinity on one hand, and laying on of hands and consignation (with or without Chrism) with a prayer for the gift of the Spirit on the other, is accomplished by including in the rite of Holy Baptism two elements from the traditional service of Confirmation: the prayer for the seven-fold gifts of the Spirit and the laying on of hands by the celebrant, signifying sealing (or marking) with the Holy Spirit.

The prayer for the seven-fold gifts of the Spirit (PrBCP, p. 308) is a revised form of the prayer in BCP which precedes the laying on of hands by the bishop at Confirmation (BCP, p. 297). It embodies the same substance as the analogous prayer in the old Roman Catholic service of Confirmation, itself at least as ancient as the Gelasian Sacramentary, which probably represents sixth century usage. The formula for sealing in PrBCP is an expansion of the Eastern Orthodox, "The seal of the gift of the Holy Spirit."

By these additions to the baptismal rite, it is intended that the rite should express everything that has been considered to be part of the initiation ceremony since the *Apostolic Tradition of Hippolytus* (ca. 200). In particular, those parts are restored to Baptism which, in the development of the western Catholic practice of initiation, were reserved to the bishop as the completion of Baptism. The rite of Baptism in PrBCP is intended to be complete and *to express that completeness as adequately as possible*.

It is not a tenable position to argue that the Holy Spirit is made present and available solely by this prayer and action added from the old Confirmation service. It is, in fact, a faulty theology of Confirmation to hold that members of the Church "receive the Holy Spirit" only at Confirmation, as if they had not in a real sense received the Spirit already at Baptism. Neither Baptism nor any sacramental action can be understood apart from the free act of the sovereign Lord, working through his Spirit according to his promises. All life in the Church is life in the Spirit. In the words of the Agreed Positions, Christian initiation expresses the accession of the Spirit from the beginning. Both BCP and PrBCP imply that in water baptism the Spirit is already present and active. For example, in BCP appears the prayer, "Give thy Holy Spirit to this child" (BCP, p. 276), and in PrBCP the prayer, "Fill them with your holy and life-giving Spirit" (PrBCP, p. 305), and in the Thanksgiving over the Water, "Now sanctify this water, we pray you, by the power of your Holy Spirit" (PrBCP, p. 307).

Moreover, in the *Apostolic Tradition of Hippolytus*, the prayer and the formula reserved to the bishop after the water baptism assume that the Spirit has been already at work in the prior action. The bishop's prayer begins, "O Lord God, who hast made them worthy to obtain remission of sins through the laver of regeneration of (the) Holy Spirit" (*Ap. Trad. Hippol.* 11.22, Easton's tr.).

We conclude that by restoring these elements of the traditional Confirmation service to Holy Baptism, we have reunified the initiatory rite, and allowed it to signify fully what the rite is universally believed to accomplish. But we have not added any new essential element to the rite. "The *essential* element of Christian initiation," as the Agreed Positions affirm in accordance with long-standing Anglican teaching, "is baptism by water and the Spirit, in the Name of the Holy Trinity." The element of an explicit sealing by the Spirit, in a phrase of Reginald Fuller's, belongs to the *bene esse*, or *plene esse*, of the baptismal liturgy. PrBCP is a rich text. It contains the amplest and most comprehensive liturgical expression of Christian initiation which we can propose. *But we do not thereby imply that the initiatory rites of other Christian fellowships lack anything essential if this element of sealing is missing.*

After water baptism and the sealing, the third element of Christian initiation is first communion. PrBCP expresses the theological connection between

Baptism and Eucharist by providing a structure which leads naturally from one to the other. The point is reinforced by the introductory rubric, "The bishop, when present, is the celebrant; and is expected to preach the Word and preside at Baptism and the Eucharist" (PrBCP, p. 298).

In PrBCP, there is no rubrical indication to suggest that any baptized person is not eligible to receive Holy Communion. There is, however, a judgment of the House of Bishops that infants should not receive Holy Communion until they have reached an "appropriate age." It falls upon the Ordinary of each diocese to set the procedure by which the determination of such age will be made.

The BCP rubric, "there shall be none admitted to the Holy Communion, until such time as he be confirmed or ready and desirous of being confirmed," has been omitted, in accordance with one of the Agreed Positions concerning a post-baptismal Affirmation of Vows. Baptism is the sole requirement for admission to Holy Communion.

The Officiant at Baptism

In Eastern Orthodox Churches, bishops authorized presbyters to officiate at the initiatory rite from a very early date. This permission extended to the whole service, including the sealing with the Spirit. In Western Churches, following a custom which originated in the city of Rome, bishops authorized presbyters to perform water baptism but reserved the final ceremony of chrismation and laying on of hands for themselves. The difference between East and West in the performance of baptism rested at the beginning on no theological differences. It was a practical decision.

In restoring the unity of the baptismal liturgy, PrBCP rests explicitly on the ancient theory that bishops may delegate some of their liturgical functions to their presbyters and deacons. The bishop, when present, is the celebrant; he is expected to make manifest his role as the chief liturgical persona. "In the absence of a bishop, a priest is the celebrant and presides at the service" (PrBCP, p. 298). In the manner of Eastern Orthodoxy, the priest performs the whole rite. There are no theological difficulties with this change. Even in the Roman Catholic Church, certain presbyters have also been allowed to confirm, using Chrism. PrBCP practice obviously represents a break with our own traditional practice, but it does not represent a break with the theology of ministry. We believe that the gains in clarity and ecumenical openness amply justify the change.

Use of Chrism

In Eastern Orthodox Churches, where this pattern of Baptism already pertains, the sealing of the Spirit is accompanied by anointing with scented oil blessed by the bishop. The origin and history of this practice is set forth in great detail in Leonel Mitchell's study, *Baptismal Anointing* (SPCK, 1966). The practice is ancient, although whether or not certain New Testament texts imply it is questionable. It was abolished in the Church of England by the Prayer Book of 1552. It has been restored during the past few decades in a number of dioceses of the Episcopal Church and other Churches of the Anglican Communion.

There is obviously considerable difference of opinion within this Church about the use of oil. Some hold that the sacramental character of the sealing with the Spirit, and the role of the bishop in the whole rite of initiation, can be safeguarded only if oil blessed by him is used during the sealing. Others hold that the ceremonial use of oil is now meaningless because oil is no longer widely used in everyday life after bathing, and the Old Testament connection between oil and the Spirit has been largely forgotten (*cf.* Isa. 61:1-4). For these persons oil has become a "dead symbol." They would resist being required to use it, and would point out that the sacramental presence of the bishop at a rite of initiation is better safeguarded by a presbyter on whom he has laid his hands than by oil on which he has laid his hands. The optional use of oil provided in DPB is intended to acknowledge uninvidiously both points of view.

Confirmation in PrBCP

As the Agreed Positions make clear, Confirmation "should in no sense be understood as being a 'completion of Holy Baptism.'" Whatever is necessary to "complete" Holy Baptism has been restored to the rite itself, as noted. Confirmation, however, retains a significance of its own. It is "an act and occasion for (more or less) mature personal acceptance of promises and affirmations made on one's behalf in infancy." Such an act, undertaken voluntarily at an age when decisions are important, represents a solemn commitment of one's life to Christ. That commitment is "expected" of "those baptized at an early age, when they are ready and have been duly prepared" (PrBCP, p. 412). It is expected, also, of those who are baptized as adults, unless such adults have been baptized in a service that includes the laying on of hands of a bishop.

The principle of reaffirming baptismal vows in the presence of a bishop has been extended, as we have seen, to other critical moments in a person's spiritual life. It is appropriate that such commitments should be made before a bishop, since the bishop uniquely represents the whole Church. And it is fitting that those making such a commitment should receive laying on of hands with a prayer for the gift of the Holy Spirit to "direct and uphold them" in new responsibilities and new circumstances.

Postscript about Satan

In PBS 18, there was only one renunciation: "Do you then renounce evil in all its forms?" It was widely felt that this single question, all-encompassing as it was, did not do dramatic or liturgical justice to the gravity and solemnity of the occasion.

PrBCP provides a three-fold renunciation (p. 302) comparable to that in ancient rites and to the BCP renunciation of "the devil and all his works, the vain pomp and glory of the world, and the sinful desires of the flesh." In the first of the new renunciations, the candidate is asked to renounce "Satan and all the spiritual forces of wickedness that rebel against God." This reintroduction of the figure of Satan has in turn provoked adverse criticism, on the ground that Satan is a purely mythological figure, no longer credible to most of those who will be required to answer the question.

Although anyone with pastoral experience might have sympathy for this point of view, there are strong reasons for restoring the mention of Satan. Christian faith has traditionally dealt with a personal and focused spirit of evil as well as with a personal and focused Spirit of God. Apart from that focus, it would be difficult to understand how the death of Jesus could be thought to have any once-and-for-all significance, expressed in important, though admittedly symbolic, language as the "conquest of Satan."

In the Biblical tradition, Satan is himself a creature, finally under God's control, a "fallen angel" (*cf.* Isa. 14:12-21; Ezek. 28:12-19; Rev. 20:1-3). Christianity does not subscribe to the radical or ultimate dualism espoused by the Satanism and demonism which have come to some prominence in recent years. Christianity is to be sharply distinguished from such teaching by its *controlled* dualism. God alone is ultimate, and even Satan is finally to be beaten down under our feet (Great Litany, PrBCP, p. 152). But Satan stands for a reality in the Christian understanding of evil, the reality of an evil beyond human control though not beyond God's control. Other more contemporary language may some day be found to express the same reality. Preachers and teachers will try to do just that. But a personal Satan appears in crucial passages of the New Testament, especially in the temptations of our Lord. Satan has been named in Christian liturgies down through the centuries. It is appropriate to keep some reference to him in the baptismal rite.

The Holy Eucharist

The full title for the eucharistic service in PrBCP is *The Holy Eucharist: The Liturgy for the Proclamation of the Word of God and Celebration of the Holy Communion.* This title recognizes formally the two parts of the service: the service of the Word and the sacramental meal. Readings from the Scripture, on the model of synagogue services, have been prefixed to the communion meal at least from the time of Justin Martyr (ca. 150 A.D.), although there was no such formal service of the Word at the original Supper in the upper room. For the first time in the history of English and American Prayer Books, a title is proposed to reflect this ancient bi-partite structure. The title of PBS 17, *The Liturgy of the Lord's Supper: The Celebration of Holy Eucharist and Ministration of Holy Communion,* is not quite so precise. The title of the service in BCP, *The Order for the Administration of the Lord's Supper or Holy Communion*, puts all the emphasis on the meal. The new title emphasizes as never before the importance of the proclamation of the Word in this central act of Christian worship.

The dropping of the title, Lord's Supper, reflects disuse of the term in our Church. The common names among us have been Holy Communion—a title which represents only half the action—or Mass—a title which probably is related to the dismissal at the end of the service. The term *Eucharist*, or *Thanksgiving*, is both ancient and descriptive of the whole, a great act of Thanksgiving to God through Word and Sacrament in their essential and inextricable unity.

The section of PrBCP entitled Holy Eucharist contains a number of elements. There is a Rite I Eucharist, prefaced by an Exhortation in language which, though contemporary, would not be jarring in a Rite I celebration, and the Decalogue and a Penitential Order in traditional language. Rite II is prefaced by a version of the Decalogue and Penitential Order in contemporary language. The Rite II Decalogue has been taken over and amended from the contemporary language services of the Church of England and the Church of Ireland. The section after Rite II, containing the Prayers of the People, is followed by a form for Communion under Special Circumstances (chiefly for sick and shut-ins). The Order for Celebrating the Holy Eucharist, indicating the sequence of events and providing two prayers of consecration, brings the section to a close.

Features Common to Rite I and Rite II

Opening Acclamations

Three opening acclamations are provided. Two are already familiar from STU and AS: "Blessed be God . . ." for ferial occasions and "Alleluia, Christ is risen . . ." for the Easter season. To these two has been added an acclamation for Lent and other penitential occasions. These forms constitute a way to mark seasonal emphases in the service from its beginning. They are optional in Rite I.

The Word of God

Three lessons are provided: a reading from the Old Testament, an Epistle, and a Gospel. The Old Testament lesson and psalmody are an addition to BCP provisions, introducing a new dimension to the eucharistic celebration. The provision of three lessons is a departure from traditional Orthodox, Roman Catholic, and Protestant practice, but it corresponds both to ancient usage and to the format of the contemporary ecumenical lectionary adopted by the Roman Catholic Church and, in principle, by most major Protestant denominations.

The lectionary itself has been thoroughly reviewed and reworked since 1973. The eucharistic lectionary in AS was felt by some to attenuate the full message of the Old Testament by concentrating too heavily on messianic and eschatological passages at the expense of narrative and prophetic sections. The lectionary of PrBCP has attempted to correct this balance.

Although this revision of Old Testament lessons has affected the ecumenical agreement of the eucharistic lectionary, an effort has been made to preserve agreement of Epistles and more especiallyof the Gospels. In the eucharistic lectionary of the 1928 BCP some 90% of the lessons were also used by Roman Catholics and Lutherans, though not always on the same Sundays. The extent of agreement is not quite so high in PrBCP, but it is still impressive. Since this lectionary is provided not only for the Eucharist, but for any main Sunday service, and since a number of other Churches, in addition to Roman Catholics, Lutherans, and Anglicans, are beginning to use it, the possibility of hearing the same set of lessons on a given Sunday wherever one goes to Church in Western Christendom is very great.

A sermon is indicated by heading as part of the Proclamation of the Word (PrBCP, pp. 326, 358). This indication is intended to be a stronger encouragement for preaching on Scripture lessons than the BCP rubric, "Then followeth the Sermon" (BCP, p. 71).

In general, the provisions of PrBCP for the proclamation of the Word of God are stronger and more ample than those in BCP.

The Nicene Creed

The text of the Nicene Creed established by the International Consultation on English Texts is provided in both Rite I (as the first option) and in Rite II. We have already discussed this text (see pages 170–171). The BCP text appears in Rite I as an option. The only emendation in the traditional text is the restoration of the word "holy" as one of the marks of the Church (PrBCP, p. 328). "Holy" was dropped from English and American books after 1549, apparently the result of a printer's error. There was no theological reason for omitting it, and since it does appear as a mark of the Church in the Apostles' Creed (PrBCP, p. 54 et al) its reappearance in the Nicene Creed does not alter but strengthens the teaching of the Book regarding the Church.

The use of the Creed is required only on Sundays and other major feasts, following the custom of the pre-Reformation Western Church.

The Order Following the Creed

In both Rite I and Rite II, in accordance with recommendations of the Lambeth Conferences of 1958 and 1968, the order of the parts of the service following the Creed has been rearranged. In both Rites, the Creed is followed by Prayers of the People, Confession, Absolution, and the Peace. Offertory and consecration together comprise the next major section, the Great Thanksgiving.

This order is somewhat different from that followed in previous English and American Prayer Books. English books after 1552 made the "Prayer for the

Whole State of Christ's Church" part of the offering. It was followed by the Confession and Absolution, which thus also became part of the offering of the people. ("Just as I am, without one plea . . . I come.") The result of this structure, however, was to separate the offering of bread and wine from the Prayer of Consecration by so much other liturgical material that any easily grasped sense of the connection between them was to all intents and purposes lost. It could be understood if explained, but it was difficult to feel. This situation still prevailed in 1928.

PrBCP has moved the offering to its pre-Reformation position just before the Prayer of Consecration, or Great Thanksgiving (PrBCP, pp. 333, 361). The connection between offering and consecration (*prosphora* and *anaphora* in Greek) thus becomes clearer. The Prayers of the People, the Confession, Absolution, and Peace have become an independent block of material, with its own weight. In fact, this position of the intercessions at the end of the service of the Word may have been oldest of all (Justin Martyr, *I Apol.* lxv).

The use of the Confession in PrBCP is the same in Rite I and Rite II. In both STU and AS, the use of the Confession was normally required in the First Service. In the Second Service, an ambiguous rubric seemed to make the Confession optional. In the amended version of AS, it was clear that a Confession was to be said most of the time, and "if the Confession is omitted, a penitential petition is to be included in the Intercession" (AS, p. 28). The rubric in PrBCP, for both Rite I and Rite II, provides that "on occasion, the Confession may be omitted." But the permission to substitute a penitential petition from one of the intercessions in place of the Confession has been dropped. These provisions are intended to insure a full general confession of sin for most services, and to recognize that on certain occasions a Confession may appropriately be omitted. For example, at ordinations, rubrics exclude a Confession; and, if a Eucharist were preceded the night before by a service of preparation including a Confession, a Confession would be omitted at the celebration. In the ancient Church, no Confession was said from Easter to Pentecost.

The Comfortable Words in Rite I follow the Absolution as in BCP rather than precede it as in STU and AS. They are designated for optional use. Although logic is on the side of hearing the Comfortable Words *before* Absolution, trial use indicated that the psychological impact of the sequence was greater in the BCP order.

The Peace fits aptly after the Absolution. Peace with God issues in reconciliation with neighbors. In that network of restored relationships, one then can offer gifts. One remembers Jesus' injunction in the Sermon on the Mount: ". . . first be reconciled to your brother, and then come and offer your gift" (Matt. 5:24).

The Holy Communion

Offering.—The close association of the Offering with the Great Thanksgiving has already been noted.

One of the contributions of recent liturgical scholarship has been a deeper understanding of the Offertory. By offering money, bread and wine, and prayers, the congregation offers representatively itself and the world. Rubrics which provide that representatives of the congregation bring bread and wine, money or other gifts, while the people stand, seek to provide action congruent to this meaning of offering. The preparation of the altar by a deacon or assisting priest (rather than by the celebrant) further underlines the fact that the Offertory is not the action of the celebrant alone (*cf.* PrBCP, pp. 322 and 354).

The force of the Offering in PrBCP, following the Absolution and Peace, is that a community of baptized persons, accepted and forgiven by God, bring the gifts they are commanded to offer, and offer themselves through these gifts, to be transformed and renewed by the Body and Blood of Christ, his very life, made accessible to them through bread and wine according to his promise. The elements thus offered are the "means effectual" of communion and grace.

The Great Thanksgiving.—The very title of this section of the eucharistic liturgy, inserted in the text of both Rite I and Rite II, represents a new appreciation of the significance of this prayer, a prayer of thanksgiving to God for all that he has done for us in creation and redemption. It echoes the prayer of thanksgiving said by gatherings of devout Jews at their daily meals, and so presumably said by Jesus at the Last Supper: "Blessed art thou, O Lord our God, eternal King, who feedest the whole world with thy goodness, with grace, with loving-kindness and with tender mercy. . . .We thank thee, O Lord our God, becausethou didst give as an heritage unto our fathers a desirable, good, and ample land, and because thou didst bring us forth, O Lord our God, from the land of Egypt, and didst deliver us from the house of bondage; as well as for thy Covenant which thou hast sealed in our flesh; for thy Law which thou hast taught us; thy statutes which thou hast made known unto us. . . ." (*Tr. Berakoth, M.* vii.5.) The central hallowing of the Eucharist is literally and deeply eucharistic, an act of thanksgiving.

Breaking of the Bread.—The breaking of the bread has been moved from the Prayer of Consecration (BCP) to a place just before Communion (PrBCP). By making this shift, it is hoped to restore to the Eucharist the ancient imagery of the breaking of the single loaf as a means of participation in the one Church and the one Christ. In the words of Bland Tucker's paraphrase of the *Didache,*

As grain once scattered on the hillsides
Was in this broken bread made one,
So from all lands thy Church be gathered
Into thy kingdom by thy Son. (Hymn 195)

Invitation.—In both Rite I and Rite II, the Invitation to Communion, which appeared in STU and AS (Second Service) as "Take them in remembrance that Christ *gives* himself for you" has been restored to its BCP form: "Take this in remembrance that Christ *died* for you."

The present tense in the trial use versions occasioned considerable criticism, on the grounds that the phrase is not Biblical, and that it seemed to undercut the once-and-for-all character of Christ's saving work. Although the Commission would hold that the present tense is theologically justifiable, that Christ is present in the Eucharist as sacrificed, as well as risen, that his self-giving is present as a liturgical and spiritual reality, the Commission does not in any way wish to be understood as calling into question the historically unrepeatable nature of the death of Jesus of Nazareth "for us and for our salvation." By the reappearance of the BCP text with its historically graphic died, we continue to emphasize that basic affirmation of our faith.

Special Features of Rite I

In comparison with the First Service of STU and AS, PrBCP Rite I Eucharist has been given new degrees of flexibility, so that it can be celebrated either in a manner nearly indistinguishable from BCP, or, if desired, in a way much more like that of Rite II.

In order to make it possible to stay closer to BCP, the 1928 text of the Nicene Creed has been added as an option, the order of Absolution and Comfortable Words has been restored as it was in 1928, and Eucharistic Prayer I, word for word, is the Prayer of Consecration of PrBCP. An additional direction on p. 408 permits the singing of a hymn after the postcommunion prayer, and hence of the Gloria in excelsis, if so desired.

Features which make it possible to conform a Rite I celebration more nearly to a Rite II celebration are these: the optional use of an opening acclamation; the provision for singing the Trisagion in place of the Kyrie, and the placement of the Gloria after the Kyrie; the option to use the ICET text of the Nicene Creed; the permission to use other Prayers of the People in place of the Prayer for the whole state of Christ's Church and the world; the presence of an alternative Confession; the optional inclusion of Benedictus qui venit; the provision of an alternative, shorter, form of the Great Thanksgiving; the optional Invitation to Communion and alternative sentences of administration; and the optional Dismissal by the deacon at the end.

In addition, by electing to address the long sentence of invitation to the congregation as a whole, the celebrant can say the short sentence of administration, "The Body of our Lord Jesus Christ keep you in everlasting life," to each communicant. The Eucharist is a corporate action of the Church; but at the time of Communion, each person can be addressed individually, in Rite I as in Rite II. Each communicant is given an opportunity to respond by saying "Amen."

Some additions to the Prayer for the whole state of Christ's Church and the world are worth comment. As in STU and AS, the petition for "Christian Rulers" has become the more inclusive "for those who bear the authority of government in this and every land" (*cf.* 1 Tim. 2:1-2, "I urge that supplications, prayers, intercessions, and thanksgivings be made for all men, for kings and all who are in high positions, that we may lead a quiet and peaceable life, godly and respectful in every way"): In a nation where separation of Church and State is a fundamental principle, and in a world of interdependent nations, it does not seem defensible to limit prayers to Christian rulers only. There is also an "ecological" petition for faithful stewardship. Such a petition was also found in STU and AS, but the wording in DPB has been considerably changed to express a positive rather than a defensive idea of stewardship (". . . that we may honor thee with our substance," replacing ". . . that we neither selfishly waste nor wantonly destroy thy handiwork.")

We should also notice the omission of certain words at the end of the Prayer of Humble Access. In the old form, the conclusion contained the phrase "that our sinful bodies may be made clean by his body, and our souls washed through his most precious blood." Although the phrase was doubtless intended rhetorically, it implies both a dualism of body and soul, and a difference in effect of the two sacramental elements, which is difficult to defend. The phrase has simply been dropped, as in Holy Communion Series 3, of the Church of England.

Special Features of Rite II Prayers of the People

Among the features of Rite II, we note the number of Prayers of the People (pp. 383-393). These prayers are all in litany or responsive form, as one way of expressing a fundamental thrust of PrBCP—maximum congregational participation in the services expressing the corporate character of the People of God. The people are given a voice in the prayers offered in their name. As in STU and AS, these prayers of intercession vary in length and style, although all conform to the basic outline of prayers indicated on p. 359 and again on p. 383. The fact that all the forms contain intercessions for this spectrum of concerns makes them all prayers for the "whole state of Christ's Church and the world," hence suitable for use in the Eucharist of the People of God.

Although revised and strengthened, they are basically the same prayers which were offered for trial use in STU and AS. However, the Good Friday Solemn Collects, which were Form VI in STU and AS, have not been printed at this place in PrBCP, but only in the Good Friday liturgy, to emphasize their special character. Any of these prayers can easily be rendered in either traditional or contemporary language (*cf.* rubric on p. 383).

Confession

The prayer of confession is a somewhat altered form of the Confession in STU and AS. The Confession proposed for trial use at this point contained no explicit expression of sorrow or repentance. The present version seeks to supply this lack, which had been widely felt. It also omits the phrase "forgive what we have been," which suggested to some that our very creation was wrong, and not our human distortion of it. (See the discussion above on pp. 174-175.)

Great Thanksgiving

Rite II provides four Eucharistic Prayers, A through D. A is the prayer printed in the Second Service in STU and AS. B is a combination of prayers A and B provided for the Order in STU and AS. C in PrBCP is C of STU and AS. D is new to PrBCP, but it was authorized for trial use in 1975. Based on ancient *anaphoras*, it is the work of an unofficial committee consisting of Roman Catholic, Episcopal, Presbyterian, Lutheran, and Methodist scholars. It is a response to the suggestion made at the General Convention at Louisville that one of our Eucharistic Prayers should correspond to one of the Roman Catholic Eucharistic Prayers. If it is accepted in all of these denominations, it will represent an ecumenical achievement of the first order.

Certain features are common to all the prayers. One is an emphasis on *creation* (see the discussion on p. 172 above). In striking contrast to Eucharistic Prayer I from Rite I, all these Rite II prayers move to restore this ancient theme of eucharist, thanksgiving to God for his creation, a theme which, as we have seen, appears in the Table Blessing which Jesus presumably used at the Last Supper (above, p. 172). In particular, in the preface to the Sanctus, God is addressed as "Father Almighty, Creator of heaven and earth," rather than "Holy Father, Almighty, Everlasting God." And we find such phrases as, "In your infinite love you made us for yourself" (A); "We give thanks to you, O God, for the goodness and love which you have made known to us in creation" (B); "Fountain of life and source of all goodness, you made all things" (D). Prayer C, of course, is an extended paean of praise to the Creator: "At your command all things come to be; the vast expanse of interstellar space . . ."

Another emphasis characteristic of these prayers is on eschatological fulfillment, the Second Coming of Christ "in power and great glory." (See the earlier discussion on p. 43.) The significance of this motif is its focus on confident hope and expectancy for the future. It is a welcome note in the eucharistic service.

Oblation (Anamnesis).—The oblation or anamnesis is the part of the Great Thanksgiving in which the saving acts of Christ are commemorated as the basis for the eucharistic offering (*cf.* BCP, p. 80). It will be noted that the anamnesis of Prayer A is ampler than it was in the Second Service of STU and AS. Although the intensity of the acclamation, "Christ has died, Christ is risen, Christ will come again," is powerful, it did not make explicit the remembering of God's action in Christ on our behalf in connection with the offering of the bread and wine. Many felt that such silence rendered the prayer weak if not defective. Consequently, in the paragraph following the acclamation, the sentence has been inserted, "Recalling his death, resurrection, and ascension, we offer you these gifts." This addition constitutes the section as a formally complete anamnesis.

Invocation (Epiklesis).—The invocation or epiklesis is that section of the Great Thanksgiving in which the Holy Spirit is invoked (*cf.* BCP, p. 81). Each of the new Eucharistic Prayers has an invocation of the Spirit both on the elements and on the congregation. This "double" invocation makes a theologically intelligible description of the sacramental transformation. As Christ was incarnate by the Spirit, but can be recognized only in the power of the Spirit ("no one can say 'Jesus is Lord' except by the Holy Spirit." 1 Cor. 12:2), so the bread and wine become for us the Body and Blood of the Son by the power of the Spirit; and also they can be recognized as such only by the power of the Spirit.

The English Book of 1549 placed its epiklesis before the Words of Institution, as in certain ancient liturgies. American Books, following the Scottish Book of 1637, have placed the epiklesis after the anamnesis, as in Orthodox liturgies. Arguments for one position or the other might be significant if one believed in a "moment of consecration." PrBCP services express no such moment, consistent with Anglican tradition. The whole service consecrates. Consequently, it is as appropriate that the work of the Spirit should be expressed near the end of the prayer (in A, B, D) as near the beginning (in C).

Atonement.—(See the discussion on pp. 172-174.)

Other Features

Consecration of Additional Elements

According to BCP, additional bread and wine could be consecrated only by the recitation of the whole Prayer of Consecration, as far as the end of the Invocation (BCP, p. 83). In both Rite I and Rite II, additional elements can be consecrated by means of a brief prayer which in the simplest way possible identifies the new bread or wine with the same intentions which were expressed over the old. It is a gain in simplicity, practicality, and confidence that "God knows our needs before we ask."

Use of the Reserved Sacrament

Rubrics in BCP, like those of previous American or English books, prohibit the reservation of the Sacrament. The reasons for this provision are well known. In the late Middle Ages the Sacrament had been reserved to be adored. The Reformers struck against what they held to be idolatry. "The Sacraments were not ordained of Christ to be gazed upon, or to be carried about, but that we should duly use them" (Article XXV).

Subsequent experience has led the Church to recognize situations when it may be desirable to reserve the Sacrament, precisely so that it may be duly used. PrBCP provides for two such situations: the communion of the sick and shut-ins of the parish; and the communion of a congregation where the services of a priest cannot be obtained.

The first situation has long been accepted by Episcopalians. Canon Wedel used to speak of the analogy to a family birthday party. If one member of the family is sick and cannot come, he or she wants a piece of the birthday cake as the next-best thing to being there. A new cake wouldn't do at all. So, especially at Christmas and Easter, priests have for a long time reserved enough consecrated bread and wine for the sick, or "others who for weighty cause could not be present at the celebration." The PrBCP rubric (p. 408) legitimates this common use of the reserved Sacrament.

PrBCP also provides that a bishop may authorize a deacon to distribute Holy Communion from the reserved Sacrament if the services of a priest cannot be obtained. This permission was first granted by the House of Bishops at their Glacier Park meeting in 1965. The liturgy for that case is carefully spelled out in another rubric on p. 408. This practice also falls under the category of "due use."

Pastoral Offices

The Pastoral Offices provide a liturgical ministry for the crucial turning points in the lives of Christians. In BCP, the first of the Pastoral Offices was Baptism, the new birth of Christians. The section continued with the Offices of Instruction and Confirmation, which was the rite to mark attainment of "years of discretion," then with Marriage, Thanksgiving after Childbirth, Visitation of the Sick, and Burial of the Dead. PrBCP follows the same pattern except in the case of Baptism, which has been moved forward as one of the Gospel sacraments, as we have seen. Certain additions to these offices have been made, which will be discussed in order of appearance.

Confirmation

Confirmation has already been treated in connection with Baptism (see pages 190-197). The essential parts of the service of Confirmation were printed along with Baptism for convenience' sake. But Confirmation is printed also in full here within the Pastoral Offices, where it has traditionally appeared in all Anglican Prayer Books.

A Form of Commitment to Christian Service

A Form of Commitment to Christian Service provides an opportunity for a member of the Church to make or renew a commitment to the service of Christ in the world, either in general terms or upon undertaking some special responsibility. The person who uses this form is expected to prepare an Act of Commitment or statement of intention, to be read at the beginning of this service, which is appointed to take place in the Eucharist before the Offertory (PrBCP, p. 420).

An essential part of this action involves a reaffirmation of baptismal promises. The service thus deals with a situation similar to that envisioned in the Reaffirmation of Baptismal Vows, included in the service of Confirmation. In this latter case, however, those who make the reaffirmation present themselves to a bishop. In the Form of Commitment, the celebrant at the Eucharist, normally a priest, represents the Church. The prayers in the two rites are nearly identical. In the Reaffirmation of Baptismal Vows, the prayer of the bishop reads,

> *N.*, may the Holy Spirit, who has begun a good work in you, direct and uphold you in the service of Christ and his kingdom (PrBCP, p. 419).

In the Form of Commitment, the prayer of the celebrant runs,

> May the Holy Spirit guide and strengthen you, that in this, and in all things, you may do God's will in the service of his kingdom and of his Christ (PrBCP, p. 420).

It is likely that the circumstances which would lead persons to present themselves to the bishop instead of a priest would entail more crucial and life-changing decisions. A prayer of the bishop, made in the name of the Church, is a solemn and weighty thing. However, it is not necessarily any more efficacious than the prayer of a presbyter. There is *theologically* no difference in what the prayers express, or in what is thought to be accomplished in the two services. There is a difference in the nature, solemnity, and weight of the occasion.

The Celebration and Blessing of a Marriage

The PrBCP form for the Celebration and Blessing of a Marriage appears at a time when the institution of marriage in our society is undergoing many changes—changes resulting from the increased ease and frequency of divorce, from the felt failures of the nuclear family, and from the consequent desire to see the new family established by marriage in the context of society as a whole. The new marriage service intends to recognize the cultural changes which are taking place, provided that they do not contradict the Christian understanding of marriage as a lifelong and monogamous union. The new service intends to affirm and strengthen that understanding in the face of forces which call it into question.

The Exhortation

In order to strengthen and clarify Christian teaching about marriage, several themes not present in the BCP service have been added to the exhortation at the beginning of the PrBCP service.

It is said, for example, that the institution of marriage belongs to the created order. "The bond and covenant of marriage was established by God in creation"

(PrBCP, p. 423). Marriage is not only a sacrament of redemption, although it is that, since "it signifies to us the mystery of the union between Christ and his Church" (PrBCP, p. 423).

A second paragraph states that marriage is first for the "mutual joy" of husband and wife; secondly, "for the help and comfort given one another in prosperity and adversity"; and thirdly, "when it is God's will, for the procreation of children and their nurture in the knowledge and love of the Lord." None of these purposes was mentioned in BCP. In this time of confusion about the purposes of Christian marriage, it is deemed wise to be as explicit as possible. The order of the phrases is carefully chosen in the face of widespread misunderstanding of the Church's teaching. It intends both to affirm the third purpose—the procreation of children—and to deny first place to it.

Declaration of Consent

The Declaration of Consent continues in traditional phrases the traditional Christian insistence that marriage is to be life-long and monogamous: ". . . forsaking all others, to be faithful to him/her as long as you both shall live" (DPB, p. 424).

The new question to the congregation, asking for its upholding of the bride and groom in their marriage (PrBCP, p. 425), is a direct recognition of the importance of the community's role in maintaining the marriage relationship.

The "giving away" ceremony has been removed to the Additional Directions, in view of two considerations: (1) it is not an essential element of Christian marriage; and (2) it is widely felt to be inappropriate that one person should be "given" to another. That act could be interpreted as disregarding the personhood of the one who is given. However, its use is still provided in two forms: the traditional "giving away" by the bride's father, and, alternatively, the presentation of either or both bride and groom by their respective parents, or others (PrBCP, p. 436).

The Ministry of the Word

The Collect (p. 425) has been reworked to emphasize, as the Collect in STU did not, the covenantal aspect of marriage, and the need for God's grace to maintain the vows (*cf.* STU, p. 313).

Lections appear in PrBCP, as they did in STU, but not previously in our Anglican tradition. The readings further express Biblical teaching about marriage—rooted in creation, blessed by God, transformed by the redemptive act of God in Christ. The use of lessons makes possible an easy transition to a celebration of the Eucharist, if that be desired, for the marriage service itself then becomes the Proclamation of the Word. Even if there is no Eucharist, the lessons enrich the rite.

The Marriage

The exchange of vows is thus separated from the Declaration of Consent by the Ministry of the Word. It becomes possible to emphasize the independent acts by which the man takes the woman's hand and promises fidelity to her, and the woman takes the man's hand and promises fidelity to him, as the essential element of the marriage. The couple are the ministers of this sacrament. The celebrant witnesses and blesses, but does not perform the marriage. The BCP rubric directing the man and the woman to say their vows "after the minister" has been reworded to read simply, "the Man, facing the woman and taking her right hand in his, says" (PrBCP, p. 427). Similarly for the Woman. The couple may read their vows or recite them from memory.

Although the exchange of rings is still the customary form of the exchange of gifts, PrBCP recognizes that in different cultures other gifts are sometimes used at this point. An additional direction allows for this possibility (PrBCP, p. 437).

The sentence which accompanied the gift of the ring in BCP suggested that the exchange accomplished the marriage. ("With this ring I thee wed.") In the new rite, the exchange of gifts has become the symbolic exchange of property and person. ("With all that I am and all that I have I honor you." PrBCP, p. 427.)

By this alteration, some of the earthiness of the old English phrase, "with my body I thee worship and with all my worldly goods I thee endow," has been restored. More significantly, this alteration makes the exchange of vows, rather than the exchange of rings, more obviously the outward expression of the wedding. The form for the blessing of the ring(s) has been reworded to express the same intent.

Each of the partners makes his or her promises "in the Name of God." If one partner is not a Christian, he or she can still make the promise with a clear conscience. The celebrant, however, pronounces that they are "husband and wife" in the Name of the Trinity. There is no compromise of the trinitarian faith of the Church; but each partner should be able to make true vows with a whole heart. It should be observed that the Trinity was not invoked at all in the exchange of BCP vows. "Man and wife" has become "husband and wife" to express better the equality of the sexes.

The Prayers

The prayers at this point of the service gather up themes and motifs which have been sounded earlier: the need of husband and wife for each other and for God's grace; the communal responsibilities of the couple, and their dependence on communal support; the sign of God's love which their love gives to a sinful world.

The Blessing of the Marriage

The prayer before the Blessing (p. 430) and the Blessing (p. 431) may be said only by a priest or bishop, in accordance with the customary Anglican understanding of the priestly office. The first of these prayers, drawn in part from ancient material and authorized for trial use in 1975, is a rich and eloquent prayer for the blessing of God.

Deacons may officiate at marriages if permitted by civil law to do so, and if a priest or bishop is not available. In this case, deacons are not authorized to say this prayer or give this blessing (*cf.* rubric PrBCP, p. 422). In the presence of a priest or bishop, deacons may, of course, participate in the other parts of the service as the rubric on page 422 allows.

The moment at the end of the marriage service when the groom customarily kisses the bride is once more recognized as the occasion for the exchange of the Kiss of Peace, initiated by the couple as ministers of the marriage. The exchange of the Peace is optional.

The Blessing of a Civil Marriage

This rite provides an orderly and explicit way to bless a marriage not previously solemnized by the Church. It provides for a common situation. It requires no theological comment.

An Order for Marriage

There are some occasions when it might be desirable to allow a couple to prepare the service for their own wedding in consultation with the celebrant. It also may be appropriate to permit a service rather different in some outward respects from the Celebration and Blessing of a Marriage. PrBCP provides an Order for Marriage, comparable to the Order for Celebrating the Eucharist, to make such occasions possible. In this way, various ethnic or cultural marriage customs may be incorporated into the rite. The life of our Church will be enriched by such opportunities. The Order, which should be strictly followed, also insures that there will be specific Christian content in the service. In particular, it specifies the vows to be exchanged by the bride and groom, since these vows constitute the essential element of Christian marriage. The wording of the vow is exactly the same as in the Celebration and Blessing of a Marriage. By making optional the inclusion of Readings from Scripture and by the provision of the optional use of the vows as they appear in BCP (p. 301f.), the Order for Marriage permits the use of the BCP Solemnization of Holy Matrimony in its entirety.

A Thanksgiving for the Birth or Adoption of a Child

This service replaces the *Thanksgiving of Women after Childbirth* in BCP. The BCP service bears the sub-title *Churching of Women*, a rite which in the medieval

Church was thought to effect the removal of the ritual impurity which childbearing was believed to entail. Through all the English and American Prayer Books, however, this service has not expressed purification, but rather thanksgiving for safe deliverance and preservation "in the great danger of Child-birth" (BCP, p. 305). In recent years, with the great improvement in medical science, it has come to be felt nearly universally that safe deliverance, though important, is not the chief thing for which a mother need be thankful on the birth of a child; and also that not only the mother, but the whole family, should have an opportunity to give thanks. The focus of the service is now on the addition of a new life to the family. A prayer for safe delivery is, to be sure, included (DPB, p. 444), but the emphasis of the service has changed.

Since the focus has become the gift of a new life to a family, it is convenient to provide within this service a form for the adoption of a child, with an exchange of promises by the parents to accept the child, and by the child (if old enough) to accept the new parents.

This service is a good example of the influence of changing social conditions on liturgical practice. The present service should be much more useful under existing conditions than its predecessor.

The Reconciliation of a Penitent

In the past, American Prayer Books have provided no form for private confession and absolution. The abuses of the penitential system in the late Middle Ages were so numerous, and the superstitions surrounding it so great, that the English Reformers made no liturgical provision for private confession except for the sick or dying. There was, to be sure, general confession; and the Second English Prayer Book (1552) made it quite clear that God "hath given power and commandment to his Ministers, to declare and pronounce to his people, being penitent, the Absolution and Remission of their sins" (BCP, pp. 7, 24). In the Anglican tradition there is no theological problem with the idea of a priest's hearing confession and pronouncing absolution.

Moreover, the pastoral use of *private* confession has been enjoined on those "whose conscience is troubled and grieved in any thing." "Let him come to me," read the priest in an exhortation at Holy Communion which has appeared in all English and American Prayer Books, "or to some other Minister of God's Word, and open his grief, that he may receive such godly counsel and advice, as may tend to the quieting of his conscience, and the removing of all scruple and doubtfulness" (BCP, p. 88). English Prayer Books encourage the sick to make a special confession to the priest, "if he feel his conscience troubled in any weighty matter," and provide a form for absolution (English Book of 1662). At the corresponding point in BCP, in place of an explicit absolution, the rubric continues, "after which confession, on evidence of his repentance, the Minister shall assure him of God's mercy and forgiveness (BCP, p. 313).

In other words, private confession has been pastorally encouraged, and priestly absolution provided, from the beginning of the Anglican tradition. The present two services for the Reconciliation of a Penitent simply make an official liturgical form for private confession available. The longer of the two forms adds to the shorter some verses of Scripture on the occasion of the confession. They are otherwise equivalent (*cf.* rubric, PrBCP, p. 446).

The same two forms for absolution are provided in each service. One is a prayer that Christ will absolve the penitent from all his sins. The other is stronger: "by the authority committed to me, I absolve you from all your sins." Neither formula implies that the priest pronounces absolution in his own person or on his own authority. What authority there is, is God's. That authority, including the authority to forgive sins, is conferred at the ordination of a priest (PrBCP, p. 531). The longer formula for absolution personalizes, or embodies, the forgiveness of God more directly than the shorter. For the penitent, it is sometimes important to know not only that God forgives, but also that some human person, bearing that word of forgiveness, can say, "I forgive." Although some priests and some lay people will undoubtedly find one form more congenial than the other, both personal and impersonal forms are theologically justifiable, and both may be pastorally useful.

Ministration to the Sick

The provisions for ministry to the sick consist of three parts: Ministry of the Word, Laying on of Hands and Anointing, and Holy Communion. These parts correspond roughly to Visitation of the Sick, Unction of the Sick, and Communion of the Sick in BCP. A collection of prayers for the sick and for use by sick persons concludes this section of PrBCP.

The Ministry of the Word contains lessons arranged for several different circumstances. There is a general set, expressing God's comfort in affliction and his power to heal through faith; a penitential set, expressing Christ's power over sin as well as over disease; a set suggested for use when anointing is to follow; and a set suggested for use when Communion is to follow.

Like the Prayer Books which preceded it, BCP made a major interpretation of sickness: it was connected with sin. The Order for Visitation begins with the antiphon, "Remember not, Lord, our iniquities; Nor the iniquities of our forefathers." The first set of propers at the Communion of the Sick in BCP established sickness as the "chastening of the Lord." This is not, to be sure, the only accent sounded in BCP's provision for ministry to the sick, but it is unmistakable. PrBCP subdues, but does not completely eliminate, this note. In the set of penitential propers, for example, the connection between sin and sickness lies close, but the power of Jesus to perfect faith is also clear. Thus, in cases when a penitential interpretation of sickness is appropriate, it is available. But in PrBCP it is not a leading accent. The power of God to restore health, and the healing work of

Christ as a sign of God's kingdom, are the chief themes. This change does represent a shift in theological outlook—a welcome one.

Ministration at the Time of Death

Some material in the BCP Visitation of the Sick seems most appropriate at the time of death: for example, the Litany for the Dying and the Commendation (BCP, pp. 317-319). These prayers have been gathered in a separate section of PrBCP entitled *Ministration at the Time of Death*; and prayers for a Vigil and prayers at the time a body is brought into the church have been added. It is hoped that these additions will be pastorally useful. They raise no theological questions.

Burial of the Dead

There are both Rite I and Rite II Burial Services. Rite II offers the possibility of a more intimate and personal service. Note the rubric at the bottom of p. 492, which provides for an informal introduction and bidding; notice also the use of names in most of the prayers, and the new litany on p. 497, with its warmer and less formal tone. Rite II can readily be adapted for use as a memorial service.

The lessons and prayers are arranged so that they may constitute a service of the Word at a Eucharist, although, as in the case of Baptism and Marriage, this material may be used separately if desired. Old Testament passages and Psalms have been supplied, and a larger selection of Epistles and Gospels than in BCP. All the BCP lections, however, are included in the PrBCP provisions. In Rite I, the Psalms are in the BCP version.

There is no special service for the Burial of a Child, as there was in BCP. In PrBCP, rubrical directions indicate a suitable choice of Psalms and lessons for such an occasion (PrBCP, p. 468). The appropriate Collect, one of the prayers from the BCP service for the Burial of a Child (BCP, p. 342), is plainly marked.

In its proclamation of hope in the destruction of death, confidence in God's victory, and expectation of the "resurrection of the dead and the life of the world to come," PrBCP burial services represent no significant change from BCP theology. If anything, these accents are heightened. "The liturgy for the dead is an Easter liturgy," runs the opening rubric in the PrBCP Order for Burial (PrBCP, p. 507). A series of anthems, partly from Eastern Orthodox sources, suggested for use as the body is borne from the church, underlines this teaching powerfully.

Episcopal Services

This section of PrBCP contains services for the Ordination of Bishops, Priests, and Deacons, as well as a Litany for Ordinations, the Celebration of a New Ministry, and the Consecration of a Church or Chapel. It is introduced by a revised Preface to the Ordination Rites. This Preface makes it clear that from the apostles' time there have been different ministries, and that three distinct orders of ministry have been characteristic of Christ's holy catholic Church: bishops, priests, and deacons.

The Underlying Concept of Ministry

The use of the word *minister* in the Christian community deserves some comment. *Minister* is derived from the Latin word *minus*, which means less. Its use in a Christian context suggests the Gospel passage, "he who is least among you is the one who is great" (Luke 9:34), and others like it. *Minister* and its cognates frequently render various forms of *diakonos*, the Greek word for servant. *Diakonos* is regularly used in the New Testament both of Christ and of those who are his. There is no suggestion in the New Testament use of the terms that there is any necessary rite of ordination to ministry as such. The whole People of God exercises ministry (2 Cor. 5:18, Eph. 4:12). There are, to be sure, special ministries (Acts 1:17, 25; 6:4; Col. 4:17).

PrBCP aims to recapture this New Testament sense that ministry is a function of the whole Church. "Who are the ministers of the Church?" asks the Catechism. "The ministers of the Church are lay persons, bishops, priests, and deacons" (PrBCP, p. 855). Thus one may speak of ordained ministers, but they are persons who express and enable the ministry of the whole People of God. All the orders are said in the Catechism "to represent Christ and his Church," in addition to, and prior to, their special functions.

PrBCP is sparing of the term *minister* to describe one who performs a liturgical function. On the one hand, it is not precise enough. A careful attempt has been made in the rubrics concerning each service to specify what may be done in that service by lay persons, bishops, priests, and deacons. On the other hand, the term *minister* describes a Christian person not only, indeed not chiefly, in liturgical function, but rather in mission to the world. Thus, rubrics speak specifically of bishop, priest, or deacon when necessary; or when a general term is required, they speak of *officiant* in the Daily Offices and *celebrant* in the sacramental and pastoral offices.

The word *minister* is used in PrBCP in three contexts: (1) to refer to ordained persons of other denominations, as in the phrase, "Ministers of other Churches may appropriately be invited to participate" (PrBCP, p. 558), or, "Neighboring ministers should be invited to participate" (PrBCP, p. 566). In this case, the term *minister* is conventional, and its use is justified by the consideration that the representative officers of the ministerial Church are ministerial. (2) In a similar vein, PrBCP refers to the *Celebration of a New Ministry*. It is designed for the institution of a priest as the rector of a parish; but "it may also be used for the installation of deans and canons of cathedrals, or the inauguration of other ministries." The ministry of a lay person might be so marked. In this case, too, the liturgical function of the persons involved is not chiefly in focus, rather their lives of service.

Consequently, they too can conveniently be called ministers, as representatives of a ministerial Church. (3) The person in charge of a congregation, regardless of order, is referred to as a minister (*cf.* first rubric, p. 453).

Episcopate and Body

The theory of ministry which underlies these services turns on the role of the bishop. These provisions for ordination are provisions for an *episcopal* Church, a Church whose polity depends on bishops. In company with every Christian body, our Church would insist that the ministry is in the first instance Christ's ministry. The Church, the Body of Christ, ministers in Christ's name and acts for him (1 Cor. 12). The ministry of reconciliation has been entrusted to the Church (2 Cor. 5:18ff). Episcopal Churches hold that this ministry is focused and summed up in the episcopate. Bishops stand for, and represent, their dioceses to the Church at large, and the Church to their dioceses (Ignatius *ad Eph.* 1.3, and *ad Mag.* 11.1, etc.; also Cyprian, *Ep.* 45, 69; etc.).

Because bishops have this representative quality, all liturgical powers were at the beginning vested in them. They were the presidents of their congregations. During the course of time, bishops have found it convenient and necessary to share some of these powers with presbyters, and with deacons and lay persons as well. There is no question about their power and right to do so. PrBCP makes an effort to be explicit and consistent in these assignments of liturgical functions, as the following discussion will seek to establish.

Some Features of the New Ordination Rites

BCP spoke of the "consecration" of bishops, the "ordering" of priests, and the "making" or "ordering" of deacons. Since these terms turn out to represent distinctions without differences, PrBCP speaks of "ordination" to all three orders, and refers to the prayer spoken during the laying on of the bishop's hands as the "consecration" in each case.

The representative character of each order is emphasized by the requirement that lay persons and priests present a bishop for ordination, and at least one lay person and one priest present a priest or a deacon. One question in each rite has to do with the fulfillment of canonical requirements.

As in BCP, ordinations are in the context of Eucharist. Each service consists of a Presentation, the Ministry of the Word, an Examination, and the Consecration. There has been no effort to duplicate the BCP provision of different places within the Eucharist at which ordination to the different orders occurs. The resulting gain in clarity of structure is considerable.

The question put in the STU ordinal, "Is he worthy?" and its answering acclamation, "He is worthy," was widely misunderstood during trial use, and occasioned a great deal of criticism. It has been altered in PrBCP to "Is it your will that N. be ordained a bishop (or priest or deacon)?" The answer supplied is, "That is our will," or, "It is." This form avoids the unintended implications of moral righteousness conveyed by the earlier version. The consecration formula in each rite is a prayer accompanied by the laying on of hands. There is no imperative statement, "Take thou authority," or "Receive the Holy Ghost," as in BCP. Since there are ancient models for the PrBCP forms of ordination, and since the eucharistic elements are consecrated by prayer, there is no reason to suppose that this form is in any way defective. In each case it is a prayer that the Holy Spirit will come upon the ordinand for the work to which the person is being ordained. The prayer used for bishops is the oldest known formulary for this purpose. Drawn from the *Apostolic Tradition* of Hippolytus, it is also now in use in the Roman Catholic Church. The forms commend themselves as being both ancient and conforming to the traditional Anglican teaching that ordination is bestowed by the laying on of hands with prayer.

Description of the Three-fold Ministry

Bishop

From the preamble to the Examination, we learn that the bishop has a primary missionary function—to be "one with the apostles in proclaiming Christ's resurrection and interpreting the Gospel;" that he should "guard the faith, unity, and discipline of the Church;" that he should celebrate and provide for the sacraments, ordain, and be "a faithful pastor and wholesome example" to the flock of Christ. The bishop is exhorted to follow him who came not to be served, but to serve.

He is to be faithful in prayer and the study of Scripture, to enlighten minds and stir up consciences by proclaiming the Gospel, to encourage and enable others in their several ministries, to take part in the government of the whole Church, to be a pastor to his clergy, and to have compassion on all, especially the poor and strangers.

This is a fuller account of the office of bishop than the BCP ordinal contains, particularly with respect to the sacraments, to guarding the unity of the Church, to enabling the ministry of others, and to being a pastor to the clergy. In particular, it is ampler than the description in the Offices of Instruction, which records simply,. "The office of a Bishop is to be Chief Pastor in the Church; to confer Holy Orders; and to administer Confirmation" (BCP, p. 294). The PrBCP Ordinal is also consistent with the PrBCP Catechism: "The ministry of a bishop is to represent Christ and his Church, particularly as apostle, chief priest, and pastor of a diocese; to guard the faith, unity, and discipline of the whole Church; to proclaim the Word of God; to act in Christ's name for the reconciliation of the world and the building up of the Church; and to ordain others to continue Christ's ministry" (PrBCP, p. 855).

Priest

From the Examination of the priest, we learn that a priest is to "work as a pastor, priest, and teacher, together with your bishop and fellow presbyters, and to take your share in the councils of the Church." He is to proclaim the Gospel, fashion his life according to its precepts, to love and serve the people with whom he works, to preach, declare forgiveness, share in the administration of sacraments; he is to respect and be guided by his bishop's direction; to study the Holy Scripture and other things which will make him a more able minister, and to persevere in prayer.

The new rite brings to expression the important and traditional function of the priest as a councilor with the bishop for the governance of the Church. This is a new and significant note in Anglican books. The difference between BCP's "Will you be diligent . . . in reading the Holy Scriptures, and in such studies as help to the knowledge of the same, laying aside the study of the world and the flesh?" and PrBCP's emphasis on "other things which will make him a more able minister" points to the larger world in which the Church must exercise its ministry in the twentieth century. Apart from these new notes, the role of a priest as envisioned in the two ordinals is virtually the same. It is primarily pastoral. In particular, it is consistent with the statement in the new Catechism: "The ministry of a priest is to represent Christ and his Church, particularly as pastor to the people; to share with the bishop in the overseeing of the Church; to proclaim the Gospel, to administer the sacraments, and to bless and declare pardon in the Name of God" (PrBCP, p. 856). By recognizing that priests have a share in overseeing the Church, the PrBCP Ordinal acknowledges that priests (unlike deacons) have collegiality with the bishop.

With the statement on the ministry of a priest in the PrBCP Catechism, one should compare the answer to the corresponding question in the BCP Office of Instruction. "The office of a Priest is, to minister to the people committed to his care; to preach the Word of God, to baptize, to celebrate the Holy Communion, and to pronounce Absolution and Blessing in God's Name" (BCP, p. 294).

Deacon

From the Examination of a deacon, we learn that the deacons are "called to a special ministry of servanthood directly underthe bishop." Their role is not collegial. Deacons are to serve all people, "particularly the poor, the weak, the sick, and the lonely" (PrBCP, p. 543). They are to study the Holy Scripture, to make Christ known by word and example, "to interpret to the Church the needs, concerns, and hopes of the world" (PrBCP, p. 543). They are to be guided by the direction and leadership of the bishop, and in all things to seek "not their own glory, but the glory of Christ" (PrBCP, p. 543).

Two items in this description deserve attention. First, there is a new charge, "to interpret the world to the Church." Although this matter, like so many of the other things involved in ordination, should not be understood to lie solely with those ordained, nevertheless deacons usually come to ordination after a fresh encounter with the world. Many deacons continue in their secular occupations.

Secondly, to an even greater degree than in BCP, the ministry of a deacon is conceived as a helping ministry. In the opening rubrics, Concerning the Service of the Church, we find the following: "The leader of worship in a Christian assembly is normally a bishop or priest. Deacons by virtue of their order do not exercise a presiding function, but, like lay persons, may officiate at the Liturgy of the Word . . . Under exceptional circumstances, when the services of a priest cannot be obtained, the bishop may, at discretion, authorize a deacon to preside at other rites also, subject to the limitations described in the directions for each service" (PrBCP, pp. 13-14). There are several liturgical functions in PrBCP which a deacon is preferentially designated to perform: at the Eucharist, the reading of the Gospel, the intercessions, the preparation of the elements, and the dismissal; and at the Easter Vigil, the recitation of the Exsultet (PrBCP, p. 288). All are matters of tradition rather than theology.

There is a small but appreciable difference between this understanding of the office of deacon and that of BCP. The BCP Ordinal permits deacons to baptize infants in the absence of priests. PrBCP requires that deacons be especially authorized by bishops to baptize infants or adults on each occasion (*cf.* PrBCP rubric, p. 312). BCP puts a stress on teaching which PrBCP transfers to priesthood and episcopate. Teaching, too, will be done by deacons under the direction of priest and bishop. We may conclude that the servant character of the diaconate is established more clearly in PrBCP than in BCP, although the catechetical definitions in the two books are virtually identical. In the BCP, it runs, "The office of a Deacon is, to assist the Priest in Divine Service, and in his other ministrations, under the direction of the Bishop" (BCP, p. 294). In PrBCP we read, "The ministry of a deacon is to represent Christ and his Church, particularly as a servant of those in need; and to assist bishops and priests in the proclamation of the Gospel and the administration of the sacraments" (PrBCP, p. 856). Unlike BCP, the new rite does not assume that all deacons will be admitted to the priesthood. In general, it may be said that PrBCP presents the diaconate as an order of great dignity, with a distinct character of its own.

Celebration of a New Ministry

This service replaces the Office of Institution of Ministers in BCP. As has already been noted, the Celebration of a New Ministry can be used at the institution of a rector of a parish, and also in many other settings. This added range of use reflects the wider understanding of ministry to which we have already referred.

The service extends considerably the number of symbolic presentations provided in BCP, in line with PrBCP's general intention to supply visible and dramatic action. The new minister's prayer for himself (PrBCP, p. 562) is a revision of the eloquent prayer in BCP (BCP, p. 573).

The Dedication and Consecration of a Church

A church building could be consecrated according to the *Form of Consecration of a Church or Chapel* in BCP only when the building was debt-free. While there was a mortgage, the building could be "dedicated," although the Prayer Book provided no form for such action. This use of words, like the vocabulary for the ordination of the three orders of ministry, turns out to involve distinctions without differences. There is no *theological* reason to prevent a church building from being dedicated or consecrated to God while parishioners are paying the mortgage.

The basic intention of the BCP service and the PrBCP service are the same—to dedicate the whole building to the service of God, and then its chief liturgical furnishings: font, lectern, pulpit, altar. The order of events in PrBCP, however, is more dramatic, for the different furnishings are dedicated as they are used in an unfolding Eucharist: lectern and pulpit before the ministry of the Word, organ before the response to the Epistle, altar before the Peace, after the Prayers of the People. There is a notable gain in clarity and force.

The Psalter

The Translation

The Psalter appears in PrBCP in a new translation, in contemporary language. The BCP version, originally that of Miles Coverdale, is used as the basis of this new text. The old wording is retained when deemed possible. In this way the BCP Psalter's dependence on the Vulgate and Septuagint has been preserved in the cases where the Latin or Greek text gives a preferable reading.

Be joyful in the Lord, all you lands;
serve the Lord with gladness
and come before his presence with a song,

is still the opening verse of the One Hundredth Psalm.

Nevertheless, the Psalter has been thoroughly reworked, with the intention of reflecting both contemporary word usage and also the results of the most recent Hebrew scholarship. Since the Psalter is to be used in both Rite I and Rite II, no word has been employed in the new translation which would not have been available to Coverdale in the sixteenth century. Thus, the first verse of Psalm 95, the Venite, reads in PrBCP,

Come, let us sing to the Lord;
let us shout for joy to the Rock of our salvation.

It is believed that this version renders the Hebrew text more adequately and poetically than BCP, but it will not sound unduly anachronistic when used with Rite I.

Divisions and Use

The traditional divisions of the Psalter for monthly recitation of all the Psalms in course at Morning and Evening Prayer have been retained in PrBCP at the request of many who read the Daily Office.

In the Daily Office lectionary, Psalms are assigned on a seven-week cycle, with seasonal interruptions. Psalms which refer to creation and the paschal mystery have been assigned to Saturday evenings and Sundays. Passion Psalms are assigned to Fridays. In the Lectionary for Sundays and Holy Days, Psalms are assigned on a topical basis. Thus, the use of the Psalter in PrBCP is approximately the same in nature as in BCP; and in view of the specific provision of Psalms or sections of Psalms at celebrations of the Eucharist in PrBCP, as was not the case in BCP, it is hoped that the Psalter will be used with even greater frequency.

Generic Terms

A careful study has been made of the generic words in the Psalter. Where at all possible to eliminate masculine nouns where a generic meaning is intended, they have been removed. No automatic formula accounts for the resulting changes. Sometimes a plural has been substituted, as in Psalm 1:1,

"Happy are *they* who have not walked in counsel of the wicked . . ."

Sometimes a different kind of substitution has been found necessary. For example, Psalm 9:20 read in BCP,

". . . that the heathen may know themselves to be but men."

In PrBCP, it runs,

". . . let the ungodly know they are but mortal."

In certain instances, where the reference is unmistakably messianic, and where a familiar New Testament allusion and liturgical implication would be destroyed by an alteration, no change has been attempted. Thus Psalm 8:5 reads,

"What is man that you should be mindful of him?
the son of man that you should seek him out?"

Prayers and Thanksgivings

The collection of prayers and thanksgivings in PrBCP comprises seventy intercessions and petitions, of which twenty-seven appeared in BCP, and eleven thanksgivings, of which one appeared in BCP. Most of the others appeared in PSB 25 (*Prayers, Thanksgivings, and Litanies*). Conversely, of the forty-two prayers in the section of Prayers and Thanksgivings in BCP and the twenty-five in the Additional Prayers at the end of the book, some 60% appear, either in this section of Prayers and Thanksgivings or elsewhere in PrBCP. Of the ten thanksgivings in BCP, only one appears in PrBCP. Evidence of trial use suggests that all the prayers and thanksgivings in BCP used with any frequency at all have been picked up in PrBCP.

The most interesting theological feature of this section is the new order of the prayers. In previous Anglican Prayer Books, intercessions began with prayers for the State, then the Church, then the social order, and finally personal life. This order, which reflects the priorities of a Church established by the State, is followed in the intercessions after the third Collect at Morning and Evening Prayer, in the Litany, and in the Prayer for the Whole State of Christ's Church in the Communion service. It also underlies the order of the prayers in the BCP collection of Prayers and Thanksgivings. In PrBCP, the order has been shifted, because the priority of concerns of those who do not live in an established Church is different. Here prayer is made first for the world, then the Church, then national life, the social order, the natural order, and family and personal life.

The range of concerns in the twentieth century is also wider than the scope of the prayers in BCP suggests. Among the prayers which have been added are a prayer for those who suffer for the sake of conscience, a prayer for cities, a prayer for towns and rural areas, one for those who are alone, one for victims of addiction. For the first time in an English or American Prayer Book there is a prayer for enemies. Among the new thanksgivings are found an alternative general thanksgiving, a thanksgiving for the Church, a thanksgiving for the nation, and one for the diversity of races and cultures.

An Outline of the Faith

(Commonly called the Catechism)

In comparison with the BCP Catechism, the PrBCP Outline of the Faith is longer and fuller. It comprises one hundred and twelve questions and answers. The BCP Catechism contains twenty-five. Even the Offices of Instruction, which contain a section on the Ministry not included in the Catechism itself, comprise only thirty-three questions and answers.

The range of material covered is also greater. The BCP Catechism is conceived in relation to the promise undertaken by sponsors at Baptism that they will "take heed that this Child learn the Creed, the Lord's Prayer, and the Ten Commandments" (BCP, p. 277). In addition to questions about the meaning of these three items, the BCP Catechism adds at the beginning some material about other baptismal promises, and, at the end, questions about the two sacraments.

The Offices of Instruction also include statements about the Church and the Ministry.

The Outline of the Faith is more inclusive, with questions about Human Nature; God as Father, Son, and Spirit; the Old and New Covenants; Sin and Redemption; the Scriptures; Prayer; and Christian Hope. Sections on the Creed, the Lord's Prayer, and the Ten Commandments are also included, to be sure—the Lord's Prayer in the longer section on Prayer and Worship.

If one were to compare the answers in the PrBCP Outline with those in the BCP Catechism on the same subject, it would be noticed that in the Ten Commandments, for example, the emphasis falls on the positive rather than on the negative implication of the injunctions. In the BCP comment on the First Commandment, one is instructed first to believe and fear God, then to love him. In PrBCP, the answer is first love, then obey. In the BCP comment on the Seventh Commandment, one learns to keep one's body "in temperance, soberness, and chastity" (BCP, p. 289); in PrBCP, "to use all our bodily desires as God intended" (PrBCP, p. 848). It is hoped that such an answer, while not so explicit as BCP, will in fact raise questions and so become "a point of departure for the teacher," as the rubrics introducing the Outline of the Faith suggest. (PrBCP, p. 844.)

The answer to the one question regarding the Apostles' Creed in BCP simply establishes the triune nature of God. PrBCP has extensive questions on each Person of the Trinity. The section on the Creeds briefly identifies each of the three creeds printed in PrBCP—the Apostles', the Nicene, and the Athanasian.

The PrBCP treatment of the sacraments begins with the familiar definition, "The sacraments are outward and visible signs of inward and spiritual grace" (PrBCP, p. 857); it deals at length with Baptism and Eucharist as "great sacraments" (p. 858), or as "sacraments of the Gospel" (p. 860). There is a section identifying and defining five "other sacramental rites," clearly distinguishing them from the two sacraments of the Gospel. The five are, of course, Confirmation, Ordination, Holy Matrimony, Reconciliation of a Penitent, and Anointing of the Sick, these titles having been conformed to those of the PrBCP Pastoral Offices.

Neither the Catechism nor the Offices of Instruction in BCP mention these other sacramental rites at all, and the treatment in Article XXV of the Thirty-Nine Articles is brief and rather negative. The attitude expressed in PrBCP is conformable to that of Article XXV, in that it clearly establishes that the five "have not the like nature of Sacraments with Baptism and the Lord's Supper," but deals with them in a more positive and detailed way.

There has been some resistance to including a catechism in PrBCP, in view of the considerable weight of opinion that the learning of answers by rote is not an effective way of communicating either knowledge or faith. It is in fact not intended that this Outline of the Faith should be committed to memory. Its very length almost precludes such an approach. The rubrics concerning the catechism establish a different style of use. "This catechism is primarily intended for use by parish priests, deacons, and lay catechists, to give an outline for instruction. It is a commentary on the creeds, but is not meant to be a complete statement of belief and practice; rather, it is a point of departure for the teacher, and it is cast in the traditional question and answer form for ease of reference" (PrBCP, p. 844). It is hoped that adult inquirers will find the new catechism helpful in describing the basic teachings of the Episcopal Church, and that members of long standing can readily remind themselves through it of the fundamentals of Christian faith.

Historical Documents of the Church

PrBCP includes five "historical documents of the Church": (1) the Chalcedonian definition of the Person of Christ, 451 A.D.; (2) the Athanasian Creed; (3) the Preface to the First Book of Common Prayer, 1549; (4) the Thirty-Nine Articles of Religion, in the form established by the American Church in 1801; and (5) the Chicago-Lambeth Quadrilateral, 1886-1888.

These documents, in addition, of course, to Scripture and creedal and liturgical formularies regularly used in worship, indicate the living theological tradition in which PrBCP has been shaped. The Chalcedonian definition is the crucial paradoxical Christological statement of the Catholic and undivided Church. It was accepted at the fourth ecumenical council, at Chalcedon, in 451, and defined the Person of Christ as "truly God and truly man . . . in two natures, without confusion, without change, without division, without separation." The Athanasian Creed is the amplest brief statement of the doctrine of the Trinity as it developed in Western Christianity. It has appeared in all English Prayer Books, although never in an American book until now. The version in the English Prayer Books is that taken up in PrBCP. In this form, Bishop Seabury desired to have it included as a document in the first American Prayer Book.

The Preface to the First Book of Common Prayer describes an attitude toward the reform of worship which has prevailed in Anglicanism from the beginning, with its respect for the work of the past, its recognition that all such good provisions can "in continuance of time" become corrupt, its emphasis on regular and thorough reading of the Scripture, and its insistence that such language be "spoken to the people in the Church, as they might understand."

The Thirty-Nine Articles of Religion is the only one of these five documents which appeared also in BCP, and is the only official statement of a theological position which the Church of England ever made. Although it is not a "confession," like the Westminster or Augsburg Confessions, a statement of belief which members of the Church are expected to affirm, it does represent for Anglicans an important marker and touchstone for belief. It is the "rock from which we have been digged." The text of the Articles is that revised for the use in the American Church in 1801. In those articles where emendations have been made of the

English text of 1571/1662, the original form of the article has been appended (*cf.* Articles VIII, XXXVI, XXXVII).

The Chicago-Lambeth Quadrilateral lists those items which our Church deems "essential to the restoration of unity among the divided branches of Christendom" (PrBCP, p. 877). Hence they are the basis of any serious ecumenical discussion. They comprise the Holy Scriptures of the Old and New Testaments as the revealed Word of God; the Nicene Creed as the sufficient statement of the Christian Faith; the two Sacraments—Baptism and the Supper of the Lord, ministered with unfailing use of Christ's words of institution and of the elements ordained by Him; and "the Historic Episcopate, locally adapted in the methods of its administration to the varying needs of the nations and peoples called of God into the unity of His Church" (PrBCP, p. 877).

These five documents help to define a characteristically Anglican theological stance, which the liturgies in PrBCP also are intended to express: at once catholic, reformed, and positively seeking the unity of the Church.

Tables and Lectionaries

Tables for finding the date of Easter and other Holy Days, which are greatly simplified versions of the BCP tables and instructions, and two tables of lessons bring the Book to a close. The Tables for finding the date of Easter and other Holy Days require no further comment, but the lectionaries need some further discussion.

The Lectionary

The first table of lessons is entitled simply "The Lectionary." It is to be used for the main service on Sundays and other major Holy Days and on special occasions. It could be conveniently described as the "main service lectionary."

Some of the features of this lectionary have been already noted. It provides a Psalm and an Old Testament lesson for each occasion, as well as an Epistle and Gospel. The Psalms and lessons are arranged on a three-year cycle instead of on a one-year cycle, as in BCP.

This lectionary has been worked out in conversations with a number of other Christian Churches—Roman Catholic, Lutheran, Presbyterian, and Methodist. It has not been taken up in exactly the same form by each body, but the extent of agreement is noteworthy. The proper Epistles and Gospels of BCP were largely common to Roman Catholics, Lutherans, and Anglicans. The present main-service lectionary bids to find even wider ecumenical usage.

This lectionary is designed to be used either at the Eucharist or at either one of the Offices, as was not the case in the Eucharistic lectionary in STU and AS. "The same lessons are to be read at the principal morning service, whether the Liturgy of the Word takes the form given in the Holy Eucharist or that of the

Daily Office" (PrBCP, p. 888). In either case, all three readings may be used. In the case of the Eucharist, one may decide between the Old Testament lesson and the Epistle. The use of the Psalm is optional though highly desirable. In the case of the Daily Office, one may decide between Epistle and Gospel.

It is difficult to be precise about the theological impact of this new lectionary. The undeniable power of hearing the same Epistle and Gospel on a given Sunday year after year is lost. On the other hand, there is an important gain in the fact that the new lectionary draws upon a much larger range of Scripture than the BCP lectionary did; and this fact would remain true even if the BCP Sunday Office lectionary were added to the eucharistic propers. In response to frequently voiced criticisms on the basis of trial use, the length of many assigned lessons has been increased in PrBCP beyond their length in AS, at least optionally; and a larger variety of Old Testament passages has also been supplied. This lectionary now represents the basic teaching of Holy Scripture as well as, and far more fully than, the BCP lectionaries for Sunday use.

The Daily Office Lectionary

The second lectionary is for use with the Daily Offices. It is arranged on a two-year cycle, and provides Sunday as well as week-day readings, in case both the Daily Office and the Eucharist are held on Sunday. The Old Testament readings on Sunday in this lectionary do not break the sequence of the weekday readings. New Testament lessons are assigned on a seasonal basis. This lectionary constitutes a fuller provision of Scripture for the Daily Office than that found in BCP. No significantly different theological emphasis is discernible.

VI. Conclusions

PrBCP is a comprehensive book. It makes provision for a wide variety of styles of Episcopal worship: simple and ceremonial; formal and informal; traditional and modern; staid and venturesome. The Book is designed so that the Episcopal Church in all its diversity will be able to use it. To include enough variety to achieve that end, a great deal of new material has been put within the covers of PrBCP. It may not be equally pleasing to everyone. A given congregation may not like or use all the liturgical possibilities which this Book makes available. But there is room in the Book for most existing Anglican customs, and there is room for growth—particularly growth in understanding and love in the face of divergent liturgical practice. If PrBCP is found acceptable, our Church may yet become that "positive hotbed of charity and humility" which Screwtape's labors managed to prevent a generation ago. (C. S. Lewis, *Screwtape Letters*, Macmillan, p. 75.) The times are ready for it.

PrBCP is an ample book. Time and again in this review, we have noticed that its treatment of certain matters is fuller than that in BCP: for example, its use of Scripture, its Catechism, the scope of prayers and thanksgivings, the description of the orders of ministry, the understanding of sickness. In these and other ways, PrBCP expands horizons.

PrBCP is an ecumenical book. In one direction, one sees the elements it has in common with Roman Catholic, other Anglican, and Protestant Churches—ICET texts, the common lectionary, the new Eucharistic Prayer D in Rite II. In another direction, one sees some of the elements it has adopted from the Orthodox liturgies—the reunification of the rites of initiation, the opening acclamations of the Eucharist, Prayers of the People I and V, as well as the concluding anthems of the Burial Service. In still another direction, much of the liturgical revision currently taking place in other Churches parallels what is proposed in this Book.

PrBCP is a pastoral book. Indeed throughout, but especially in the Pastoral Offices, a number of human needs are recognized for the first time in an American Prayer Book: reconciliation of a penitent, adoption of a child, prayers for use by sick persons, and the Rite II Burial Service with its provision for greater intimacy and warmth.

Above all, PrBCP is a eucharistic book. Its major services center and issue in the great Christian act of thanksgiving.

The General Convention of 1976, judging by the impressive majorities given the Book in both Houses, believes that this is the right Book for our time. We trust that in years to come, it will facilitate the task of this Church, described in the Preamble to our Constitution as "upholding and propagating the historic Faith and Order as set forth in the Book of Common Prayer." It is offered now to the Church for the praise and glory of Almighty God, and we pray that it will nourish the Church and its individual members as richly as its predecessors have done in their time.

www.ingramcontent.com/pod-product-compliance
Lightning Source LLC
Chambersburg PA
CBHW061347300426
44116CB00011B/2021